IN THE
SHADOW
OF VESUVIUS

IN THE SHADOW OF VESUVIUS

A Life of Pliny

Daisy Dunn

WILLIAM COLLINS

William Collins
An imprint of HarperCollins*Publishers*
1 London Bridge Street
London SE1 9GF

WilliamCollinsBooks.com

First published in Great Britain in 2019 by William Collins

1

Lines from 'The Barn' from *Death of a Naturalist* by Seamus Heaney reproduced
courtesy of Faber and Faber Ltd.

A catalogue record for this book is available from the British Library

ISBN 978-0-00-821109-7

Maps by Martin Brown

Typeset in Electra by Palimpsest Book Production Ltd, Falkirk, Stirlingshire

Printed and bound in Great Britain by CPI Group (UK) Ltd, Croydon CR0 4YY

MIX
Paper from
responsible sources
FSC   **FSC® C007454**
www.fsc.org

This book is produced from independently certified FSC™ paper
to ensure responsible forest management.

For more information visit: www.harpercollins.co.uk/green

For my grandparents, Don and Wendy Short

Contents

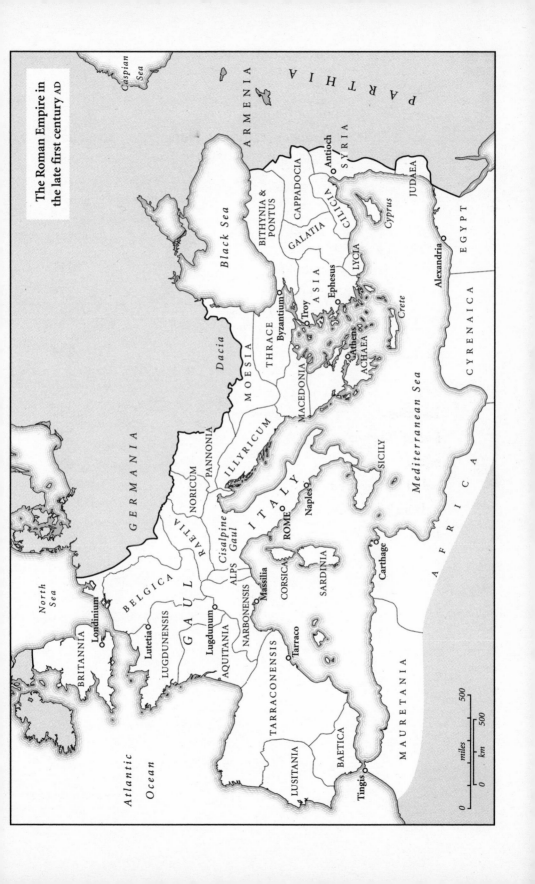

The Roman Empire in the late first century AD

Caspian Sea

ARMENIA

PARTHIA

Black Sea

BITHYNIA & PONTUS

CAPPADOCIA

GALATIA

CILICIA   Antioch○   SYRIA

ASIA   LYCIA   JUDAEA

Troy   Ephesus○   *Cyprus*

Byzantium○

THRACE

Dacia

MOESIA   MACEDONIA   Athens○   ACHAEA   *Crete*

Alexandria○

EGYPT

CYRENAICA

ILLYRICUM

PANNONIA

NORICUM

RAETIA

Mediterranean Sea

GERMANIA

Cisalpine Gaul   ALPS

SICILY

ITALY

ROME○   Naples○

North Sea

BELGICA

G A U L

LUGDUNENSIS   Lutetia○   Lugdunum○

NARBONENSIS   Massilia○

CORSICA

SARDINIA

Carthage○

A F R I C A

BRITANNIA   Londinium○

AQUITANIA

Atlantic Ocean

TARRACONENSIS   Tarraco○

LUSITANIA   BAETICA   Tingis○

MAURETANIA

miles   0   500

km   0   500

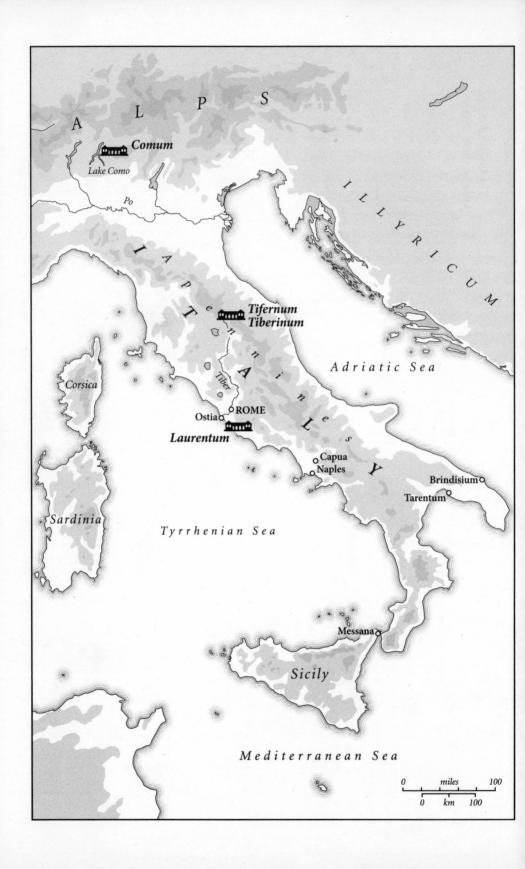

A L P S

Comum

Lake Como

Po

I L L Y R I C U M

A P E N N I N E S

Tifernum
Tiberinum

Tiber

Adriatic Sea

Corsica

Ostia ○ ● ROME

Laurentum

○ Capua
Naples ○

○ Brindisium

Tarentum ○

Sardinia

Tyrrhenian Sea

Messana ○

Sicily

Mediterranean Sea

0   miles   100

0   km   100

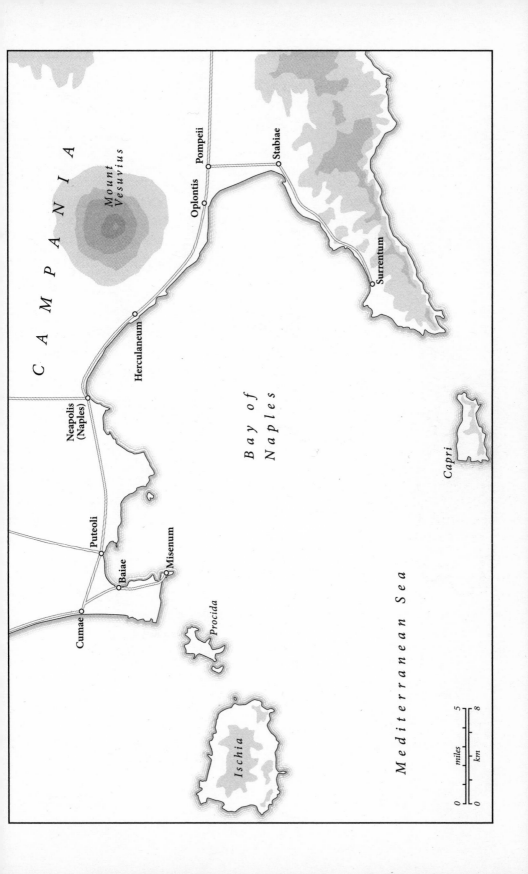

Nota

This book explores the ways in which the Plinys – Younger and Elder – thought about life, death and the natural world. At its heart is a biography of the younger, better-documented Pliny, whom I have pursued through his *Letters* together with his uncle Pliny the Elder's extraordinary encyclopaedia, the *Natural History*. It is also a celebration of the enduring appeal of both men, their work and the treatment of their ideas through the passage of time.

Reading the *Letters* and *Natural History* in Latin is very involving and requires much to-ing and fro-ing between sources – from Roman histories to satires; from ancient Greek poetry and medical tracts to the writings of the Church fathers. Among Pliny the Younger's regular correspondents were the historian Tacitus and biographer Suetonius, whose celebrated accounts of the emperors post-date his letters by a number of years and supplement several of his descriptions of events in Rome. There are also a good many surviving but largely forgotten inscriptions and archaeological remains which are relevant to the lives of the two Plinys. I have brought these together with the literary sources in order to provide a three-dimensional view of the world from which they came. All translations from the Greek and Latin are my own, unless indicated otherwise.

In the spirit of both Plinys, I have eschewed a strictly chronological narrative and followed rather the seasons of the Younger's life, while drawing on the *Natural History* throughout. The shape of the book gives a flavour of Pliny the Younger's year, which was structured slightly differently from ours. Julius Caesar had reformed the calendar in the first century BC because it had fallen out of step with the seasons – the discrepancy caused by the fact that it was based on the cycle of the moon. Caesar had it replaced with a solar calendar. There were now twelve months divided into thirty or thirty-one days each, with the exception of February which, as today, had twenty-eight, or twenty-nine every leap year. Although Pliny the Elder confessed that there was still little exactitude in ascertaining the proper time for a star to appear, or in marking the beginning of a new season when change is so gradual and weather so unpredictable, the Julian Calendar offered a stable framework. Pliny the Elder had winter begin on 11 November, spring on 8 February, summer on 10 May and autumn on 8 or 11 August.

PART ONE

AUT-

Darker than Night

Lucky, I think, are those men with a god-given gift for doing what deserves to be written about or writing what deserves to be read – and very lucky are those who can do both. Through his own books and yours, my uncle will be one of these.

Pliny the Younger to Tacitus, Letter 6.16

The crisis began early one afternoon when Pliny the Younger was seventeen and staying with his mother and uncle in a villa overlooking the Bay of Naples. His mother noticed it first, 'a cloud, both strange and enormous in appearance', forming in the sky in the distance. Pliny said that it looked like an umbrella pine tree, 'for it was raised high on a kind of very tall trunk and spread out into branches'. But it was also like a mushroom: as light as sea foam – white, but gradually turning dirty, elevated on a stem, potentially deadly.[1] They were too far away to be certain which mountain the mushroom cloud was coming from, but Pliny later discovered it was Vesuvius, some thirty kilometres from Misenum, where he and his mother Plinia were watching.

The cape of Misenum was famous for its sea urchins and even more so for its harbour, which was home to one of Rome's two imperial fleets.[2] Its name preserved the memory of Misenus, trumpeter of Aeneas, who fought alongside Hector in the Trojan War and escaped the burning citadel only to perish 'in a death he did not deserve'. 'In his foolishness,' said Virgil, 'he happened to fill the waves with sound by blowing into a seashell, and summon the gods to a song contest.'[3] Triton, son of the sea god Neptune, drowned him in his envy. It was in the course of gathering wood for Misenus' funeral pyre, in the volcanic region of Cumae, that Aeneas discovered the golden bough that secured his entry to the Underworld.

Pliny the Elder, Pliny's maternal uncle, was admiral of the fleet, in charge of maintaining and fitting out the boats which served predominantly 'as protectors' of the seas off Italy.[4] On the morning the cloud appeared, he had risen early as usual, bathed, lunched, and was working when, at around midday, his sister came to tell him what she had seen. Abandoning his reading and calling for his shoes, he made his way to a higher vantage point for a better view.

Pliny the Elder was a historian and a naturalist as well as an admiral. He had recently finished writing his thirty-seven-volume encyclopaedia on natural history, a few passages of which were concerned with the world's volcanoes. He had described Mount Etna in Sicily glowing through the night and 'covering in frost the ash it ejects' when snow lay over its surface.[5] He had described, too, the volcano Cophantus in Bactria, north of the Hindu Kush, and Mount Chimaera in Lycia (in southern Turkey), where the fires allegedly grew when it rained but could be extinguished by earth or manure. He had written of a crater in Babylon that threw up flames like fish, and of volcanoes in Persia, Ethiopia, and the Aeolian islands. But not of Vesuvius. In the *Natural History*, Vesuvius is simply a vineyard-covered mountain watered by the River Sarno and visible from Pompeii.[6]

If Pliny the Elder knew it was a volcano at all, he thought it was extinct.

He gave the impression that the region of Campania was too green and well-watered to burn, with 'plains so fertile, hills so sunny, glades so safe, woods so rich in shade, so many bountiful kinds of forest, so many mountain breezes, such fertility of crops and vines and olives, fleeces of sheep so handsome, bulls with such excellent necks, so many lakes, and rivers and springs which are so abundant in their flow, so many seas and ports, the bosom of its lands open to commerce on all sides and running out into the sea with such eagerness to help mankind!'.[7] 'Lucky Campania', mused Pliny the Elder, was where Nature had gathered all her gifts.

The grapevines were especially famous. An ancient wall painting from the region shows the wine god Bacchus, dressed in a handsome bodysuit of grapes, surveying the vines on the lower slopes of a mountain – in all likelihood Vesuvius itself. An enormous snake, the 'Good Spirit' of vineyards, is depicted in the foreground of the painting. It was by snapping off these long, trailing vines, weaving them into ladders, and lowering themselves onto a plain beneath the slopes of Vesuvius that Spartacus and his men had managed to launch a surprise attack on the Romans, drive them back, and take over their camp during their uprising in 73 BC.[8] Almost a century after Spartacus was defeated, the Greek geographer Strabo noted the presence of blackened stones towards the summit of the mountain and suggested that the ash of fires 'since quenched' had contributed to the fertility of the soil, as it had upon Mount Etna.[9] If fires were responsible for the success of Vesuvius's grapevines, however, there was no suggestion that they had not been extinguished for good. Vesuvius first erupted about 23,000 years before and had now been dormant for approximately 700 years

– dormant, but as alive as the crops which enveloped it.[10] Like a snake, it was now sloughing its skin.*

The process had begun perhaps two hours before Pliny's mother first noticed it. A relatively small eruption had presaged the larger one that formed the cloud.[11] Taller and taller the pine tree grew, propelled from its chamber and sucked up into the sky through convection.[12] At its peak, it would reach a height of thirty-three kilometres.[13] Pliny the Elder decided that this 'phenomenon' warranted further investigation. After taking in what he could from his lookout point he made up his mind to leave Misenum to draw nearer to its source. Earlier in the day he had given his nephew something to write. When he now asked him whether he wanted to accompany him, Pliny refused, insisting that he would prefer to stay behind with his mother in order to work. Pliny the Elder would go without him. He gave orders for a boat to be fitted out and was just leaving the villa when he received a written message from his friend Rectina, who lived beneath Vesuvius. Terrified, she was begging for his help, for there was now 'no escape except by boat'. It was then, Pliny recalled, that his uncle 'changed his plan and what he had begun as an intellectual pursuit he completed with all he had'.[14] Admiral Pliny had the entire fleet at his disposal and launched the quadriremes – large, but surprisingly swift ships equipped with two banks of rowers, two men per oar – with the intention of bringing help not only to Rectina, but to as many on that populated shore as he could.

For several hours, the fleet held course across the Bay of Naples. Despite heading in the very direction whence others were now fleeing, Pliny's uncle was said to have been so fearless that 'he described and noted down every movement, every shape of that evil thing, as it appeared before his eyes'.[15] To any sailors

---

* The volcano known as 'Vesuvius' today is the inner cone that formed inside 'Monte Somma' – thought to be the remains of the older volcano that erupted in AD 79.

who survived to tell the tale of their admiral's fortitude, the chance of reaching land in safety must have seemed increasingly remote as they proceeded across the water. First ash rained down on them, then pumice, then 'even black stones, burned and broken by fire'. This was no hail storm. The fall of grey-white pumice is thought to have lasted eighteen hours in total.[16] On average, it was falling at a rate of 40,000 cubic metres a second.[17] By the time the quadriremes had come within sight of the coast, the pumice had formed island-like masses on the sea, impeding them from advancing any further. When the helmsman advised turning back, Pliny the Elder adamantly refused. 'Fortune favours the brave,' he said.

Although the pumice prevented them from reaching Rectina, they determined to put in where they could. Stabiae, a port town just south of Pompeii, lay about sixteen kilometres from Vesuvius. A contemporary image reveals the town's harbour to have had long elegant promontories, criss-cross balustrades, sand-coloured pediments and towering columns crowned with sculptures of men.[18] By the time the fleet arrived here, the columns would have been mere shadows, with evening falling across the bay.

As ash and pumice continued to pour down, Pliny the Elder went to find a friend, Pomponianus, who had already stowed his possessions aboard a ship, 'set on flight if the opposing wind settled'. Pliny the Elder embraced him and requested a bath before joining him for dinner. 'Either he was content,' Pliny speculated later, 'or he showed a semblance of contentment, which was just as great-hearted.'[19] As his host and his household watched flames leaping from the mountain and lighting up the night sky, Pliny the Elder told them that they were witnessing merely 'the bonfires of peasants, abandoned through terror, and empty houses on fire'.[20] As if soothed by his own deception, he soon fell asleep. He was fifty-five years old, corpulent and had a weak windpipe.[21] As the hot ash and pumice began to mount up on the pavement outside the doorway, his raw and narrow airwaves – call it asthma – for once proved to be a blessing. He might have been trapped inside had his noisy breathing not alerted Pomponianus' household to his continued presence inside the house. Rousing him from his bedchamber, they gathered to make a final decision as to whether to stay put or leave while they still could. The weight of the pumice and repeated earth tremors had now begun to cause buildings to collapse. If they remained in the villa they might be crushed. If they ventured outside, then the pumice could still throw other structures down on top of them. About two metres of it would fall on the town of Stabiae alone.[22]

The inhabitants of Campania had felt the tremors for days, but they were used to these movements, this background noise. As Pliny observed, 'they were not particularly frightening because they were so commonplace'.[23] Over sixteen years had passed since the last truly devastating earthquake had struck, demolishing temples, baths and municipal buildings in Pompeii and the surrounding towns.[24] Some citizens had fled after that earthquake and vowed never to come back.[25] More had stayed, only to witness their neighbours wander in a sort of madness, their livestock – over 600 sheep – dying as noxious gases permeated the atmosphere.[26] It would not occur to the people of Campania to connect these events with the eruption that was now taking place. It must have been inconceivable that what was unravelling so quickly had been set in train so many years earlier.

The earthquake of AD 63 had been as unexpected in its timing as it had in its force. Striking on 5 February, when Pliny the Younger was little more than a year old, it made a mockery of the ancient belief that earthquakes never happen in winter.[27] Theories put forward over the past 600 years for the cause of earthquakes ranged from wrathful gods to the movement of water beneath the earth and activity of fire or air.[28] Pliny the Elder, for his part, subscribed to a theory of 'opposing winds'.[29] He believed that the earth and all things upon it were full of life-giving breath; that winds lurked deep beneath the ground in even the darkest hollows and ravines. Left alone, these winds were quite content within their burrows. They would make room for any fresh air that tried to insinuate its way into their caverns by leaving through chinks in the earth.[30] Strato of Lampsacus, a philosopher from the school of Aristotle, had discovered that hot and cold repel one another. The winds beneath the earth would do all they could to recede from the cool, incoming air. If they could find no chinks through which to escape, however, and air continued to filter in, then a mighty struggle would ensue. It was in the midst of this battle between winds that the earth burst open to relieve the pressure mounting inside. Neither Pliny the Elder nor anyone else yet knew of the existence of tectonic plates, but his theory showed an understanding of the role that opposing forces play in triggering earthquakes.

The winds theory even partially accounted for what happened next. It was rightly presumed that the sheep that died in AD 63 did so as a result of bowing their heads so close to the earth from which gases such as carbon dioxide and sulphur were now emanating. The death of livestock is a common occurrence in volcanic regions. In the spring of 2015, over five thousand sheep died in Iceland as a result of intoxication by volcanic sulphur. Humans hold their heads sufficiently high to inhale the poison in smaller doses. Their heady confusion tends to pass. But what no one realised in AD 63 was that this earthquake and gaseous release was evidence not of winds moving beneath the earth but of magma rising within Vesuvius. Earthquakes had continued to plague southern Italy over the next sixteen years of the younger Pliny's life as – slowly – the volcano began to wake.

As the earthquakes started to intensify across the Bay of

Naples, buildings seemed both to be swaying on their foundations and collapsing from their debris-laden roofs. Pliny the
Elder remained sufficiently rational to realise that to stay inside,
while the earth shook and the sky fell in, would be fatal. He,
Pomponianus and the other men and women in the house at
Stabiae gathered up pillows, strapped them to their heads, and
ventured out into the darkness. Pumice is light and porous –
formed, as it is, when gas bubbles expand and burst inside the
rising magma, which then solidifies and rapidly cools – but a
large piece of rock might easily have felled them.[31]

Back in Misenum, Pliny and his mother had made a similar
decision. Pliny had gone to bed early only to be woken from a
short sleep. Although pumice and ash were yet to fall here, the
tremors had become so strong that objects and furniture were
'not only being moved, but turned over'.[32] Fearing accident or
worse, they went outside and sat on a terrace that overlooked
the sea. On the previous day Pliny had been too absorbed by
his work to accompany his uncle out of Misenum. On this night,
being absorbed by his work might have been – might yet be –
his salvation. Summoning a slave to bring him Livy's *Ab urbe
condita*, a recondite history of Rome, Pliny resumed his note-
taking. As he read about the foundation and development of
Rome and its people – and as the earth continued to shake –
Pliny focused solely on the work in hand. With retrospect he
asked himself whether this was not an imprudent thing to have
done (he was sufficiently circumspect to realise how he must
have looked – to be scribbling while masonry was crashing to
the ground), but in his heart he never doubted the wisdom of
his act. He was doing precisely what he imagined his uncle
would be doing, wherever he was.

Morning was now rising over Stabiae, but it was unlike any
morning the people had known. It was like night, only 'blacker
and denser than all the nights there have ever been'.[33] It was

then that Pliny the Elder took a torch and made his way to the shore to see whether there was any chance of escape. The sea was wild. The wind was against them. And so he lay down on a cloth on the beach. He called out once, then a second time, for some cold water. He drank. Then something happened.

Fresh flames appeared and with them 'the smell of sulphur that suggested there were more flames to come'. The people of Stabiae fled, among them Pliny the Elder's companions. They had probably sensed the onrush of a nuée ardente – an avalanche-like 'burning cloud' of ash, gas and rock.[34] The pine-tree cloud that Pliny and his family had witnessed from Misenum on the previous day had now collapsed into itself, too dense to be supported on its trunk any longer.[35] Released from this collapse, a series of nuées ardentes had begun to sweep Campania at a minimum of a hundred kilometres an hour, making debris of whatever lay in their path.

Neither Pliny nor his uncle knew that deadly surges had already overwhelmed the town of Herculaneum. Pliny, sitting with his mother at Misenum, and his uncle, lying on a beach at Stabiae, were comparatively distant from the volcano. Stabiae lay sixteen kilometres to its south-east; Herculaneum, just seven kilometres to its south-west. Although Herculaneum had experienced little pumice-fall owing to the direction of the wind, the earthquakes had been catastrophic. In a bid to take cover, hundreds of its residents had made their way to the shore where a series of arched vaults, probably boat stores, was set back from the coast. Each vault was barely three metres wide by four metres deep. Those who could not fit inside one or reach their shelter in time – many men ceded their places to women and children – remained exposed on the coast.

The people of Herculaneum saw the avalanche coming. Huddled beneath the arches and spread out over the beach, they clung to each other. They were entirely helpless. As floods of volcanic matter hurtled towards them, they died upon impact with its heat. In its second stage, a nuée ardente produces pyroclastic flow, a current of magma and gas of around 400 degrees Celsius. Struck by a series of volcanic surges and flows, Herculaneum was buried deep beneath the layers of debris. The arches under which its inhabitants lay became their funeral vaults, shrouding their remains for the next two thousand years.

The panicking crowds at Stabiae were now witnessing what was probably the last of six pyroclastic surges. Two had already struck Herculaneum, a third hit Pompeii, a fourth overwhelmed any Pompeians who remained, and the fifth buried their city.[36] Roused from his blanket on the beach, Pliny the Elder got up, leaning on two slaves for support. He managed to stand, but then he fell, defeated.*

Pliny later reasoned that his uncle died because the thick fumes and air had obstructed his fragile airways. He was probably right. The surge cloud from a nuée ardente is low in oxygen and would have filled his lungs with ash, asphyxiating him.[37] When his body was discovered a few days later, it was said by whoever found and reported it to be intact and unharmed, with the look more of sleep than of death. The body of a victim of thermal shock does not look peaceful. It is rigid, the hands typically clenched like a boxer's, the result of tendons contracting in the heat. Many of the bodies later uncovered at Pompeii would show signs of thermal shock.

Pliny and his mother were further away from the volcano and better placed to escape. By daybreak, the earthquakes at Misenum had become so severe that they threatened to bring the villa down on top of them, and they quickly decided to leave the town. As mother and son made their way through the streets

---

* In a surviving fragment of a biography attributed to Suetonius, it is said that some people thought Pliny the Elder was in fact killed by a slave, whom he urged to hasten his death in the agonising heat.

they found themselves followed by a crowd, 'favouring someone else's plan to their own, which in moments of fear is akin to prudence'.[38] Crowd mentality steered the refugees clear of the falling buildings and into the possibility of safety.

Pliny and his mother proceeded by carriage. They were joined by one of Pliny the Elder's friends who had recently come to visit from Spain. As the earth tremored, they darted one way then another, their vehicles twisting and turning. Over the course of their journey, they witnessed scenes which defied explanation. The sea seemed to 'be absorbed back into itself and sort of be pushed back by the earthquake', leaving a trail of marine life stranded in its wake.[39] This was either the beginning of a tsunami or simply a further effect of the force of the earthquakes. Inland, meanwhile, 'a terrifying black cloud, burst by twisting, quaking flickers of flame, began to gape to show long fiery tongues, like lightning, only bigger'. The cloud descended upon the earth and covered the sea until neither the island of Capri, nor even the promontory of Misenum itself, was visible on the horizon. Ash began to fall, only lightly, and hardly noticeable at all against the thick gloom that pressed them from behind, spreading over the earth like a torrent. Pliny did not know it, but the cloud was very probably the edge of the nuée ardente that had already killed his uncle at Stabiae.[40] Pliny the Elder's friend urged Pliny and his mother on before fleeing the danger himself: 'If your brother, if your uncle, is alive, he would want you to be safe; if he has died, he would have wanted you to survive him. So why do you hesitate in your escape?'

There was now little time. Pliny's mother begged – ordered – her son to leave her behind, knowing she would slow him. She told him that she was 'heavy in years and body and could die happy, if only she was not the cause of [his] death'.[41] Reflecting on this moment, Pliny thought of Virgil and his description of the fall of Troy. In the poem, Aeneas' wife, Creusa, follows behind him as they make their escape. By the time Aeneas reaches safety, she has gone.

Pliny's mother stayed close by him as the ash fell. He took her firmly by the hand so as not to repeat Aeneas' mistake. Leaving the carriages behind, they hurried on by foot while there was still enough light to see. At Pliny's suggestion they left the main path so as not to be trampled by the crowd in the darkness. At one point they paused to rest and the cloud made night of day.

This day, which had struck the people at Stabiae as blacker than any night they had ever experienced, seemed to Pliny 'not so much a moonless or cloudy night, but as if the lamp had gone out in a locked room'. He might still have been in his study had it not been for the screaming:

> You could hear the wailing of women, the cries of babies, the shouting of men. Some were calling for their parents, others for their children, others for their partners, trying to make out their voices. Some wept for their own fate, others for those of their relations. There were some who prayed for death through fear of death. Many raised their hands to the gods; more reasoned that there were now no gods anywhere and that the night would last forever and ever across the universe.[42]

Was this the end of the world? Was this the *ekpyrosis* the Stoic philosophers feared, the fire that closed one life cycle and opened another? Was this the moment 'Titan Sun casts out day' and 'a kind of death and chaos overcomes/ all the gods together and/ death sets itself upon itself . . . ?'[43]

Pliny's uncle had feared the coming of the conflagration. He had noticed that sons were now shorter than their fathers and taken this as a sign that the human seed had begun to dry in

14

the approaching flame.[44] If anyone needed proof of how dramatic the shrivelling of man had been, then he provided it in his description in his encyclopaedia of an ancient corpse measuring twenty metres tall that had been uncovered in a mountain on Crete. Split open during an earthquake, the mountain appeared to have yielded the body of a giant. Some believed it was Orion, whom Jupiter, king of the gods, placed in the sky as a constellation. Others said it was the remains of Otus, son of Neptune. But could it not have been human? The body of mortal Orestes, son of Agamemnon, had already been exhumed and measured at over three metres tall.*

Pliny the Elder had resorted to myth to explain the inexplicable and now the younger Pliny imagined himself inhabiting epic. The desperate women and infants of Campania were like the souls of the Virgilian Underworld. Pliny was Aeneas, who in Virgil's poem is surrounded by the 'overwhelming sound of wailing/ and weeping spirits of infants, whom the black day/ stole away, ripping them from the breast at the very threshold/ of sweet life, and plunged into bitter death'.[45] He was in a living hell. He was not even particularly close to the volcano. He could only have imagined the depths of hell others had now entered. Pliny was as much a visitor to Misenum as Aeneas was to the Underworld. If only his escape could be as easy.

The people of southern Italy were not alone in their fear. The effects of the eruption were felt thousands of kilometres away, 'the amount of dust so great, all in all, that some reached Africa and Syria and Egypt, and some reached Rome, and filled the air above and cast the sun in shade'.[46] This dust would later spread 'sickness and terrible pestilence' among the survivors. Its sudden appearance overhead was bewildering, even to the people

---

* The discovery of the 'bones of Orestes' at Tegea, in the Peloponnese, was described by other ancient historians, too, including Herodotus in the fifth century BC. The bones probably belonged to a mammoth.

of Rome, who 'did not know and could not imagine what had happened, but considered that everything had been turned upside down, and that the sun was vanishing into the earth, and the earth being raised to the heavens'.[47] Some spoke of giants in the darkness, or spread false stories of the extent of the destruction. Others merely panicked. Pliny and his mother carried on, shaking themselves free of the ash that settled on their shoulders to avoid being 'smothered and overcome by its weight'.[48] Unlike so many of the people around him, Pliny did not cry, because even in these dire moments he could reason, and in reasoning, he found something close to belief. His belief became his consolation when he told himself, 'Everything is dying with me, and I am dying with it.'

It was a few days before the darkness lifted. As it did, there was a glimmer of sunlight and Pliny's vision was restored. His first impression, upon turning back to Misenum with his mother to await news of his uncle, was that 'Everything had changed, buried deep in ash as if in snow.'[49]

ONE

Roots and Trees

Paper is made from papyrus that is cut into strips with a needle so as to be as wide as possible but very fine . . . Every sheet is woven on a board dampened with water from the Nile. The muddiness of the liquid serves as a glue.

Pliny the Elder, *Natural History*, Book 13

There was a time when it was thought there was only one Pliny, a curious conflation of the Elder, who died in the eruption of Vesuvius in AD 79, and the Younger, who survived it. The most important contribution the elder Pliny had made to history was his multi-volume encyclopaedia. The *Natural History* was astonishing for its breadth. Believing that 'no book is so bad that there is nothing to be taken from it', Pliny the Elder had crammed facts from as many as 2,000 different volumes into its pages, citing the research of Greek and Roman geographers, botanists, doctors, obstetricians, artists, and philosophers.[1] Offering observations on everything, from the moon, to elephants, to the efficacy of ground millipedes in healing ulcers, Pliny the Elder had left behind an indispensable compendium of knowledge.

His nephew was no less versatile. Though commonly confused with his namesake through Late Antiquity and the Middle Ages, Pliny the Younger was an important figure in his own time.[2] He survived the Vesuvius disaster to become a lawyer, senator, poet, collector of villas, curator of drains, and personal representative of the emperor overseas. He was also a prolific writer of letters, a couple of which contain his account of the eruption. It took a priest at the cathedral of Verona in the early fourteenth century to disentangle the orator who wrote these letters from the historian and admiral of the fleet who produced the encyclopaedia and perished beneath the volcano.[3] Giovanni de Matociis, the author of a book on empire from Rome to Charlemagne, produced a critical essay which, though laden with errors, made the essential point. There was not one Pliny but two.

In around 1500, a complete manuscript containing over three hundred of Pliny the Younger's letters – far more than de Matociis had known of – was miraculously uncovered in an abbey in Paris. The papyrus dated to the fifth century, making it one of the oldest classical manuscripts ever found (six leaves of it still survive in a library in New York). Aldus Manutius, one of the great publishers of Renaissance Venice, acquired it to produce a book of Pliny the Younger's correspondence, for which there was now a considerable appetite.[4] The discovery in 1419 of an incomplete manuscript in Verona (or possibly Venice) had prompted the first printed edition of the younger Pliny's letters in 1471, two years after his uncle's encyclopaedia was first published in print.[5] The release of books by two Plinys in as many years was met with considerable emotion across Italy.

No sooner had the books been published than an intense intellectual dispute broke out between the cities of Verona and Como (ancient Comum) over the birthplace of the uncle and nephew. The Veronese priest de Matociis had been in no doubt that the pair were native to his home town. In the preface to his encyclopaedia, Pliny the Elder invoked Catullus, the love poet born in Verona in the first century BC, as his 'fellow countryman'. Verona and Comum both formed part of former Gaul. The

Veronese now seized upon these words as proof that Pliny the Elder was one of them. Rattled by their presumption and haughtiness, the people of Como, a town some 150 kilometres to Verona's north-west, retrieved their copies of the *Natural History* and threw open its covers to reveal what was written in the frontispiece. Early editions of the encyclopaedia were prefaced by a biographical note which identified Pliny the Elder explicitly as a man of ancient Como.[6] The Veronese refused to back down. The horror of having witnessed scholar after scholar, poet after humanist – Petrarch, Flavio Biondo, Lorenzo Valla, Niccolò Perotti – come out in support of Verona's rivalrous claim eventually drove the people of Como to more extreme measures.[7] In their determination to win this contest they commissioned a sculptor to produce larger-than-life-size statues of both Plinys, which they displayed prominently in their town centre. The Veronese responded by erecting a statue of the elder Pliny on the rooftop of their council building. If they could not have both Plinys they could at least have one. Standing among the most famous sons of ancient Verona – Catullus and Cornelius Nepos, the dedicatee of his poetry book, the architectural writer Vitruvius, and the poet Aemilius Macer – Pliny the Elder would watch over Verona's Piazza dei Signori for ever after.[8]

If the people of Como were going to settle this dispute, they had no choice but to produce a definitive portrait of the lives of the Plinys in their ancient town. The task was taken up in the sixteenth century by a pair of polymaths: Paolo Giovio, a collector of art, advisor to the art historian Giorgio Vasari, and physician to Pope Clement VII, and his brother Benedetto, a notary, classical scholar, and historian.[9] Gifted and imaginative, if not also highly impressionable, they were precisely what Como needed. Paolo put aside his copy of the *Natural History*, picked up the *Letters* and began to dream of constructing a novel kind of museum-villa in memory of Pliny the Younger. Meanwhile Paolo's brother sought to deconstruct the Veronese claims to Pliny the Elder on textual grounds and to re-establish the connection of Pliny the Younger to the town through archaeology. It would take time and ingenuity but the Giovio brothers would prevail. The Plinys were men of ancient Como – and they were worth fighting over.

Pliny the Elder was born Gaius Plinius Secundus in Comum in AD 23 or 24. His family was of the second highest social order, the equestrians, which meant that he was wealthy, but not so illustrious in his birth as the Julii or Claudii or any of the other great patrician families who had filled the Roman senate for centuries.* He began his career, as was customary for a man of his class, with a spell of military service, which he took to with assiduity. In AD 47, thirty years prior to his appointment as admiral of the fleet, he joined a campaign off what is now the Netherlands and found himself waging 'a naval battle against trees'.[10] He was on the lakes when he saw them. They were not rolling over the surface of the water, but floating towards him as upright as ships' masts. It was terrifying. He recalled that the trees often took the men when they were least prepared, 'driven by the waves as if purposely against our prows when we were moored at night'. The men had no choice but to confront the huge trunks head on.

It was typical of Pliny the Elder to seek an explanation for the peculiarities of the landscapes he encountered on his tours: it was because the trees on the banks attained such heights in their 'determination to grow' that they could be borne along vertically on their roots when they were torn up by the wind and waves. The description sounds fanciful but it is perfectly possible for a current to carry trees along on their roots. Many stumps were carried erect down river during the eruption of Mount St Helens in Washington State in 1980.[11] It is thought that the petrified

---

* To be an equestrian one needed to possess property to the value of 400,000 sesterces. The property qualification for the senatorial class was a million sesterces. A labourer typically earned about 1000 sesterces a year.

forests of Yellowstone National Park may also have developed as a result of trees being carried upright through water.[12]

The curiosity that drew Pliny the Elder towards Mount Vesuvius, and his death, was the product of a lifetime's fascination with the natural world. Already as a young soldier he was making observations which he would incorporate into his *Natural History*. His description of trees floating across the lake was included in a section on the forests of Germania. It was a rare piece of reflection, for Pliny the Elder seldom paused to reminisce on his own experiences, and an important one, for it was in these woods, so thick that they 'add to the cold with their shade', that the Romans had suffered one of their most crushing defeats in recent history.

At the end of the previous century, the first Roman emperor, Augustus, had sent the Roman army into German territory in the hope of pushing their frontier north beyond the Rhine towards the River Elbe.[13] Drusus, son of Augustus' third wife Livia, enjoyed some formidable early successes in the campaign, but died in 9 BC following a fall from his horse. About fifty years later, Pliny the Elder dreamed that he had been visited by Drusus' ghost. According to Pliny the Younger, it was as a result of this encounter, in which Drusus begged to be saved from 'the injustice of being forgotten', that his uncle went on to produce a twenty-volume account of the German Wars.[14] The work is sadly now lost but proved useful to later historians, who referred to its passages on Agrippina the Elder, mother of the emperor Caligula, and her attainment of more power over the Roman army than the generals themselves.[15]

After Drusus died, his brother Tiberius, who would precede Caligula as emperor from AD 14 to 37, worked hard to pacify the Germanic tribes, but was recalled before the Romans could conquer all the territory they desired around the Rhine. The most catastrophic setback came in the autumn of AD 9 when a Roman legate named Varus was leading three legions through

21

the thick Teutoburg Forest near the River Weser. Varus fatefully put his trust in a Germanic chieftain, who had formerly served with the Roman auxiliary, only to be attacked by his tribesmen.[16] The Roman legions were destroyed. Although the Romans lost the land they had gained to the east of the Rhine, they managed to create a zone of provinces beneath the Danube and had made sufficient inroads to maintain troops across the Rhineland with centres at modern Mainz and Cologne. Over the following decades, insurrections, mutinies and plundering became increasingly common among the Germanic tribes, and it was in the interest of quelling the so-called Chauci that Pliny the Elder had found himself waging a war against trees in AD 47.

The Romans at home came to know the Germans by repute. They learned that they had wild blue eyes, reddish hair, large strong frames, little tolerance of thirst and heat, but natural resistance to cold and hunger owing to their climate.[17] Their tribes did not live in cities but 'scattered and far apart, wherever a fountain or plain or grove took their fancy'.[18] Pliny the Elder at least had the good fortune to be confronting 'the very noblest of the Germans, who elect to preserve their greatness through justice'.[19] The Greater Chauci lived between the Elbe and Weser rivers and the Lesser between the Weser and the Ems. As the Romans' commander, a severe but capable man named Gnaeus Domitius Corbulo, led the triremes up the Rhine channel, the rest of the fleet proceeded through a network of estuaries and canals.[20] Pliny the Elder took one look at the territory and concluded that the Chauci were 'a miserable people' to inhabit country so flood-prone.[21] He likened them in their huts on higher ground to sailors aboard a ship and then, as the waters receded, to victims of a shipwreck.

As he and his fellow soldiers set about sinking the tribesmen's ships, Corbulo succeeded in subduing the neighbouring tribe of the Frisians, and made after the leader of the Chauci.[22] No sooner had he put him to death than he received orders from Rome to withdraw his troops to the near bank of the Rhine.[23] Rome was now ruled by Claudius, son of Drusus who had died in Germania. His rise to power had come about almost by accident when, in AD 41, the Praetorian Guard murdered his nephew Caligula and supported him to take his place. Though sickly, stammering, and frequently taken for a fool, Claudius was highly astute. The last thing he wanted was to stir up war among the very tribes he hoped to pacify. The Roman empire now stretched from Hispania in the west to Pontus (north-east Turkey) and Judaea in the east, and he had ambitions of extending it further still. By the end of his rule, Claudius would have succeeded in annexing Thrace, Lycia (in southern Turkey), Noricum (Austria with some of Slovenia) and Mauretania in north Africa. In the period when Pliny the Elder was in Germania, Claudius' attentions were firmly focused on Britain. Knowing that it would be a tremendous coup to succeed where Julius Caesar had twice failed – in conquering the 'remotest island in the west' – Claudius had launched an expedition to Britain in the summer of AD 43 and returned to Rome in triumph the following year.[24] Although it would be another forty years before the Romans had truly conquered England and Wales, Claudius had set the process in motion.

Germania, meanwhile, remained unsettled. In around AD 51, Pliny the Elder returned to the region to quell the agitations of another tribe, the Chatti. It was probably in this period that he began writing his book *On Throwing the Javelin from Horseback*. Like his histories of the German Wars, the work is unfortunately lost, but presumably set out the military techniques he had learned on the battlefield. His experiences might well have commended to him the German technique of hurling javelins at close quarters over the Roman tradition of firing them at long range.[25] Later, in his *Natural History*, Pliny the Elder provided the merest glimpse into how he might have soothed his aching limbs after these exercises. There were hot springs at nearby

Mattiacum, modern Wiesbaden, where the water, he wrote, remained warm 'for three days'.[26]

Not everyone would have found military life conducive to writing, but Pliny the Elder happened to be posted under a commander who had literary ambitions of his own. Pomponius Secundus would one day be celebrated for the 'erudition and polish' of his plays, one of which was inspired by the story of Aeneas.[27] Pliny the Elder later described him as 'a poet and very distinguished citizen' who was so self-restrained that he never belched.[28] Although Pomponius failed to achieve war against the Chatti, he was greeted in Rome with triumphal honours, which were but 'a fragment of his fame in the eyes of posterity, among whom the glory of his poems prevailed'.[29] On visiting him at home, Pliny the Elder was impressed to find official papers in his collection dating from almost two hundred years earlier.[30] These, and his experience of his command, left a lasting impression; a biography of Pomponius Secundus, written in his memory, is among Pliny the Elder's other lost works.

Having returned from Germania, Pliny the Elder went to see Claudius put on a magnificent naval battle on a lake beside a mountain he had had bored through in central Italy. Keen to display his muscle against the backdrop of this spectacular feat of engineering, the emperor had the Roman triremes and quad-riremes drawn up and boarded by an extraordinary 19,000 servicemen. Crowds from the nearest towns and from as far away as Rome arrived and filled the banks and hills 'in their cupidity or duty to see the emperor'.[31] Pliny the Elder's eye, however, was drawn not to Claudius but to his fourth wife (and niece), the empress Agrippina the Younger, for she was dressed in a 'cloak of woven gold without any other material'.[32] Pliny the Elder never failed to notice a glint of luxury. He paused on Agrippina's cloak as if it held a clue to her true character.

He would be among several historians to suggest that Agrippina was responsible for Claudius' death a few years later. In the autumn of AD 54, the empress was said to have ordered Claudius' plate of *boleti* (bolete, perhaps porcini) mushrooms to be poisoned because she feared he was grooming his natural son Britannicus as his successor rather than her own son Nero, whom she had had him adopt.[33] Succession under the Julio-Claudian emperors was never without drama. Even the emperors who were fortunate enough to have natural sons had reason to fear the emergence of rival heirs. Pliny the Elder incorporated the rumour of Agrippina's machinations into his encyclopaedia as little more than an illustration of the dangers of mushrooms. It was his belief that, if mushrooms were not spiked by a scheming empress or poisonous by Nature, then they could still become deadly by absorbing whatever happened to be in the soil where they sprang up. The nail from a soldier's boot, a piece of old rag, even the breath of a snake in the soil could render a mushroom noxious as it rose 'lighter than sea foam' from its womb-like tunic.[34] As far as Claudius' mushrooms were concerned, the poison only spread. Agrippina's act, Pliny the Elder quipped, gave the world a new 'poison' in the form of the teenage emperor Nero.

While initially Nero put on an honourable front – arranging an elaborate funeral for Claudius, abolishing some taxes and reducing others, hosting extravagant entertainments for the people – he soon lived up to Pliny the Elder's assessment of him.[35] First he had his stepbrother Britannicus poisoned. Then, after several failed attempts, he dispatched his controlling mother to her death. Then he killed his aunt. He then kicked his pregnant wife Poppaea to death when she reproached him for returning home late from the races.[36] Around sixty years would pass before Suetonius recounted these murders in his *Lives* of Rome's rulers, from Julius Caesar to Domitian. The Algerian-born biographer (he is thought to have come from the Romanised town of Hippo Regius) was head of the libraries at Rome and had access to the imperial

25

archives. Even allowing for some bias in his account, it is clear that the latter part of Nero's rule was deeply unsettled. If Pliny the Elder had hoped that he would have more freedom to pursue his literary interests after returning from his Germanic expeditions, then Nero's impulsiveness showed him otherwise.

When a fire broke out in Rome in AD 64, the emperor was among those suspected of starting it. Nero is in fact thought to have been outside the city when the fire started, but this did not stop some historians from speculating as to why he might have been so eager to destroy it. 'As if offended by the ugliness of the old buildings and by the narrow winding streets,' wrote Suetonius, 'he set fire to the city so openly, that several men of consular rank caught his attendants with tow and torches on his own estate but did not arrest them.'[37] The city burned for six days and seven nights. To deflect blame, Nero selected a scapegoat. He became the first Roman emperor to persecute Christians, whom he was said to have punished less for the conflagration than for their 'hatred of the human race'.[38] 'Believers' were wrapped up in animal pelts and bitten by dogs, fixed to crosses, and used as human torches to light up the night sky over the imperial gardens. Amongst the Christians to die in Nero's reign were the apostles Peter and Paul.

It was not only the early Christians but the Roman senators who feared for their lives as their role became increasingly redundant in the face of Nero's autocracy. Political *delatio* or 'informing' became a profitable business in Pliny the Elder's lifetime and would continue to plague Rome after his nephew entered the senate in the late eighties AD. A man who laid an accusation against another could achieve political advancement as well as money. If he succeeded in informing upon someone for *maiestas*, or treason, then he was entitled to at least a quarter of the defendant's property (further funds went to the state treasury).[39] An unscrupulous emperor was only too happy to accommodate such activity if it resulted in the downfall of a senator who threatened his power. Stability in Rome had always depended upon its citizens' willingness to monitor each other. Informers might have stolen the people's 'commerce in speaking and listening', but for some men that was a small price to pay for an emperor's protection and the opportunity for self-advancement.[40]

Such was the climate when, in AD 65, a group of senators, equestrians, and members of the Praetorian Guard came together to hatch a plan to blot out Nero's poison for good. Intent on killing him during the coming games, the conspirators gathered round a popular senator named Gaius Calpurnius Piso, who might have made an honourable substitute for Nero, if only the details of their plot were not leaked before it could be executed.[41] No sooner had Nero learned what awaited him than he made after the conspirators. Among those to die for their alleged involvement in the plot were Nero's former tutor, Seneca the Younger, Seneca's poet nephew Lucan, and that 'arbiter of elegance' Petronius, a satirical writer who was accused of being friends with one of the conspirators.[42]

Pliny the Elder played no part in the conspiracy but grew increasingly cautious about what he wrote down. In the mid to late sixties AD, when 'every kind of study that was a little freer or more creative was rendered dangerous by the servitude of the times', as his nephew later put it, Pliny the Elder resorted to writing only what he was certain could not offend: an eight-book treatise on *The Ambiguities of Grammar*.[43]

Pliny the Younger, known here onwards as 'Pliny', was born in about AD 62 under Nero, the last of the Julio-Claudian emperors, matured under the Flavian dynasty – Vespasian, his elder son Titus, and younger son Domitian – and peaked under the emperors Nerva and Trajan. We know far more about him than we do his uncle because he wrote so profusely of his experiences. One of the great chroniclers of life, Pliny could be rather pompous and self-regarding, but he was also highly sensitive to the world around him. His surviving letters, which range from a couple of lines to several pages of Latin, provide a rare insight into the habits of his uncle and an unparalleled portrait of his own life at the very centre of things in the first and early second centuries AD.

This was a period in which an equestrian could advance very quickly through the ranks of society. One hundred and fifty years earlier, Cicero had felt marginalised as a 'new man' – the first in his family to enter the senate – in a world dominated by aristocrats. Pliny seems to have experienced no such prejudice as he proceeded in his career. He became a senator and went on to document what it was like to live and work under an emperor's nose. Of the many rulers he lived under, Domitian, who reigned from AD 81 to 96, and Trajan, who reigned from AD 98 to 117, shaped his experience the most. Pliny's letters post-date Domitian but frequently refer back to the events of his rule. Generally despised by the historians who described him, Domitian caused Pliny considerable unease, but must have supported him for him to have risen through the senate as he did. Pliny's letters reveal his struggle to distance himself from the detested Domitian in the wake of his death. Trajan, by contrast, was an immensely popular ruler, his rise to power hailed in his own times as the beginning of 'a very happy age' in Rome's history.[44] Pliny exchanged over a hundred letters with the ruler and honoured him with an extravagant speech. The *Panegyricus*, which Pliny delivered in the senate house in AD 100, is highly prized because it is the earliest complete speech to have survived from ancient Rome since Cicero's *Philippics* against Mark Antony of 43 BC.[45]

Pliny's letters contain another important first: the earliest pagan sources on the tension between Romans and Christians.[46] Pliny encountered what he called the 'depraved and unbridled *superstitio*' – a subversion of what he understood by 'religion' – after Trajan dispatched him to Bithynia, on the south coast of the Black Sea, one of the many provinces now ruled from Rome, in the last years of his life.[47] Although Pliny could never have predicted that by the fourth century Christianity would be the central religion of the Roman empire, his understanding of its resilience as a faith must have influenced the way he engaged with the Christians he met.

After his uncle's death in AD 79, Pliny became his beneficiary and worked hard to sustain his memory. He inherited his agricultural estate in the upper Tiber valley (in modern Perugia), and personal effects including 160 of his notebooks, double-sided and written in 'the very smallest handwriting'.* Pliny the Elder had once rejected an extraordinary offer of 400,000 sesterces for his notebooks in favour of leaving them to his nephew. And, as Pliny later reflected, 'there were rather fewer' notebooks at that time than there would be by AD 79. He also bequeathed his nephew his name.[48] Pliny the Elder had no children by the time he died and Pliny had lost his father as a boy. Pliny the Elder therefore adopted him posthumously by bequest of his will. It was in recognition of his adoption that Pliny the Younger tended to use the name 'Plinius', after his maternal uncle, rather than 'Caecilius', after his natural father.

Pliny might have struggled to remember all the facts the *Natural History* contained, but through his uncle's words he gained a certain perspective on the world and impetus to establish his place within it. Despite professing to be 'very lazy' by comparison with the elder Pliny, he was deeply influenced by his methods for dedicating as many hours of each day as possible to scholarship. Pliny was in a sense haunted by his uncle and the scale of his achievements, which seemed to exceed what was possible in a single lifetime. The *Natural*

---

* Pliny the Elder was evidently admiring of small handwriting. He recorded in his encyclopaedia that Cicero had known of a complete manuscript of Homer's *Iliad* that was so tiny it could be enclosed in a single nutshell. This fact, included in the seventh book of his *Natural History*, is thought to be the origin of the phrase 'in a nutshell'.

History, Pliny the Elder's sole surviving work, was a seminal achievement. Although the Greeks had produced compendia, and at least two Roman writers anticipated him in creating encyclopaedic collections of their own, the *Natural History* was of another order entirely.[49] The oldest extant encyclopaedia from the Graeco-Roman world, it is indigestible in its enormity. Pliny the Elder claimed that it featured 20,000 pieces of information – though it is now known to contain far more. He included a list of contents in an attempt to make it navigable. The labourer might turn to the pages on 'Viticulture', the artist to the sections on pigments. The *Natural History* was a book for everyman.

Pliny the Elder was in the midst of a discussion of insects when he paused to confess, 'I am forever watching Nature and persuaded to think that nothing about her should be deemed impossible.'[50] In many ways a testament to that thought, his encyclopaedia was a celebration of the peculiarities of Nature over the corrupting influences of materiality. Wealth in this period was concentrated in the hands of the varied few (senators, equestrians, fortunate freedmen – former slaves), but Pliny the Elder still feared for the damage it might cause the wider world.

Perhaps the most vivid symbol of temptation and human corruptibility in the encyclopaedia was the oyster. Pliny the Elder returned to it often, revealing its qualities and health benefits as well as its dangers. He had seen men plunder the earth for gold and gems as well as oysters and feared for the earth's future stability. If fire, war and general collapse did not lead to the destruction of the world, then he believed that man's greed would.[51] He witnessed emperors construct monumental edifices, Nero's Golden House with its revolving dining room epitomising the needless opulence to which the affluent might aspire. Meanwhile, treasures were being carried home from overseas and whetting – or so he imagined – Roman appetites for even more. Pliny the Elder recognised that 'globalisation' could bring improvements, particularly in knowledge, but also challenges. Just as we have come to realise that technologies and antibiotics can be destructive when we rely too heavily upon them, he believed that the easy availability of resources and foreign medicines would weaken Rome.

In his *Natural History* he encouraged his readers to preserve the natural world from destruction by explaining how it could help them. Concerned that knowledge of the healing properties of plants was by now broadly confined to 'the rustics and illiterate', he had undertaken to study as many specimens as he could first hand to describe to his more urban readers. 'With the exception of a few,' he inspected them under Antonius Castor, 'the greatest authority in that art in our age', who lived beyond his hundredth birthday.[52] Pliny the Elder enjoyed some success in his mission to promote natural remedies over strange concoctions from the East. Many of his treatments and cures would be extracted and republished as early as the fourth century as the *Medicina Plinii*. Structured predominantly '*a capite ad calcem*' – from head to heel, an arrangement that became standard in medieval medicine books – the *Medicina Plinii* survived into the fourteenth century and beyond and was even known in medieval England. Several guides from this date recommended the wearing of amulets made from animal body parts to prevent pregnancy. Contraceptive advice found in Pliny the Elder's *Natural History* included the insertion of parasites from a spider's head into a deer hide worn on a woman's arm.[53]

In his uncle's writings, therefore, Pliny inherited not only his pearls of wisdom, but also his warnings against the destructive forces of wealth and greed. Pliny was descended on both sides of his family from the Comum elite. Estimated to have been twice as wealthy as the average senator, he was forever at risk of descending into the life of luxury that his uncle had censured.[54] But while Pliny was not immune from indulging in his wealth, he recognised that there was more to life. He is often at his most interesting in his letters when pondering the sort of life he wants to lead. While perennially attracted to the idea of a quiet retirement spent enjoying books, baths and country air, he also savoured the spice of Rome and had ambitions of becoming a famous poet. In addition to the agricultural estate that he inherited from his uncle, he had a home on the Esquiline Hill in Rome, another on Italy's west coast, and several in his native Comum. He was forever darting between the city, coast, countryside and lake and adapting his daily routine to each. It felt as natural to him to change houses and rooms through the year as it did to the Roman general who asked Pompey the Great, 'Do I seem to you to have less common sense than the cranes and storks and thus not to change my living arrangements in accordance with the seasons?'[55] Believing that a man is happiest when he can be confident that this name will live forever, Pliny was strategic in the ways he divided his time. The problem was that he wanted eternal fame *and* daily contentment. His life would be in many ways an exercise in how to achieve both.

Pliny published most of his letters in his lifetime and arranged them himself, not chronologically, but 'however they came to hand'.[56] The opportunity to cast himself in the best possible light was not one he always took. It is impossible to tell what Pliny added to his letters during the process of editing, but some of what he took out is obvious. There are no addresses, no measurements for the buildings he commissioned, and – most noticeably of all – no dates. Some of the letters can be dated on internal evidence, but a significant proportion of them cannot.[57] If we can wager a reason as to why Pliny ensured that they could never be arranged in precise chronological order, it would be that he wanted his life to be seen for the unpredictable journey that it was. Read out of order, his letters evoke a life of ups and downs, uncertainties, and questions rather than certain progress. How does one survive when all around are falling? Is suicide ever the best course? What separates necessity from excess? Pliny does not always find the answers, but he has a way of opening minds to the unexpected.

PART TWO

WINTER

TWO

Illusions of Immortality

I have not yet, indeed, thought of a remedy for luxury. I
am not sure that in a great state it is capable of a remedy,
nor that the evil is in itself always so great as it is represented.

Benjamin Franklin, *On Luxury, Idleness,*
and Industry, 1784

Pliny counted the historian and lawyer Cornelius Tacitus
among his close friends. Born around AD 56, probably in
southern Gaul, in the region of modern Provence, Tacitus was
five, perhaps six years Pliny's senior and, as Pliny noted, 'excep-
tionally eloquent'.[1] He wrote a study of *Germania* and a piercing
account of the second half of the first century before embarking
upon his celebrated *Annals* of the early Roman emperors. He
was also a couple of steps ahead of Pliny on the senatorial
ladder. Although Pliny did not consider himself a historian, he
saw in Tacitus someone he would do well 'to imitate'. He told
Tacitus that they were of a similar nature and that, if he could
only follow in his successes, then he might achieve his dream
'to be considered "second best but by a long way"' to him.[2]
The quote came from Virgil's *Aeneid* and described the position
of a Trojan soldier in a footrace. Competitive and admiring in
equal measure, Pliny would write more letters to Tacitus over

the course of his life than to anyone else except the emperor Trajan, to judge from what survives.

The lives of Pliny and Tacitus frequently crossed. After he lost his father as a boy, Pliny was appointed a mentor, Corellius Rufus – a senator he 'always referred everything to' – and a legal guardian, Verginius Rufus. When Verginius passed away many years later, at the age of eighty-three, it was Tacitus who delivered his funeral oration. Pliny was still grieving when he went to hear it. 'I think of Verginius,' he confessed, 'I hear him and talk to him and I hold him.' He had known Verginius almost his whole life. His native Comum bordered Verginius' Mediolanum (Milan), and their families owned adjoining property.[3] A successful military man, Verginius had thrice been consul and might even have been emperor, had he heeded popular pleas to accept the role at the end of Nero's reign. To Pliny he had been less a hero than a guiding light, showing him 'the affection of a father' and helping him as he embarked upon his career before resuming an honourable retirement on the coast of Etruria in Italy. 'He read the poems which were written about him,' recalled Pliny, 'he read histories, and was part of his own posterity.'[4] Such scrolls, however, could be heavy, especially for an elderly man. It had been Verginius' misfortune to drop a scroll on a polished floor, slip, and fracture his hip while attempting to retrieve it. The injury weakened him and he died.

Pliny's grief was still raw ten years later when he visited Verginius' former home and discovered that his tomb had not been finished, the man in charge of completing it too idle to have troubled himself over such a humble monument. 'A mixture of anger and misery come over me,' wrote Pliny, 'that his ashes lie neglected without name or epitaph, although his glorious memory still wanders the world.'[5] Tacitus' oration, sadly now lost, had done much to perpetuate Verginius' achievements. It was so exemplary and well pitched that Pliny had anticipated accurately that his prayers for Verginius to remain 'in the memories of men and in conversation' would be granted. No one could replace Verginius, but in honouring his accomplishments as beautifully as he did, Tacitus became a model for Pliny in his own right.

One day, about thirty years after the eruption of Vesuvius, Pliny took the bold step of writing a letter to Tacitus expressing his desire to be featured in his work. His books will be 'immortal', Pliny predicted, 'this is why (I'll freely admit it) I am so keen to be inserted into them'.[6] By the very next line he had launched into a detailed report of his prosecution of a Roman general for corruption. Tacitus was generous towards Pliny but craved something more profound from him. The historian was anxious to 'hand down to posterity a faithful account' of the eruption that had killed Pliny's uncle.[7] Buoyed by the idea that the death of the elder Pliny (not to mention his own survival) might achieve 'immortal glory', Pliny cast his mind back to his youth. In the first of two letters to Tacitus he described the course of the eruption before concluding on a cliffhanger: 'My mother and I, meanwhile, were at Misenum – but that is of no historical consequence and you only wanted to know about my uncle's death.' It had the desired effect, and Tacitus now politely requested from Pliny an account of his own experience of Vesuvius. Pliny was only too happy to oblige: 'You will read these parts without intending to write about them,' he prevaricated in a further letter, 'for they're not remotely worthy of history; indeed, if they strike you as unworthy even of a letter, then impute it to the fact that you requested them.'[8]

This was the first and last time Pliny wrote of his mother in his letters, the earliest of which date to almost twenty years after the disaster, by which time she had presumably died. Conscious of how much time had passed, Pliny vowed in his accounts to draw on what he had witnessed himself and what he had heard immediately after the eruption, 'when the truth is most remembered'.[9] The sole eyewitness reports of the disaster to survive antiquity, Pliny's letters have long been admired for their detail. The passages in which he described what he had experienced for himself are particularly valuable, his account of the stages, range, and appearance of the eruption broadly consistent with the archaeological evidence.[10] The picture he paints of a rising ash column followed by prolonged pumice fall is in fact so well observed that volcanologists now classify such eruptions as 'Plinian'. It is more difficult to substantiate what Pliny described of his uncle's bravery, but then, whatever he wrote was always going to be open to doubt. As Umberto Eco asked in 1990: 'One wonders whether Pliny would have preferred a Reader accepting his glorious product (monument to the Elder) or a Reader realising his glorifying production (monument to the Younger)?'[11]

Readers have, for the most part, accepted Pliny's account of the eruption as both a remarkable tribute to the dead and a stirring enticement to adventure and risk. In the seventeenth century, the scientist and statesman Francis Bacon demonstrated just how readily Pliny the Elder's example could be revived in the modern world.[12] Bacon had held high office as Lord Chancellor and Privy Councillor under King James I and was the author of a work of natural history of his own, the *Sylva Sylvarum*. Although scholars had by now begun to discredit many of the so-called facts of the elder Pliny's ancient encyclopaedia, Bacon was fascinated by its author and his fate and, in 1626, determined to present himself as his successor for his inquisitiveness.

Bacon was travelling north through London towards Highgate on a snowy day when the thought occurred to him that snow, like salt, might provide an effective means of slowing the decay of flesh. As his coach rattled slowly on, he surveyed the whitening roads and conceived a plan for testing his theory. After gathering what snow he could, he stopped at 'a poore woman's howse at the bottome of Highgate hill' and presented her with a hen to disembowel (where he acquired the bird he did not say).[13] The poor woman did as she was told, and Bacon proceeded to stuff the carcass with the snow. Unfortunately, soon after conducting the experiment, he became unwell. When he started vomiting he was unsure 'whether it were the stone, or some surfeit, or cold, or indeed a touch of them all three'.[14] He only knew he was too unwell to make it home. He therefore travelled the short distance to the house of his friend, the Earl of Arundel. Although the earl was not home, the housekeeper was 'very careful and diligent about [him]' and installed him in a guest bed with a warming pan. Bacon, however, quickly deteriorated. The bed had not been slept in for over a year and was damp, apparently leaving him with a graver chill than the one he had come in with. 'In 2 or 3 daes,' wrote John Aubrey, 'he dyed of suffocation.'[15]

'Suffocation' was more enterprising a death than pneumonia or opium-poisoning, now considered the likelier causes of Bacon's demise.[16] It evoked most readily Pliny the Elder, being suffocated by the volcanic ash which Pliny had so memorably compared to snow. Scholars have studied closely the letter Bacon wrote on his deathbed in Highgate, likening himself in his quest to experiment with 'the conservation and induration of bodies' to Pliny the Elder, 'who lost his life by trying an experiment about the burning of the mountain Vesuvius'.[17] The elder Pliny had died after launching a mission to rescue people from the eruption, but that mission, as Bacon recalled, had originated as a quest to observe the phenomenon at close quarters. The parallel between preserving flesh through snow and rescuing flesh from fire was not lost on Francis Bacon, who concluded that there were less honourable ways of losing one's life than by experimenting with methods for preserving it.

Five years after Bacon's death, Vesuvius erupted in the largest and most catastrophic explosion recorded since AD 79.[18] Between three and eighteen thousand people were thought to have perished in the Plinian cloud and ensuing pyroclastic flows. Francis Bacon might have missed his chance to inspect the kind of ash that had extinguished his idol, but there were many more men like him who took the latest eruption as a cue to explore the history of the volcano. Across Europe, the eruption awoke new interest in the lives of the two Plinys. That Vesuvius had shown itself to be as deadly as Pliny claimed in his letters to Tacitus offered adventurers an unprecedented impetus to prove their daring. Inspired by Pliny's visceral descriptions in his letters, Englishmen began to travel to Naples in increasing numbers and test their resolve in the shadow of the crater.

Among them was Sir William Hamilton. The future husband of Emma, mistress of Lord Nelson, Sir William had begun his career in the military before becoming MP for Midhurst in Sussex and being dispatched as British envoy to Naples. Upon arriving in the region in the 1760s, he witnessed a series of volcanic eruptions, which he determined to document in detail. The explosions were relatively small but even so their force surprised him. He was in his villa one morning when he saw a cloud rise from Vesuvius in 'the exact shape of a huge pine-tree, such as Pliny the younger [sic] described in his letter to Tacitus'.[19] When he was sure the lava had been released and it was safe enough to leave the house, he ventured outside to explore. Just as he was examining the lava, there was a bang, the mountain split once more, and 'a fountain of liquid fire shot up many feet high, and then, like a torrent, rolled on directly towards us'. As the sky grew dark and the smell of sulphur became 'very offensive', he and his guide turned on their heels and 'ran near three miles without stopping', the ground trembling all the while beneath their feet.[20]

Pliny the Elder was not alone in his fascination with natural phenomena. A banker named Lucius Caecilius Iucundus adorned the household shrine of his villa in Pompeii with scenes from the devastating earthquake of AD 63. A temple of Jupiter, Juno and Minerva and an archway to the forum are shown swaying on their foundations.

Hamilton sent observation after observation of the volcanic activity to the Royal Society, of which he was a fellow. His letters later formed the basis for a book. Hamilton's *Campi Phlegraei*, on the 'flaming fields' of Campania, was illustrated with colour prints by an artist named Pietro Fabris, who captured perfectly the sense of complacence that such a beautiful landmark could inspire in those who lived beneath it. Here was flame-crowned Vesuvius, billowing puffs of smoke into the pale skies of Italy while finely attired ladies looked on casually from across the water.

Hamilton had arrived in time to observe some of the excavations which had begun at Pompeii. It had long been known that cities lay hidden underground. Already in Francis Bacon's time, an Italian architect had chanced upon the ruins of Pompeii while digging a canal. There is evidence that people had begun tunnelling through the ancient layers of Herculaneum too, as early as the thirteenth or fourteenth century.[21] But it was only in the decades before Hamilton arrived, and at the instruction of King Charles III of Spain, that the process of

41

uncovering the cities began in earnest. Excavations were first undertaken by a Spanish military engineer named Rocque Joaquin de Alcubierre in Herculaneum in 1738 and at Pompeii a decade later. As Hamilton noted, the ancient villas of Pompeii were 'covered about ten or fifteen feet, with pumice and fragments of lava, some of which weigh three pounds'.[22] Excavators at both sites made a priority of removing precious objects and wall paintings from the layers. Like the poor and displaced who had returned to the buried cities in the immediate aftermath of the disaster and squeezed into the villas to claim whatever Vesuvius had failed to, the excavators worked more greedily than methodically. Their digs were haphazard, sporadic, and limited in scope, with little thought given to stabilising the structures underground.

Preserved within the snow-like layers were imprints of the victims of the disaster of AD 79. The shapes of human bodies frozen in time were more palpable than fossils, but proved far less easy to extract from the ground. It was only some decades later, in the mid-nineteenth century, that a Neapolitan numismatist and archaeologist named Giuseppe Fiorelli developed a technique for preserving what remained of the ancient dead. Fiorelli was appointed director of excavations at the University of Naples in 1860 following a tumultuous period in his life. Arrested and imprisoned on charges of colluding with revolutionary forces, and deprived of his research notes, he was fortunate to have been released a short time later and made secretary to the Count of Syracuse.[23] Following archaeological work at Cumae, he arrived in Pompeii, and was a few years into his new post when he poured plaster into the cavities which the shapes of the dead had left behind in the volcanic deposit. The process enabled whole bodies to be cast in the positive.

Fiorelli went on to make dozens more casts through the same

technique. He came as close as anyone could to raising the dead from their undignified tombs and reinstating them among the living. His casts gave each victim an identity. These were not just men, women, children, dogs. Every cowering shoulder and clenched fist represented an individual's response to the tragedy. Each position captured something of their personality, or at least you imagine that it did; it is easy to forget that each cast is more than a work of art. The flesh had decayed over time but, in his casts, Fiorelli created the illusion of having preserved it forever.

Excavations are still ongoing in the Bay of Naples. Significant parts of Pompeii and Herculaneum are yet to be uncovered, but the process of sifting through the layers has already called into question when precisely in AD 79 Vesuvius erupted. Of all the details Pliny provides in his accounts of the eruption, the date has proven the most contentious. The manuscripts of his letters offer a range of dates, of which 24 August is the most secure textually.[24] But while there is evidence in the concretised ash that trees were still in leaf and the broad beans of summer still fresh at the time of the eruption, other signs suggest a later date.[25] Among the material remains discovered in the layers are olives, plums, figs and pomegranates, which are harvested principally in September and October.[26] Braziers were positioned in such a way as to heat rooms in some of the villas. Summer clothes had made way for the warmer coverings of winter.[27] Was Pliny mistaken over the date, or were these the fruits of another harvest, the preparations for an unseasonably cold August, the heaviest fabrics the victims could find to protect their skin from burning pumice?

The object most commonly cited in support of a post-August date is a single coin from a hoard discovered in the 'House of the Golden Bracelet' in Pompeii, where two adults and two children were also preserved in their final tragic moments. So embedded in the volcanic layers that it could not simply have been dropped at the site after the eruption, the coin features an inscription that led scholars to date it to post early September AD 79. The coin, however, is very poorly preserved, and a recent re-examination has revealed that its legend was misread by the original interpreter. The coin has now been dated to July or August AD 79.[28] The strongest evidence today for a later eruption date is the fact that the volcanic matter was dispersed in a south-easterly direction; the winds in the Bay of Naples seldom blow south-east in August.[29]

It is entirely possible that the scribes made an error in copying the manuscripts and that 24 August was not the date Pliny orig-inally recorded.[30] Of all the days the volcano could have erupted, however, this was perhaps the most dramatic. In the Roman calendar, 24 August was the day after the Vulcanalia, an annual autumn festival during which worshippers constructed towering bonfires in honour of the fire god and tossed fish from the Tiber raw into its flames. Fire and water: give Vulcan what was ordi-narily out of his grasp, and he might be persuaded to spare the crops for harvest season. It was a cruel and insatiable god who fanned the flames of Vesuvius just a day after receiving his feast of fish.

We may never know whether Pliny was mistaken over the date of the eruption or, more likely, there was an error in the transcription of his letters. The merest possibility that Pliny might have been wrong is surprising because he was by nature extremely meticulous. His was a logical rather than a creative mind: attuned to detail and hard fact, obedient to protocol. Where his uncle was creative, Pliny was pedantic. You can tell from his prose how much care he took in finding the right phrase to express himself. Whereas Pliny the Elder was economical with his words but prone to write in sentences which changed direction with his every thought, Pliny favoured a more methodical and measured style, which reflected his occupation and approach to life more generally.

Less than a year after the eruption, at the age of eighteen, Pliny embarked upon a career as a lawyer in the Centumviral Court.[31] The centre for civil cases, the court was based within the Basilica Iulia, a beautiful multi-storeyed building in the Forum Romanum. Although it was eclipsed in Republican times by other courts, the Centumviral was now considered one of the most important in Rome.[32] Its work was highly technical and required Pliny to examine disputes arising over wills and inheritance and tackle cases of extortion and fraud. Though nominally a 'Court of One Hundred Men', who were arranged over four tribunals, the number of jurors often by now reached 180, and there was plenty of space besides for spectators.

There were few places where oratory counted for so much, for it was the jury who cast votes to determine the verdict of each case. There was a board of 'Ten Men' to preside over the panels of the court, and an interested emperor could overturn a verdict if he believed that it had been unfairly influenced, but responsibility for the delivery of justice lay principally with the lawyer and jury. Pliny was elected to the presiding board but also delivered speeches for the prosecution or defence. The main principles of the law he practised dated back to the fifth century BC, and although, as a senator, he had a role in shaping new laws authorised by the emperor into decrees, the focus in his letters is rather on his speeches and the characters he encountered in the courtrooms.[33] Pliny called the Centumviral Court his 'arena', evoking the world of blood sports.[34] There was no having recourse to the kind of statutes used today. His success depended on his strength of argument and performance.

'Risk-taker' was not the first word anyone would have used to describe Pliny, but as an orator this was what he aspired to be. He viewed his profession as an opportunity to spread his name far and wide, and understood that his reputation depended upon what people remembered of his speeches.[35] He likened the sort of rhetoric he tried to write to both the tightrope walker's art and the helmsman's skill for daring. Just as a tightrope walker summons gasps whenever she looks as though she may fall, so the orator who soars to a precipice and hovers on the very edge of possibility thrills the crowd, for the riskiest feats carry the richest rewards. The same is true of the helmsman. The one who sails a calm sea, said Pliny, will find no one waiting for him at harbour. But the one who puts in with his sail ropes shrieking, his mast bent, his rudder groaning, is 'almost put on a level with the gods of the sea'.[36]

The difficulty for Pliny was that the Court of One Hundred rarely attracted the most spectacular cases. Its work was necessary but, by Pliny's own admission, very often tedious. He despaired of the 'unknown youths' it employed as much as he did of the applauding rent-a-crowds who received bribes for attending 'in the middle of the basilica, as openly as if they were being given in the dining room'.[37] Only occasionally did Pliny land an opportunity to thrill the masses. He was once presented with a case involving a woman named Attia Viriola, her octogenarian father, and her father's new lover. Following a ten-day romance, the elderly man had brought home 'a step-mother' for Attia, whose patrimony he now sought to take away. As Pliny prepared to speak in Attia's defence, 180 jurors and almost as many spectators arrived at the basilica and proceeded to fill its benches and galleries. Pliny was surprised to find the members of the jury as divided as they were, some wholly sympathetic to the daughter, others unable to conceal their admiration for her spry father. But then he delivered his speech which, by his own account, was as intricately crafted as the

46

armour that Vulcan forged for Aeneas in Virgil's epic. With an eye to capturing the vividness of the poet, Pliny had composed a long speech 'sustained by the amount of material, and its expressive structure, and the many little flights of narrative, and the variety of the style'.[38] It was a triumph. The case was settled in favour of the daughter.

For all its shortcomings, the Court of One Hundred offered Pliny a valuable arena in which to rehearse his most daring oratorical leaps. He modelled himself on not only Virgil but the greatest orators of history: Demosthenes, Cicero, and Calvus. Demosthenes had been a politician and formidable orator in fourth-century BC Athens and established himself as the master of the comprehensive but perfectly structured argument. Calvus had flourished as both an orator and a poet in Catullus' set in the first century BC and impressed Pliny with the sheer force of his words. For 'rhetorical flourishes', meanwhile, Pliny turned to Cicero.[39]

When Pliny wasn't mining the orators' texts for inspiration, he was looking to the weather. Snow was best. 'Driven and continuous and plentiful, divinely inspired and heavenly,' it seemed to offer itself up as a model for the daring speech-writer.[40] First came the blizzard, the storm of words. Then the let-up in the spate that allowed the finest phrases to melt into a jury's ears. Finally, ice might be extracted from the slush and driven into them 'like a sword at the body – for so a speech is impressed upon the mind by equal thrust and pause'.[41] Snow may be incessant, but it is too varied in its consistency to be monotonous. Just as no one can stem snowfall, so Pliny believed no one ought to limit an orator or cut him short mid-flow.

He liked to remember how Odysseus stood as stiff as a skittle in the *Iliad*, but when he 'spoke from his big chest his words were like the snowflakes of winter, and no other mortal could then rival Odysseus'.[42] Such was the power of his words that they also turned those who heard them into melting snow. On returning home to Ithaca, as Pliny knew, Odysseus came before his wife Penelope in the disguise of a beggar and told her a false story that made her weep in remembrance for the husband she thought was lost to her:

> As she listened her tears fell and her complexion melted.
> Just as snow melts away on mountain peaks when the
> West Wind pours it down and the South-East Wind melts it
> And as it melts the rivers swell and flow,
> So tears snowed down and melted her beautiful cheeks
> As she wept for the man who was at her side.[43]

Odysseus was a perfect model for Pliny. He showed him that, if the most innocent skies can deliver the greatest snowstorms, then the most unprepossessing men can deliver the greatest speeches. A slight man himself, Pliny took considerable comfort in the idea that even epithet-rich Odysseus cut an unpromising figure of an orator to begin with.

Indeed, Pliny liked to throw what little weight he had into his delivery, as if conscious to avoid Odysseus' stiffness. He would imagine that he was planting ideas as he spoke like the seeds he sowed each winter: 'barley, beans and other legumes'.[44] Pliny received his initial training under a teacher of rhetoric named Quintilian who was a firm believer in the power of hand gestures. In a detailed treatise he described several which involved bringing the fingers into contact with the thumb in a sort of plucking motion.[45] By stretching out his arms, plucking seeds from the air, and scattering them over an invisible trench, Pliny would give a visual demonstration of what little law and landowning held in common. It was rare he could bring his worlds together, but here he tried, combining what he had learned in the fields of his country estate near Perugia with what he had learned in the rhetoric schools of Rome. Nature had taught him to treat his oratory as he did his grain so as to prepare himself for every eventuality. 'There are no fewer unanticipated and uncertain stratagems for the judges than there are for the weather and soil,' he explained to Tacitus.[46] And so in the courtroom he would reach around, scattering his enquiry as widely as the seeds upon his farms, and reaping whatever happened to take.

In Pliny's eyes such thoroughness was a virtue because it guaranteed that he would alight upon all the important aspects of a case and bring justice to bear. For others, his conscientious approach suggested a blindness, a lack of instinct, an inability to get to the heart of the matter through intuition alone. Marcus Aquilius Regulus, one of Pliny's contemporaries at the Court of One Hundred, thought fit to taunt him:

'You think all angles ought to be pursued during a case, but I see the jugular straight away, and go for it.'

'But what you think is the jugular might well be the knee or the ankle,' Pliny wittily retorted. 'I can't see the jugular,' he continued, with less embarrassment than pride, 'so I try everything, explore everything, "I leave no stone unturned", as the Greeks say.'[47]

Of all the many things that troubled Pliny about the court in which they both worked, Regulus troubled him most of all. He despised him and his aggressive jugular-grasping approach to the law. In his boyhood Regulus had seen his father go into exile and his property be handed over to his creditors.[48] As far as Pliny could discern, Regulus had spent the rest of his life trying to compensate for his early losses, acquiring as much money as possible by the least ethical means possible. He had been little more than a youth when he informed upon some of the most prominent men in Nero's senate and saw three of them put to death. The senator who proceeded to try to prosecute

Regulus in turn went so far as to accuse him of literally having an appetite for human flesh. Senator Montanus, whose party trick was to distinguish 'at first bite' whether an oyster came from the Lucrine Lake, Circeo (between Anzio and Gaeta in Italy), or from Richborough in Kent, made the incredible claim that Regulus had so despised the brother of one of the senators he had informed upon that he had paid his assassin and proceeded to take a bite out of his corpse's head.[49] Defended in court by his own brother, Regulus had been dismissed without charge.

A contemporary once called Regulus 'the most obnoxious of all two-footed creatures', which seemed about right.[50] Pliny told a story in which he characterised him as a ruthless legacy hunter. He described Regulus forcing a lady to open her will and stealing the clothes off her back. He recounted how he encouraged some doctors to prolong a man's life just long enough for him to change his will before asking them why they persisted in 'torturing' the poor man by keeping him alive.[51] 'Legacy-hunting' – known to the Romans as *captatio* – was a common enough crime for Pliny's words to have had the ring of truth. Members of the Court of One Hundred had a responsibility to protect the sanctity of wills, not corrupt them. Pliny's gossip about Regulus showed just how deeply he cared about some of the less sensational work of their court.

Pliny could never understand how Regulus managed to attract to the courtroom the crowds he did. He had 'weak lungs, garbled speech, a stammer, he is very slow to make connections, has no memory, indeed he has nothing except a mad creativity'.[52] He was jittery and pale and so bad at memorising his speeches that he relied upon writing them down.[53] Pliny disapproved of reading speeches aloud because he believed that an orator needed his hands and eyes to be free in order engage the crowd.[54]

Regulus cut not only a dull figure but a ridiculous one; he insisted on wearing an eye patch – over his right eye if he was speaking for the prosecution and over his left if for the defence. A sign of gross superstition, his patch also had the useful effect of reminding him which side he was speaking for.[55] He used to consult soothsayers on the outcome of his cases and examine livers for signs of future prosperity. Pliny once caught him in the process of divining his own fortune. Having discovered a double set of entrails inside a sacrificial animal, Regulus boasted that he would not be worth 60 million sesterces, as he had originally predicted, but twice that. Pliny did not doubt him.[56] He was considerably richer than Pliny. Among his many properties Regulus kept gardens with exquisite statues and enormous colonnades on the banks of the Tiber.[57] One day he was very nearly killed by a collapsing colonnade on the 'road to the chill heights of Herculean Tibur, where white Albula is vaporous with sulphurous waters'.*

But for all Pliny cared, Regulus might have been crushed and 'dispersed' like the columns 'in a cloud of dust'.[58]

---

* When later Regulus passed away, Pliny said: 'Regulus did well to die; it would have been better if he had died sooner.'

THREE

To Be Alive is to Be Awake

If you have a garden in your library, you'll lack nothing
Cicero, Ad Familiares, 9.4

Pliny the Elder had lived as breathlessly as he died. An exception to his own rule that 'there is nothing in Nature that does not like the change provided by holidays, after the example of day and night', he had worked through darkness and daylight.[1]

He was not like the beasts of burden who 'enjoy rolling around when they're freed from the yoke', or the dogs who do the same after the chase, or the tree that 'rejoices to be relieved of its continuous weight, like a man recovering his breath'. Believing that a moment away from his books was a moment wasted, Pliny the Elder had developed an extraordinary ability to study in any situation: not only while he ate and while he sunbathed, but even while he was rubbed down after his bath (he used to pause only for the bath itself). On one occasion when he was taking notes over dinner, a guest deigned to correct the pronunciation of the slave who was reading to them from a book: 'But you must have understood him?' Pliny the Elder asked. 'Then why did you make him repeat the word? We have lost at least ten verses because of your interruption!'[2] Pliny remembered how he used to chastise him for walking everywhere when he might have travelled by sedan chair, as he did, 'You could avoid losing those hours!'

After his spell of writing inoffensive grammar books during the latter years of Nero's reign, Pliny the Elder had found a new direction in his studies, completing a history of modern Rome begun by a historian named Aufidius Bassus and finally getting down to work on the *Natural History*. The change in his routine had come about with the rise of a new dynasty of emperors under Vespasian in AD 69. The scion of an 'obscure' family of tax collectors, Vespasian was a senator and exemplary military man and one of the most capable of Nero's generals. He had already commanded a legion in Germania and conducted a tour of Britain – where 'he brought under [Roman] control two very powerful tribes and over twenty towns and the Isle of Wight, which is next to Britain' – when Nero sent him east to quell a Jewish uprising.[3]

Tensions had been escalating ever since Emperor Augustus established Judaea as a Roman province in AD 6. Claudius had attempted to relieve hostilities between Jews and Gentiles across Alexandria and Caesarea, and granted power over Judaea to King Herod Agrippa, grandson of Herod the Great. But the death of the king in AD 44 and reversion of Judaea to a Roman province had deepened the troubles both there and in Rome, and in AD 66 the Jews, long frustrated at being subject to Roman control and taxation, finally revolted.[4] The trigger to what would be known as the Jewish War came when Nero's governor seized funds from the Temple of Jerusalem. In a bid to restore stability amid the ensuing riots, the Roman governor of Syria led his forces towards the city but ultimately withdrew in defeat. The Romans could delay no longer.

Pliny the Elder was probably in Rome when Vespasian left for Galilee with intentions of proceeding south and eventually capturing Jerusalem.[5] He was about a year into the war when his forces laid siege to Jotapata (Yodfat). The commander of the Jews, Josephus, later recounted the events in his *Jewish War*.[6] He described how he avoided being killed by his men for his desire to surrender to the Romans rather than die. If the Romans were willing to show mercy and spare them, he said, then they ought to show mercy to themselves. The circumstances in which suicide might be considered permissible would continue to be debated by Jews down the centuries, as indeed they would in the Christian Church (the most sustained argument against Christian suicide would come in St Augustine's *City of God* in the fifth century).[7]

Josephus presented suicide as a crime against nature and impiety against God: since the soul is immortal and part of the divinity, and life a gift from God, then it ought to be God's decision as to when to take it away. His description of Jewish suicides entering the darkness might well have reminded Romans of the souls of suicides wandering Hades in Virgil's *Aeneid*. Josephus failed to shake the Jews of their resolve. He therefore suggested that they take lots to kill one another so as to avoid dying by their own hands. Lots were duly taken, but when Josephus emerged as one of the last two to have to die, he ensured he did not have to by surrendering to the Romans. As if in possession of a divine prophecy, he addressed Vespasian as though he were already emperor, allegedly thereby sowing the seed of his ambition.

Around a year later, in AD 68, came news that Nero had died. Years of cruelty and overspending had left him isolated. Abandoned by his guard, he was recalled to Rome only to be declared an enemy of the state by the senate. He avoided brutal execution by taking a dagger to his own throat. Nero's death without issue left a power vacuum into which men poured like lava. AD 69 went down in history as the 'Year of the Four Emperors' and 'almost the last year of the state', as civil war broke out over the succession.[8] First to succeed Nero was Galba, governor of Hispania Tarraconensis, the easternmost of Rome's provinces in Spain. The Praetorian Guard assassinated him after seven months and installed his deputy, Otho, in his place. Otho ruled for three months. The Roman legions replaced him with their commander Vitellius. Finally, Vespasian was hailed emperor by his troops. He was fortunate enough to have the support of the governors of Egypt and Syria and the benefit of a strong army, who defeated Vitellius' men at Cremona in northern Italy. As Vespasian assumed power with the blessing of the senate at Rome, his son Titus set about completing the conquest of Judaea.

Pliny the Elder had come to know Titus well as a young man. Born in about AD 39 to Vespasian and his wife in a 'pokey dark bedroom' in a 'squalid' seven-storeyed building in Rome, he had grown up at the imperial court with Claudius' son Britannicus in a rare conferral of honour.[9] Although the young Titus was said to have been rather too keen on eunuchs and parties, he soon redeemed himself through his military prowess.[10] Having impressed everyone around him with his 'receptiveness to learning almost all the arts of war and peace' and skill in arms and horsemanship, he left for Germania, which was where he met Pliny the Elder.[11]

Following his campaign against the tribe of the Chatti, Pliny the Elder had returned to the region once more with the Roman army. In the course of his travels he came to Vetera, modern Xanten, near the Rhine, the very camp where Drusus had established his headquarters in 11 BC. Remarkably, some horse trappings bearing Pliny the Elder's name and post were discovered at the site in the nineteenth century. Made of brass overlaid in silver, the adornments are exquisitely detailed. Several roundels, four of which feature portrait heads, are connected by chains which would have fitted to the harness of the horse. The roundel inscribed with Pliny the Elder's name has at its centre a portrait of a wide-eyed man with a fringe. Was this a stylised portrait of Pliny the Elder? Could the roundel have hung from his horse? It is very tempting to picture the trapping flapping around Pliny the Elder's shins as he stormed through the thick German forests. While it is possible that the portrait does indeed show Pliny the Elder, it is more likely to depict Emperor Claudius or the young Nero.[12] Inscribed with the names of two further men besides, the trappings might well have belonged to Pliny the Elder before being passed down to officers stationed under his command.[13] Whether the object passed through Pliny the Elder's hands or not, it is a tantalising relic of the authority he had attained in the Roman cavalry at the time he met the young Titus.

When Pliny the Elder came to write his encyclopaedia, he reflected fondly on Titus as his former *contubernalis*, or 'tent-mate'. It is a pity that he did not describe in his *Natural History* the kind of life they shared in Germania. The period was evidently instructive for them both, and Titus would not forget Pliny the Elder when he became emperor two decades later. In the short term, his experience in a German camp must have been valuable preparation for the military career that he pursued under his father in the Jewish War. Once Vespasian had embarked upon his duties as emperor, Titus was entrusted with leading the legions to besiege Jerusalem, where fighting had broken out between rival groups of Zealots. As a struggle ensued between the Jews and Roman forces in AD 70, the Temple of Jerusalem was set alight. Treasures salvaged from the flames were carried to Rome and paraded the following year when Titus and Vespasian celebrated a joint triumph for their efforts. By the time the Jewish War ended with the siege of Masada in AD 73–4, hundreds of thousands of Jews, maybe more, had lost their lives. Josephus, the Jew who had predicted Vespasian's rise, enjoyed the rare privilege of living out the rest of his life in Rome as a Roman citizen.

Pliny the Elder did not describe the atrocities of the Jewish War in his encyclopaedia. The closest he came to acknowledging the destruction the Romans wreaked was when he referred to the former town of Engadda as 'second to Jerusalem in fertility and palm groves, now another funeral pyre'.[14] Masada was merely 'a fortress on a rock'. Judaea was evoked to provide context for descriptions of the discovery or trade of plants such as its native balsam.[15] Pliny the Elder did however experience Vespasian's rule from close quarters. The death of Nero and return of relative stability to Rome after the catastrophic Year of the Four Emperors enabled him to emerge from his quietude and earn a place on the imperial council. Every morning in the city, *clientes* ('clients') paid a formal greeting or *salutatio* to their patrons in the halls of their homes. Pliny the Elder, who made a habit of rising soon after midnight in the autumn and winter months, was among those who attended the emperor. An 'early riser' himself, Vespasian received his greeting before he had so much as put on his shoes.[16] Once the meeting was adjourned and he had dealt with any necessary business, Vespasian would return to bed, usually with one of his concubines (he was already a widower when he came to power).

Having re-established control over Judaea, Vespasian was determined to put the empire back on an even keel. Increasing – and in some cases doubling – the tribute which the provinces owed Rome, he earned a reputation for cupidity, but went some way towards recovering the financial losses Rome had suffered through Nero's profligacy.[17] Pliny the Elder played an increasingly important role in his administration. In the seventies AD, he was appointed to a series of civil posts or 'procuratorships' overseas. Although the details of his employments are unknown, he is said to have 'conducted very splendid and continuous procuratorships with the utmost integrity', one of which took him to Tarraconensis, the largest Roman province in Hispania, to oversee the imperial finances.[18]

Between his work for the imperial council and his promotion following his procuratorships to the admiralty of the fleet, Pliny the Elder had little time for conducting his own research. He had no more opportunity to pursue his own interests when, in AD 79, Vespasian died at the age of sixty-nine, anticipating his posthumous deification with the words: 'I think I'm becoming a god.'[19] His successor, Titus, was only too pleased to retain his former tent-mate in the imperial administration. Pliny the Elder had little choice but to persevere with his studies in the rare hours he had to himself. As he explained to the new emperor, he dedicated his days to him, and his nights to producing his encyclopaedia.[20]

A furious night-writer, Pliny the Elder was fortunate to possess what his nephew called 'a sharp intellect, incomparable concentration, and formidable ability to stay awake'.[21] There were moments when he nodded off during the day, but these were as nothing to the time other people wasted. If his passion for night-writing was born of necessity, then it was driven by the need he felt to make the most of the time he had. Humans are not wronged by the fact that their lives are brief, he wrote, but do wrong by spending the life they do have asleep. For to sleep is to lose half of one's allotted time – more than half, given that infancy, ailing old age, indeed the hours lost to insomnia, cannot truly constitute living.[22] He went so far as to establish a memorable formula to express these beliefs. *Vita vigilia est*, he wrote: 'To be alive is to be awake.'[23]

The idea was a logical solution to a theme found in Homer. If wakefulness was life, then it was because sleep was akin to death. The Homeric epics taught that Sleep and Death were brothers. When Zeus's mortal son Sarpedon falls at Troy in the

Iliad, Sleep and Death carry his body from the battlefield. A painting of them straining beneath the weight of the warrior's bleeding corpse became the unlikely adornment for a wine bowl in the late sixth century BC.[24] The brothers are formidable figures, with richly textured wings, armoured body plates and long dark beards. One grasps Sarpedon's legs, the other his gigantic shoulders, while blood gushes from his wounds like wine from a ruptured wine skin. Distributing his weight between them, Sleep and Death raise him from the ground as the god Hermes watches. There is life in Sarpedon's tendons yet, but his head is slumped, the final insult to the divine father who could not save him. To preserve what is left of his dignity, Sleep and Death must carry his body to his native Lycia for burial.

Sleep and Death were united in Pliny the Elder's mind in the same way as they were on the archaic pot. They were strange and inimitable brothers, shadows of one another, complementing each other in their work. To embrace Sleep as the brother of Death was to recognise wakefulness as the sister of life. It was by doing precisely this that Pliny the Elder was able to complete his encyclopaedia in time to dedicate it to Titus. 'You are to me such as you were in camp as my tent-mate,' he wrote to him in the preface. 'Not even the improvement in your fortunes has changed you, except in so far as you can now bestow as much as you want to.'[25]

Titus was given the opportunity to prove his generosity when, just a few months after he succeeded his father as emperor, Vesuvius erupted. Faced with the cruel task of recovering his empire from ruin, he proved himself to be a man of the utmost pragmatism. Although there was no straightforward way of rebuilding the cities when the foundations were so unstable, Titus hastened to the disaster zone and appointed a pair of senators to plan the restoration of the few salvageable buildings and oversee the construction of new ones. The property of those who had died without issue was harnessed to fund the relief effort. The imperial purse made no profit from the tragedy.[26] Titus' clemency in the wake of the disaster was the kindest tribute he could have paid the learned friend who, after a lifetime of being awake, had finally been carried off in the arms of Sleep and Death.

Pliny the Elder had pushed the boundaries of mortal achievement. His publication of over 20,000 pieces of information exceeded anything his predecessors had produced. His encyclopaedia was an attempt to overcome the frailty of human life and human memory: a record of everything man had learned and risked losing through neglect and the passage of time. It was his most precious legacy, evidence of how much one could do when one's life was structured in a certain way.

Pliny longed to establish a comparable legacy for himself. 'Day and night,' he wrote, as often quoting Virgil, 'I think "how I too might raise myself from the earth"; for that would fulfil and indeed surpass my prayer "to fly victorious over the lips of men".'[27] Another man might have been anxious to keep such ambitions to himself, but Pliny felt no shame in front of his friends and relatives. The poet Martial had found him bent over his desk enough times at his home on the Esquiline Hill to issue a warning to others against disturbing him in the middle of the day. In a poem Pliny recorded in his letters, Martial advised his reader:

> Don't you knock on his clever door
> Drunk and whenever suits you.
> He gives all his days over to gloomy Minerva
> While he prepares for the ears of the One Hundred
> This speech, which the coming ages can
> Liken to the pages of Cicero himself.
> Safer to go when the lamps burn low.
> This is your hour, when Bacchus is frenzied,

When the rose is triumphant, the hair wet with unguent.
At that hour even a dour Cato would read me.[28]

Martial's teasing poem provided Pliny with further incentive to exchange unguents for ink. For all that Pliny admired his wit – he was 'original, incisive, and sharp' – he doubted whether Martial would achieve his own dream of living forever 'on the lips of men'.

Almost a quarter of a century Pliny's senior, Martial came from Bilbilis, in the Aragon region of modern Spain, but had established himself as a keen satirist of Rome. He wrote as enthusiastically of everyday life in the city – its dinners, its gossip, its most notorious fiends – as he did of its architecture. His poetry captured the rhythm of the times with an ease and humour that is often absent from Pliny's letters. Yet Pliny could not help but wonder what interest there would be in the characters Martial skewered in his poems when he was dead and gone. Martial might reasonably have wondered how he fared in Pliny's estimation and would no doubt have been surprised at his modest hopes for his legacy. Pliny was so outwardly supportive of him that he even paid for him to make a journey home. Perturbed that poets no longer received money or promotion for their praise poetry, as they had in ancient times, Pliny had endeavoured to compensate Martial, if only 'out of respect for our friendship and the verses which he had composed about me'. It is little thanks to Pliny that Martial remains one of the most popular poets of ancient Rome.[29]

Had Martial followed his own advice and waited until the lamps burned low in Pliny's house, he would still have found him working. Bacchus was seldom frenzied when Pliny was in Rome. He was still stoppered and, if Pliny had his way, destined to remain so for as long as there were hours he could steal from night and day. Inspired by his uncle's choice of life over deadly sleep, Pliny had established a rigorous routine of his own. In the winter months he rose early, albeit some hours later than his uncle, and worked continuously throughout the day, dispensing with both the afternoon siesta and after-dinner entertainment he normally enjoyed in summer in order to persevere with his notes. His uncle had shielded his hands from the cold with gloves, 'so that not even the bitterness of the weather could snatch any time away from his studies'.[30] Pliny relied on his underfloor heating.

There is no clearer reflection in Pliny's letters of the kind of orderly, upright and morally unblemished life he aspired to live than in his descriptions of his occasional dinners. Pliny was almost irritatingly exacting about their composition. However much he tried to make light of it with his friends, there was no concealing the pedant inside him:

To Septicius Clarus,

How dare you! You promise to come to dinner, but never show up? Here's your sentence: you shall reimburse the full costs to the penny. They're not small. We had prepared: a lettuce each, three snails, two eggs, spelt with honeyed wine and snow (you shall pay for this too, a particular expense since it melts into the dish), olives, beetroot, gourds, onions, and many other choice items. You would have heard a comedy or a reader or a lyre-player or – if I was feeling generous – all three. But you no doubt chose instead to dine with someone who gave you oysters, womb of sow, sea urchins and dancing girls from Cadiz . . .

Plinius.[31]

Lettuce, snails, eggs, spelt, snow, olives, onions: these were Pliny's hors d'oeuvres. Too frugal to be particularly appetising and too precise in their arrangement to put a man at ease, they were the plate form of his considered and compartmentalised life.[32] Lettuce, sown upon the winter solstice, was served to aid digestion, promote sleep, and regulate the appetite ('no other food stimulates the palate more while also curbing it').[33] Eggs soothed the stomach and throat. Olives were picked for salt, and onions sliced for sweetness. Not too much of anything. Each ingredient was self-contained and recognisable to the Roman eye, the snow alone seeping everywhere.

Snow imagery was not uncommon in Pliny's work in the years following the eruption of Vesuvius. At once a symbol of force and frailty, snow acquired a fresh resonance in his life, featuring as prominently in his oratory as it did on his dinner plates. On one level, Pliny permitted this 'particular expense' because it illustrated his commitment to variety. Long before William Cowper declared, in his poem of 1785, that 'Variety's the very spice of life,/ That gives it all its flavour', Pliny forged a culinary metaphor for the merits of alternation. He had a friend who seemed to spend his life doing nothing. 'For how long will your shoes go nowhere, your toga be on holiday and your day be completely empty?' Pliny asked him.[34] 'If I were to make you dinner,' he continued, 'I would mix the savoury and spicy foods with sweet.'

In reality, Pliny struck more balance in his menus than he did in his daily routine. Like his uncle before him, he prioritised work over everything else, food included. The snow was his one extravagance which, in its habit of losing form and metamorphosing into valueless water, must have reminded him of how consuming but unstable life and its luxuries could be. The Romans used both snow and ice to refrigerate food during transit but also, as Pliny did, to chill their drinks. Pliny the Elder found the use of snow to chill wine in summer particularly offensive because to 'turn the curse of mountains into a pleasure for the throat' in this season meant that thought had been given as to how to keep the snow cold for the other months.[35] This made the serving of snow not a simple act of recklessness, but a conscious and determined inversion of Nature.

In the sixteenth century, the essayist Michel de Montaigne observed that the ancients also had 'cellars of snow to cool their wine; and some there were who made use of snow in winter, not thinking their wine cool enough, even at that cold season of the year'.[36] Among the classical quotations Montaigne had inscribed upon the roof beams of his chateau in Bordeaux was the following, adapted from the *Natural History*:

> *solum certum nihil esse certi*
> *et homine nihil miserius aut superbius*

> The only certainty is that nothing is certain
> And nothing more miserable or arrogant than man.

These words hung over Montaigne's meditative life.[37] They spoke as hauntingly to him in Renaissance France as they did to their first readers, encapsulating the idea that, of all living things, man alone struggles to accept the capriciousness of fate. Man's desire and quest for certainty is presumptuous and arrogant; his eternal failure to achieve it, a recipe for misery.

Given his thoughts on uncertainty, we might have expected Pliny the Elder to have been the one to promote snow as a paradigm for human fortune. But it was to his nephew's credit that he went beyond his uncle's moralising to present snow as not merely a luxury, but as something as changeable as life itself. Pliny the Elder and Montaigne saw man's successes in preserving snow throughout the seasons. Pliny saw rather his failures. He might strive for certainty, protecting his snow from the heat so that it retained its shape, but as someone who served snow at dinner parties, he knew only too well that even the best efforts failed. Whether it took one hour or one day, snow always melted away.

For all his uncle's distaste for it and the similarity it bore to the ash that had eventually killed him, snow did not develop in Pliny's mind the negative associations that it might have done. Pliny reserved his disapproval instead for the luxuries he believed to be more damaging to morality. Snow seemed less offensive in this regard than the fruits of the sea it was sometimes served with, in what his uncle viewed as a wanton 'mixing of mountaintops and seabed'.[38] In his encyclopaedia, Pliny the Elder had expressed a particular dislike of the combining of oysters and 'snow' – probably in this case crushed ice – as a delicacy. Ignoring the benefits of snow as a preservative, Pliny the Elder focused on how extravagant and unnatural it was that anyone should intrude upon two ends of the earth for the sake of satisfying his stomach. An oyster at the bottom of the ocean is no more likely to encounter snow than a snow-capped mountain is to host an oyster.[39]

Pages and pages of the *Natural History* were dedicated to expounding the dangers and ubiquity of seafood. In the fourth century BC, a poet from Sicily named Archestratus had published a collection of exotic recipes for shellfish in his Greek poem, 'On the Life of Luxury'. Shellfish had been spreading their poison across the Greek world and into Rome for centuries. 'It wasn't enough,' Pliny the Elder despaired, 'that the gifts of the sea were being pushed down our throats before they were worn on the hands, ears, head, and all over the body by men as much as by women.'[40] The sea creatures corrupted with their treasures as much as with their taste: oysters yielded their glistening pearls to grasping fishermen, while one species of predatory murex mollusc secreted a substance, which was used by the wealthy to dye their garments 'Tyrian' purple.

Pliny the Elder related that Alexander the Great and his men had encountered oysters a foot long in the seas off India. Although the Romans had not yet been so fortunate, they knew of oysters large enough to merit the name 'Three Bites'.[41] The encyclopaedist had studied oysters closely and concluded that their growth depended not only upon the moon, which controlled the tides, but also upon the progress of the seasons. The oyster as he describes it in his encyclopaedia opens its shell at the beginning of summer, as the heat of the first sun penetrates the water. As it does so, it is as though it is 'yawning', an image that is all the more striking for the fact that the oyster's head is 'indistinguishable' and lacks eyes.[42] In the heat, the oyster begins to swell with a milk-like juice – a sort of dew that it absorbs and incubates to produce pearls. (In actual fact, oysters can be hermaphroditic and switch between the two genders, developing pearls when layers of nacre build up around foreign bodies trapped in their shells.)

Oysters in deeper waters are small, wrote Pliny the Elder, because it is dark and 'in their sadness they look less for food'.[43] Their depression was presumably only deepened by the fact that they were also the first to be searched for fine pearls (the finest were often found far beneath the surface). Quite the best thing about pearls is that no two are the same: in Latin, a pearl is sometimes called simply *unio*, 'uniqueness', whence 'onion', a vegetable of iridescent layers. A pearl, said Pliny the Elder, may take on the cloudiness of morning sky or be aborted or 'miscarried' by a storm; the oyster is so alarmed by thunder that it will slam its shell shut before the pearl is fully formed. If the weather is sunny, the pearl may develop a reddish hue, losing its whiteness 'like the human body' suffering sunburn.[44] (He similarly believed that Ethiopians had been scorched by their proximity to the sun, while inhabitants of icy climates had white skin and fair hair.[45]) On this logic, Pliny the Elder attributed reddish pearls to sunny Spain, tawny pearls to Illyricum, in the Balkans, and black pearls and oyster shells to stormy Circeo in Italy.[46]

Pliny the Elder could not take credit for being the first man to speak of the oyster and pearl's susceptibility. Over a century before him, Sergius Orata, the first Italian to cultivate oyster farms at decadent Baiae in the Bay of Naples, had taken to transporting oysters from Brundisium (Brindisi) in Italy's heel and depositing them in the Lucrine Lake in Campania.[47] Once the oysters, ordinarily farmed on ropes, had absorbed the lake's delicious waters, it did not matter where they started life. Their high price depended on people's belief in their ability to absorb the richness of their surroundings.

Pliny the Elder had not liked the idea of Romans risking their lives to retrieve oysters from the depths when they might have grown all they needed in simple kitchen gardens. If he quaffed the occasional one it was not because he aspired to eat 'the palm of our tables'.[48] Provided an oyster was good – sealed, not too slimy, not too meaty, more striking for its thickness than diameter, caught neither in mud nor on sand but on a hard surface like a rock – he believed that the odd one might benefit his health. Oysters, he said, can settle the stomach and soften the bowels, restore the appetite and plump the skin, purge ulcers from the bladder, chase chilblains from the toes, and reduce the size of swollen glands.[49] The oyster was therefore a paradox. Luxurious on the one hand and healing on the other, it defied the kind of clear moral classification that Pliny the Elder liked to apply to the things around him. While the oyster was multifarious enough to earn his interest, Pliny the Elder was on balance reproachful: 'There is no greater cause for the destruction of morals and rise of luxury than shellfish.'[50] Given his friends' manners, his nephew Pliny was inclined to agree.

In his abstemiousness and censoriousness towards shellfish, Pliny proved himself to be very much his uncle's son. When his friend and fellow equestrian Septicius Clarus failed to show at his snow-and-spelt dinner, he assumed it had been because he had gone after the oysters and sea urchins on offer elsewhere. It was not like him to be tempted away by oysters: Pliny counted no one in his acquaintance 'truer or more straightforward, accomplished or trustworthy'.[51] On close enough terms with Pliny to have him assist in promoting his nephew to the senate, Septicius must have taken his teasing letter in good grace. Sue him for every morsel of food he had missed? He must be joking. The few surviving details of Septicius' life shed light on his respectability. He was named as the dedicatee of Pliny's collected letters as well as the most important biographical work of the age, Suetonius' *Lives of the Caesars*.

Some years after Pliny's death, Septicius Clarus and Suetonius travelled to Britain. Following their landings under Claudius, the Romans had suppressed the revolt of Boudicca in AD 60 or 61 and worked their way steadily northwards to conquer much of England and Wales. In AD 122, Trajan's successor, Hadrian, launched an expedition to settle pockets of unrest and begin work on the wall that would eventually stretch from the east coast to the west and mark the northernmost frontier of the Roman empire. Septicius was praetorian prefect, Suetonius private secretary to the emperor. Both were powerful roles into which they appear to have relaxed only too easily. In the course of the British campaign they were dismissed from their posts, both allegedly on grounds of overfamiliarity with Hadrian's wife.[52] It was a late and fallible source that cited the reason for their dismissal, but it may just be that Septicius finally got his comeuppance for the shameless social climbing Pliny had scolded him for.

As for Suetonius, Pliny would have been surprised he had it in him. Before becoming a prolific author, Suetonius had cut a shy and self-doubting figure, at least when Pliny was around. He was less than ten years younger than Pliny but emerges almost boy-like from the *Letters*.[53] Reticence was his defining characteristic. Pliny once helped him to secure a small estate and, as a first step towards public office, a military tribunate, or junior post, which Suetonius passed on to a relative.[54] While Septicius Clarus 'often urged' Pliny to publish his letters, Pliny practically implored Suetonius to publish work of his own. Prior to his *Lives*, Suetonius completed a biographical compendium of famous men, including Pliny the Elder, which Pliny must have been eager to see released into the world.[55] Within their circle of mutual encouragement, Pliny confessed to being 'hesitant about publishing', but Suetonius outdid 'even' him in his 'dallying and delaying'.[56]

By the time Suetonius decided to try his hand at law, he was suffering from nightmares. He must have been in his late twenties when he wrote to Pliny seeking an adjournment to a trial on the basis of having had bad dreams. A more bullish lawyer might have told him to pull himself together, but Pliny was sympathetic. A perfectionist who was 'never so prepared as to not rejoice at a delay', Pliny had also experienced dreams in the past which appeared to augur ill for his cases.[57] Around the time he embarked upon his legal career Pliny married for the first time. Nothing is known of his first wife, but he recalled in a letter how he was about to proclaim against 'very powerful citizens and even friends of the emperor' when he dreamed that his mother-in-law got down on her knees and begged him not to go through with the trial. The Romans believed that dreams merited deep consideration on the basis that they might have some bearing upon waking life. Like the Greeks before them, they realised that, while some dreams come to pass, others presage a less obvious result.

Any dream involving a mother figure was always ripe for discussion. *On the Interpretation of Dreams*, a definitive guide in five volumes, was published a generation after Pliny died and laid out what could come of nightly visits by matriarchs. The book was an important influence on Sigmund Freud, who read it before writing his *Interpretation of Dreams* in 1899, and described a number of possible scenarios. A senator like Pliny who might dream of having sex with his mother had reason to rejoice, provided he had adopted the missionary position; the mother symbolised the state, and one who governed his partner sexually could be sure to govern well politically.[58] But a man of fragile health who dreamed of having sex with his mother on top, might predict his own death – for earth, Mother Earth, does not lie above the living. Such earthy thoughts could not have been further from Pliny's conscious, but at their root lay the old idea that, for all the many things a dream can symbolise, Sleep is little more than a shadow of Death.

Since adjournments were not permitted in the Court of One Hundred, Pliny had had no choice but to ignore the warning of his dream and go through with his trial. The words he had used to reassure himself then were the words he used now to reassure Suetonius: 'The best thing is to fight for one's country.'[59] With this hearty expression of patriotism, a quote from Homer's *Iliad*, the young Pliny had stormed into the basilica, confronted the opposition, and promptly won his case. He recommended that Suetonius did the same. If his dream rendered the prospect of doing so too frightening, then Suetonius was well advised to interpret it to a better outcome. As Homer had illustrated, dreams were meaningful or meaningless depending on which of two gates they issued from. There was a gate made of horn and another of ivory. Dreams which poured through the ivory gate, according to Odysseus' wife Penelope, were empty. But those which passed through the horn gate 'bring the truth to pass whenever a mortal sees them'.[60] It was to the gate of ivory, through which 'the spirits of the dead send false dreams towards the sky', that Aeneas and the Sibyl were led as they prepared to leave Hades in Virgil's *Aeneid*.[61] By departing through the gate of false dreams it was as if their journey to the land of the dead had never happened.

Pliny anticipated that Suetonius might still struggle and told him that he would attempt to delay his case. 'It's difficult, but I'll try,' he promised, for as Homer said, 'a dream is from Zeus.'[62] The line was a wry comment on the difficulty of interpreting one's own dreams, for as he knew only too well, even dreams from Zeus could be deceptive. In the *Iliad*, Agamemnon, commander of the Greek army, was famously deceived into thinking that he could take Troy at once after the King of Pylos appeared to speak to him in a dream.[63] On waking he decided first to test his men's resolve by encouraging them to abandon the war and return home, since they had no hope of sacking Troy. Far from rejecting his plan and rallying to fight all the more defiantly, his soldiers shamefully got up to leave. It was up to Odysseus to talk them into staying. There was no chance of concluding the war after nine years in a single day. The dream was false. *Vita vigilia est.*

FOUR

Solitary as an Oyster

'You are fettered,' said Scrooge, trembling. 'Tell me why?'
   'I wear the chain I forged in life,' replied the Ghost. 'I
made it link by link, and yard by yard; I girded it on of my
own free will, and of my own free will I wore it. Is its pattern
strange to *you?*'
        Charles Dickens, A *Christmas Carol*, 1843, Stave I

The festival of the Saturnalia was for most Romans, though
not for Pliny, 'the very best of days'.[1] A week of wine and
banquets, presents and practical jokes, it took place around the
solstice each December and honoured Saturn, the Roman god
of time and the seasons. Work ceased, togas were hung up, festive
robes and caps put on, bottles opened, meat sliced, dice thrown,
and roles reversed.[2] Pliny had a couple of choices as to where
to spend the holiday. He could stay in Rome and look at flamingos
from the Nile, pheasants from Georgia, guinea fowl from
Numidia (all the birds his uncle had discouraged Romans from
travelling the world to see), while feasting – in the presence of
dwarves and female gladiators – on nuts from Pontus, dates from
Palestine, plums from Damascus, figs from Ibiza, and jars upon
jars of wine.[3] Or he could travel thirty kilometres south-west to
the coast of the Tyrrhenian Sea and recline alone in a room that

'not the voices of the younger slaves, nor the murmur of the sea, nor thunder nor lightning, nor light of day could reach, provided the windows were not open'.[4] Pliny chose the latter.

There was something of Scrooge to Pliny come midwinter, 'secret, and self-contained, and solitary as an oyster'.[5] The arrival of the Saturnalia each year was his prompt to retreat to his 'Laurentine' villa and its most isolated rooms. Lying just south of Ostia, on Italy's west coast, Laurentum was close enough to Rome that he could retire there for the season 'when the day was done'.[6] Built in the early first century on layers of oyster shells – sand, mortar, oyster shells, mortar again, pottery sherds, more crushed oyster shells – the village was delightful in its rusticity.[7] Since the roads were liable to become too sandy to drive a carriage over, Pliny thought it best to complete the final leg of the journey from Rome by horse. On horseback one would gain sufficient height to see the crowns of the trees which grew in the woods inland. Emperor Tiberius had kept an elephant menagerie and guild of gamekeepers in woods around here, while an orator named Hortensius had created his own game preserve, to which he would invite friends for dinner and watch as his musician, Orpheus, summoned forth a parade of deer and wild boar to provide 'no less distinguished a spectacle . . . than when the hunts of the aediles [junior politicians] take place in the Circus Maximus without African beasts'.[8]

Elephants had always struck Pliny's uncle as closest to men in sensibility. Though less faithful than dogs and horses, they were intelligent, obedient and fired by 'a desire for love and glory'.[9] It was Pliny the Elder who first recorded their fear of mice.* He had drawn on the research of Aristotle, who had undertaken an investigation into 'the nature of animals' for his

---

* Though, according to modern research, elephants are in fact most terrified of bees, whose stings cannot penetrate their skin but can hurt their eyes and the insides of their trunks.

pupil Alexander the Great, in the fourth century BC.[10] Using information gathered from thousands of animal keepers and hunters across Greece and Asia, Aristotle had produced a comprehensive study of animals in almost fifty volumes, which Pliny the Elder commended to his readers. Aristotle described the elephant as the most well tempered and easily tamed of species, a view borne out in Pliny the Elder's description of Romans teaching the beasts to walk tightropes, memorise the Greek alphabet, and engage in gladiatorial contests in the circus.[11] Pliny, for his part, rarely found these entertainments anything other than disappointing. There was an occasion when one of his friends put on a show of exotic beasts in the amphitheatre at Verona. But owing to bad weather, the African panthers he was promised never arrived.

Victor Emmanuel II, the first king of unified Italy, is credited with rediscovering Pliny's village in 1874 when Laurentum had again become a royal hunting preserve.[12] While in Pliny's time the villa-lined seafront was said to have borne 'the appearance of many cities', the village itself was revealed to be fairly compact and unimposing. More recent excavations have exposed part of the town plan as it developed. Beyond the houses was a road that led to Rome, some public baths (Pliny said there were three), and a forum so small that a visitor might easily have missed it.[13] A few temples, a colonnade of shops, a meeting house, a restaurant with a winsome view over a fountain and public sculptures – Laurentum 'met one's basic needs'. Land near Pliny's villa provided pasture for horses, cattle, and sheep, so there must have been milk and cheese. And though the sea off Laurentum was not 'abundant in good fish', it did have sole and prawns. For more extravagant things Pliny could always go to Ostia but, for all it might have seemed otherwise, it was never for extravagance that he came here.

Laurentum was where he wrote the most.[14] He called it his

Μουσεῖον after the 'Seat of the Muses' which contained the library of ancient Alexandria, but it was distinctly Italian.[15] The Romans traced their origins to the landscapes of Laurentum. In Virgil's epic, Aeneas is said to meet his bride Lavinia here. The place was named after the laurel tree, sacred to the poetry god Apollo, that grew in the courtyard of Lavinia's father's palace.[16] Laurentum was for Pliny, too, a place of beginnings. He was descended from the Oufentina, a former tribe established in 318 BC and named after the river Oufens which flowed through it.[17] If he could not write in a villa built upon the laurel-rich land-scapes of the Romans' ancestors (not to mention his own), then he might as well have given up.

The library of his Μουσεῖον was located in the winter quarters of his villa near some bedrooms and a dining room that was angled in such a way as to retain the sun's heat, but keep out the sound of all winds 'except those which bring in the clouds'.[18] During the Saturnalia, however, not even these rooms were quiet enough. Leaving his slaves to send their 'festive cheer' echoing through the halls, Pliny retired instead to the living room, snug, bedroom with folding doors, and darkened cell which together comprised a sort of Saturnalian suite. It was this wing of his villa – not the D-shaped portico, nor the covered courtyard, nor the dining room with a view through bay windows 'as if over three seas', nor the ball court, nor the larger bedrooms, nor the walkway that 'stretched almost to the size of a public monument', nor the baths, nor the two towers with the dining rooms, bedroom and granary they contained – that he liked best.[19] He had commis-sioned the suite himself and it was his 'true love'.

Scrooge had his dark set (sitting room, bedroom, lumber room) and Pliny his private suite. The fact that the Saturnalia fell upon the solstice, when the day is that much shorter than the night, did nothing to dissuade Pliny from shutting himself away.[20] Like a diligent schoolboy concealing his prep, he would pretend to

friends that he was having a high old time revelling in the cele-
brations.[21] Not to be fooled, Tacitus sent him a book to critique,
knowing full well that it would reach him while he was still at
his desk. Tacitus assumed, if not the role of guardian to Pliny,
then that of idol and teacher, and Pliny was only too happy to
play along. He wrote back to Tacitus at once, feigning outrage
at being called 'back to school' in the middle of the holiday. For
all Pliny fantasised about posterity reflecting in wonderment that
'two men more or less equal in age and repute . . . should have
nurtured each other's work', for much of the time he felt that
he was indeed little more than Tacitus' pupil.[22] And so he sat at
his desk, fretful that he had not produced enough work to send
and thereby punish him for so knowingly summoning him back
to the classroom in midwinter.

It was tradition during the Saturnalia for slaves to be dismissed
from their chores and waited on by their masters. But not in
Pliny's house. The satisfaction of working when no one else was
seems to have outweighed any pressure Pliny felt to engage with
his staff over the holiday. His decision was perhaps more practical
than selfish. He owned at least 500 slaves across his various
properties by the time of his death.[23] Rather than spoil them
once a year he showed them his favour in other ways. Whenever
he was looking to employ one, he would make a point of relying
on his 'ears rather than eyes', believing that reputation was a
more accurate measure of a man than the state of his hair and
clothes. Every slave who entered his service was then allowed
to leave a list of instructions for his belongings to be shared
among other slaves in the household after he died.[24] Pliny was
not always kind, but he never chained his slaves, and throughout
his life freed a great many of them. He even paid for one of his
freedmen to travel to Egypt and Gaul in order to recuperate
when he became ill and started coughing up blood. Such acts
of generosity more than compensated for his reluctance to

partake in their 'idle gossip' over the Saturnalia. The slaves were free to keep their holiday in their way, provided they let Pliny keep it in his: ensconced in rooms so secret, self-contained and solitary, that he felt like he had 'left the house entirely'.[25]

The darkened rooms of the Laurentine villa proffered few distractions and, after a while, Pliny came to depend on them. At some point in his life, he developed a weakness in his eyes, a sensitivity that seemed to have been aggravated by bright light. In his efforts to soothe them he ceased reading and writing for a while and employed a slave he could dictate to instead.[26] He took long baths as if the steam might alleviate the ache. He ate a plump chicken, an unorthodox medicine sent to him by a friend. He even took to travelling in a darkened carriage and enveloping his Laurentine villa in shadow.[27] The windows of its lower walkway were closed. Heavy curtains were pulled over other offending apertures, stilled from the sea breeze and weighed down, perhaps, by the pear-shaped clay baubles which have since been excavated from the waterfront.[28]

His home became a burrow worthy of a mole, the most 'condemned' creature to have featured in his uncle's encyclopaedia. In the Natural History, the mole is likened to 'the buried dead', living as it does in perpetual blindness in the darkness underground.[29] For Pliny the Elder, the eyes were not only mirrors of the soul – an idea he borrowed from Cicero – but 'the most precious part of the body, because through their use of light they distinguish life from death'.[30] He meant this both transitively and intransitively: the eyes enable men to distinguish what is animate and what inanimate, and being able to see distinguishes a living person from a corpse. If to be alive is to be awake, then one needs eyes one can open to the light. In Latin this idea was far clearer, for lumen meant both 'eye' and 'light', and when it meant 'light' it could also mean 'life'. Both a blind man and a dead man could be said to have had 'the light stolen from him'.[31] Lamps were often placed in the tombs of the dead as if to light their journey to the Underworld.

'Lamp', too, was *lumen*. An extensive collection of lamps was discovered at the site of Pliny's villa near Perugia. Lamps made of bronze and clay. Lamps adorned with gladiators and hunters. Lamps with wild boar, deer, and dogs running round their bases. One even featured a detailed study of a nude woman reclining seductively on a bed.[32] The warm glow of these oil lamps may have been less offensive to Pliny's sore eyes than sunlight, but it did nothing to elevate him among the living. The seven sisters of the Pleiades, which were said to appear in the sky in winter, at the beginning of summer, and at the coming of plough time, were too dim to brighten the mole-like hole of his Laurentine set.[33] Even with 'the remedy revealed by Nature for the darkness' – the light of the moon – Pliny was working largely in the dark.[34] Never did it occur to him that his sensitivity to daylight might be a symptom of his eye pain, and reading in the dark, its cause. Although the worst of the discomfort appears to have subsided, it is doubtful Pliny's eyes recovered fully as he persisted in working by night.

That so thin a veil should exist between life and death had not frightened Pliny the Elder, who had come to believe that, when we die, we are as sensationless of body and soul as we are before we are born. Were we not, he asked, then what rest would we ever find?[35] It was a pertinent question for a man who never rested in his lifetime. Pliny the Elder took a dim and unforgiving view of those who believed they could come back after they died, because to believe that this was possible meant believing that humans are at least partly immortal, and to believe that was plain *vanitas*.[36] Insisting that it was better to reduce anxiety over death by remembering that we felt no anxiety before birth, he poured scorn on many stories of supernatural activity. 'Mortals,' he said, 'are ingenious at fooling themselves and drawing deceptive conclusions.'[37] Whether we speak of spirits wandering the earth or of gods taking human forms, we are forever coaxing ourselves into more comfortable modes of existence.[38]

In his trenchant dismissal of the notion of life after death, Pliny the Elder was in sympathy with the teachings of Epicureanism. Though never particularly popular in Italy, the Greek philosophy was being read at Herculaneum at the time of the eruption. A number of carbonised scrolls, as crumpled as tree bark, have been removed from the so-called Villa of the Papyri and either unravelled or read under infrared light to reveal the influence of Epicurus.

Here was a philosophy for banishing fears, particularly fears of death, which had found an important Roman proponent in the poet Lucretius in the first century BC. In a work dedicated to the fundamentals of life, Lucretius had suggested that ghosts were not proof of an afterlife but purely scientific phenomena. Pliny and his uncle would have been familiar with Lucretius' explanation, which was all to do with vision. We see the objects around us, Lucretius said, because they give off a kind of film of atoms, which strikes our eyes and prompts us to see.[39] Just as smoke is released from fire or winter coats shed by cicadas or skins sloughed by snakes, there are everywhere floating through the air simulacra or images given off from the surface of things. But these atomic streams can also penetrate the body, awake the mind, and stir the senses within. We suppose we are seeing a ghost when in fact our mind is responding to mere simulacra. These images are so thin that they can collide with one another in the air and combine, so that when a man says he has seen a centaur what he has actually seen is the image of a horse stuck to an image of a man. We might see such images when we are awake or when we are asleep, but they are often more frightening in our dreams because we are insufficiently alert to rationalise what is in our mind's eye.

Such theories held little appeal for the younger Pliny, who, like many Romans, believed in the existence of ghosts. Fascinated by the idea that the dead might haunt the world, he took to telling ghost stories with the zeal of an early novelist, relishing the drama of their twists and turns. He never doubted the veracity of the tale of Drusus' ghost appearing to his uncle in his sleep. The episode suggested that, while sleep might carry dreams which augured death, it could also bring dreams which carried back the dead. Sleep and Death were, as often, closely united. Pliny the Elder had rejected the idea that our futures are preordained ('Stars are not . . . as is commonly thought, assigned to each of us, shining brightly for rich, dimly for poor and weak'), while accepting that phenomena such as the paling of the sun could be significant, occurring as it had upon the death of Julius Caesar and during the civil war of Mark Antony.[40] Pliny, by contrast, clung to the idea that sleep offered the dead a conduit to the living and found the possibility that ghosts might exist to warn us of our future fates utterly compelling.

Perhaps his eyes were weak enough for the shadows to play tricks on them, or perhaps he was inspired by curious activity upon the winter solstice, when 'the herb of dried pennyroyal, suspended from the ceiling, comes into flower' as if to order.[41] Whatever it was that convinced Pliny of the existence of ghosts, it was not something tangible that he could easily explain. While he accepted that the idle mind will conjure its own sights and sounds, he had heard too many stories to shake off his suspicion that there existed, too, beyond the mind, ghosts with 'a shape and power of their own'.[42]

Pliny told a particularly thrilling tale about a philosopher named Athenodorus and his haunting by the spirit of a man in chains that reads like an early draft of Charles Dickens's *Christmas Carol.*

Athenodorus has moved into an old house in Athens which is said to be haunted by the ghost of a petulant old man, 'emaciated and dirty, with a long beard and matted hair, wearing fetters on his legs and shaking chains in his hands'.[43] Athenodorus resolves to wait up for the ghost in the hallway of the house with his lamp and books beside him. Just as 'a clanking noise . . . as if some person were dragging a heavy chain over the casks in the wine-merchant's cellar' announces the arrival of Jacob Marley's spirit in Charles Dickens's tale, so in Pliny's story, 'through the silence of the night, the clanking of iron could be heard and, if you listened more closely, the sound of chains, distant to begin with, but then close by'. Dickens probably drew inspiration from Pliny's description.[44] Like Athenodorus, Scrooge is haunted by the noisy chain-bearing ghost of a man at the dead of night. Like Athenodorus, he tries to avoid meeting his gaze. In his introduction to Dickens's Christmas Books, the nineteenth-century novelist and critic Andrew Lang described the 'old-fashioned phenomenon of clanking chains' of Dickens's story as 'derived from classical superstition'.[45] In Dickens's library at Gadshill Place, his country home in Kent, was a copy of a book that contained a translation of Pliny's ghost story. Entitled *The Philosophy of Mystery*, the volume was concerned with faith and scepticism, apparitions and dreams, and was written by a surgeon named W. C. Dendy two years before *The Christmas Carol.*[46]

In Dickens's, story, Scrooge eventually converses with Marley's ghost, but in Pliny's tale, Athenodorus does his best not to engage with the approaching spirit. Fixing his eyes firmly on his work, the philosopher tightens his grasp on his stylus and concentrates on not imagining the things he fears. The clanking noise grows nearer and then the ghost reveals itself to him in all its hideousness, standing 'and sort of summoning him with his finger'. Like the young Pliny reading Livy in the middle of the eruption of Vesuvius, Athenodorus endeavours to sharpen his focus on his studies, but this proves impossible when the phantom starts shaking his chains aggressively over his head. Confirming Pliny's suspicion that ghosts are more than 'manifestations of our fears', the manacled old man draws so close to Athenodorus that it becomes impossible for him to carry on. When the ghost summons him to the courtyard of the house, he follows. The ghost then disappears. At a loss as to what else he could do, Athenodorus crouches down and marks with leaves the precise spot where the ghost paused, and then goes back to bed. On the next day he gives orders for the terrace to be dug. Beneath the ground he finds bones in chains – the remains of an unfortunate old slave. The bones are given due burial and the ghost is never seen again.

Ghost stories with happy endings may have been the equivalent of what Pliny the Elder called 'the soothing you'd give a child', but they also represented an attempt to understand the capriciousness of fate and to perpetuate the memory of those who had lost their lives to it. Pliny's ghost stories created illusions of immortality in much the same way Fiorelli's plaster casts of the eruption victims had in the nineteenth century. They kept the past alive when events contrived to bury it.

FIVE

The Gift of Poison

Human brutes, like other beasts, find snares and poison in the provisions of life, and are allured by their appetites to their destruction.

Jonathan Swift, 'Thoughts on Various Subjects', 1727

Pliny returned to Rome from Laurentum one January and joined Tacitus in speaking for the prosecution of Marius Priscus, a Roman senator accused of extortion during his governorship in north Africa.[1] Pliny would prosecute a number of crooked governors for extortion in his lifetime, and while the letters in which he described those trials are not always the most scintillating, they attest to the difficulties which confronted the Romans as their empire approached its largest extent. The emperor could not be everywhere at once. He needed governors he could trust to keep order in the provinces, but the wider and more complex Rome's power base became, the more opportunity there would be for abuses to go undetected. Towards the end of his life, Pliny would experience the challenges of governing a province for himself. In his younger years, he took seriously his duty to represent those provincials who carried reports of mismanagement by Roman officials.

Since the defendant in this case was a senator and it was his professional conduct that was being called into question, the trial was scheduled for the senate house rather than the Court of One Hundred. Senatorial trials, in which senators voted to determine the fate of their colleagues, often roused Pliny's anxieties, for he knew how willing senators could be to protect their own. If the general nature of the trial did not fluster him, there was the fact that it was taking place at the beginning of the new political year, when Rome was at its busiest, and in the presence of the emperor.

The trial got off to an unpredictable start. First, Marius Priscus pleaded guilty and even appeared willing to pay back the 700,000 sesterces he had embezzled. Then there was a problem with one of the witnesses. Of the two called in connection with the case, one was alleged to have issued a bribe to secure the exile of a fellow Roman and the death of seven of his friends, while the other was said to have paid for a Roman equestrian to be struck with a club, condemned to the mines, and then strangled to death in prison. The first witness died before the case even commenced.

When, finally, it did, Pliny was granted twelve large water clocks against which to lay out his prosecution (Tacitus would speak on the following day in response to the defence). Every eighteen minutes or so, the final drops of one water clock would swirl away and another begin. Pliny kept on talking even after the twelve clocks were spent. During his preparation for the case he had discovered that the defendant had not only committed extortion, but also accepted bribes to put innocent north Africans to death. The law stipulated that people guilty of extortion should in most cases leave for exile, which in effect entailed relinquishing their Roman citizenship, rights, and possessions, but those who accepted money for killing someone should receive capital punishment or indefinite exile.[2] Twelve clocks did not reflect the severity of this case. It was only when four more clocks had run dry that Pliny finally stopped talking. By then, he had spoken for almost five hours.

This was not the longest speech Pliny had ever given. He once spoke in court for seven hours straight. 'Rejoice! Rejoice!' he exclaimed upon reaching the end and realising that he still had an audience. In front of him stood a lone man in ripped clothes; the throng that had gathered at the beginning of the reading had torn them in their eagerness to escape.[3] While Pliny admired the vigour of a short speech he was convinced that nothing equalled a long and weighty delivery. Few sights delighted him more than that of a speech transformed into volumes of text. He did not believe that slim books looked as authoritative as thick ones, which was one reason he liked to declaim at such length. *Brevitas*, while popular with the crowds, also carried the risk of a miscarriage of justice.[4]

Pliny braced himself for the worst, in spite of his extraordinarily long speech. The possibility that Marius Priscus might get away with merely paying back what he had taken was still weighing heavily upon him as his fellow senators began to make their way across the floor of the house to vote. To Pliny's relief, the members voted that the defendant and surviving witness should both go into exile. Although the satirist Juvenal proceeded to write mockingly of Marius Priscus enjoying a sojourn in which he 'drinks from the eighth hour on and revels in the anger of gods while you, triumphant province, you weep', Pliny had scored a relative triumph with his long speech.[5] The defendant's junior, another senator, was put on trial on a separate occasion and merely exempted from promotion.[6] His crimes included receipt of 10,000 sesterces from one of the crooked witnesses, which was logged 'under the most shameful heading of "perfumes"'.[7]

Perfume was not the most offensive of the luxuries to feature in Pliny the Elder's *Natural History* but it was the most evanescent.

Roses, oil, saffron, cinnabar, reeds, rushes, honey, salt and ox-tongue herb with wine together produced a simple fragrance.[8] Particularly welcome in winter, when flowers were in short supply, perfume was said to benefit everyone except the person wearing it, who could not smell it at all. While Pliny the Elder admired its purity, the very inability of the wearer to enjoy the perfume on their own body convinced him of its wastefulness.

Observing how fervently even Roman soldiers had taken to dousing themselves in it, Pliny the Elder had been quick to characterise it as a foreign import. The earliest he came across in his research was a case Alexander the Great had carried away from Persia following his defeat of King Darius III in the fourth century BC, and by the time perfume became ubiquitous at Rome, its associations with imperial expansion and eastern decadence had been fixed. Rome spread its influence over the globe but it always brought something back. Pliny the Elder dated the birth of luxury in Italy precisely to 189 BC, when a Roman general returned in triumph from Asia carrying gold crowns, ivory tusks, and 137,420 pounds of silver with him.[9] Pliny the Elder could not deny that 'communication, established throughout the world through the greatness of the Roman empire' had led to advances in people's lives by facilitating commerce.[10] He drew consistently and proudly in his encyclopaedia on knowledge that had come to Rome from overseas. The arrival of chests of foreign treasures, however, seemed destined only to precipitate a moral decline and loss of identity in Rome. Of all the luxuries the Romans could carry home, perfume offered the best metaphor for globalisation, its steady diffusion from the east revealing the Romans for what Pliny the Elder had long suspected them to be: conquerors conquered. 'The Roman people in its greatness,' he explained, 'lost its traditions, and through defeating others we were defeated ourselves.'[11] The metaphor ran the other way, too, for while

Rome lay at the centre of the empire, for a Roman, success meant spreading one's scent as far away from it as possible.

Emperor Augustus had advised his successors to maintain the empire inside the limits that had been established at the time of his death in AD 14.[12] Although the Romans of this era were in general less expansionist than they had been during the Republic, as they focused on maintaining stability in their existing provinces, they failed to honour Augustus' will.[13] Vespasian had overseen the annexation of Lycia to Pamphylia in the south of what is now Turkey and, with his son Titus, demonstrated how emperors could continue to leave their mark upon the world by converting foreign treasures into a display of Roman might. Spoils from their Jewish War helped to finance the construction of the magnificent Flavian amphitheatre in Rome. The 'Colosseum' stood not only as a symbol of victory and strength but also as a memorial to the prowess of the first Flavian emperors. It was more or less complete when, in AD 81, Titus died suddenly at the age of forty-one having ruled for just over two years.

Reports of the cause of Titus' death varied wildly. Suetonius said that Titus was seen weeping at the end of a session of public games and contracted a fever later in the day. Taken up in a litter, he gazed at the sky and complained that his life was being taken away from him undeservedly. His younger brother, Domitian, had long plotted against him, said Suetonius. On learning that he had been taken seriously ill, the envious Domitian 'ordered him to be left for dead'.[14] Later writers went further and accused Domitian of hastening Titus' end by plunging him into a chest of snow or poisoning him with a sea hare (a type of gastropod mollusc).[15] On the first theory, offered by the historian Dio Cassius in the early third century AD, Titus falls ill and takes his brother's advice to have a cold bath. Domitian's intentions are villainous but he has the benefit of popular medicine on his side. A doctor from ancient Marseilles had recently introduced the Romans to iced baths, which they proceeded to take even in winter, 'becoming stiff with cold just for show'.[16] Domitian has a tub prepared accordingly with fresh snow until it is full to the brim, lifts his brother into it, and leaves him there to soak. Meanwhile he makes his way to the barracks, bestows upon the soldiers 'as much as his brother had given them', and takes up the name and authority of emperor. Titus dies, leaving behind a daughter, Julia, but no son. On the second theory, proposed by an Athens-born writer named Philostratus in the early third century, Titus is killed after Domitian takes objection to his kindness and feeds him a sea hare, whose ink is considered so noxious (it is in fact harmless to humans) that an oyster, cooked crab, or seahorse must be ingested to neutralise it.[17]

The Colosseum is thought to have acquired its name in the Middle Ages because it was built near the site of a colossal, 30-metre bronze sculpture of Nero, which Pliny the Elder witnessed being made. This rare coin, which dates to AD 81, features one of the very earliest representations of the amphitheatre and celebrates its astonishing capacity.

The stories which spread of Titus' death – by immersion in snow, poisoning with rancid shellfish, or, more likely, from natural causes – were such as to inspire outlandish rumours of fratricide hundreds of years later.

The death of Titus and accession of Domitian marked the beginning of a difficult period in Pliny's life. Though conscious that he was succeeding a man who had been immensely popular with the people – who had now taken to mourning 'in public no differently from how they would for a loss in their own household' – Domitian was by nature highly reclusive.[18] Suetonius described how he would spend much of his time in seclusion, stabbing flies with his stylus. Pliny pictured him rather as a monster of Hades, hiding in his lair, licking his lips with the blood of relatives, and plotting bloodshed for the noblest men in the city.[19] What Pliny described of Domitian's rule in his letters amounted to nothing less than a reign of terror. Domitian was 'that most savage beast'. He was a 'destroyer and executioner' of upstanding citizens.[20] Writing some years after his death, Pliny diagnosed him with 'a hatred of mankind'.[21] No one wanted to get too close to him; but no one wanted to be shut out of his affairs either: there was no healthy distance.

Domitian, who had been born in AD 51 on Pomegranate Street, on the northernmost of Rome's seven hills, seemed to spend his life striving, Persephone-like, to escape from the shadows.[22] His biographers explained that while his brother Titus had been raised at the imperial court, Domitian had grown up in relative poverty. Although Pliny did not describe Domitian's background, he did profess to see a look of disgruntlement in his face: anger in his eyes, arrogance about his brow, a feminine pallor to his skin and a ruddiness to his cheeks.[23] Pliny had nothing but criticism for fellow writers who praised Domitian. The poet Silius Italicus may have been 'the glory of the Castalian sisterhood [the Muses]', but Pliny could not abide his flattery.[24] His poem on the Second Punic War extended to a tremendous seventeen books and over 12,000 lines, but Pliny said it lacked inspiration. The work contained references to Domitian the 'Conqueror of Germany', who would outdo the achievements of his father and brother – which struck some readers as unedifying and dishonest when, of Domitian's few, unremarkable foreign expeditions, his campaign against the Germanic tribe of the Chatti was 'unnecessary' and his triumph 'a sham'.[25]

Pliny the Elder had described his encounters with the Chatti in the time of Claudius. Endowed with 'robust bodies, straight limbs, threatening faces, and a marked vigour of spirit', the Chatti were logical and skilful 'for Germans' and excelled as infantrymen, but had in that period occupied one of the Roman bases and taken to heavy plundering.[26] Pliny the Elder's commander, Pomponius Secundus, had split his men into two columns, one of which worked to entrap the tribesmen, while the other attacked.[27] The Romans had had good reason to hope that they might engage the tribe in a war. 'You see others go to battle,' wrote Tacitus, 'but the Chatti, to war.' The Germans, however, had feared being surrounded by the Romans and a hostile neighbouring tribe, and sent legates and hostages to Rome to sue for peace. They were seemingly still unsettled when Domitian declared war upon them more than thirty years later, in the eighties AD. Though little is known of the campaign, the Romans are thought to have made their first attack in the winter months, when the tribesmen were most pressed for supplies.[28] Domitian was among the invading troops, but returned to Rome to celebrate a triumph for his own achievements long before the war had been concluded. His jubilation may have been premature but it was not entirely vain. As a result of the campaign, the Romans managed to lay a new fortified boundary line and formally establish two Roman provinces west of the Rhine.

The problem for Domitian was that he gave the impression of begrudging his men their successes in favour of his own renown. Tacitus accused him of acting out of jealousy when he recalled a highly successful governor of Britain named Agricola.[29] Agricola was Tacitus' father-in-law. He had conquered the island of Mona (Anglesey) and pushed north into Caledonia (Scotland) to score an impressive defeat over the local tribesmen at the so-called Battle of Mons Graupius, only to find himself under orders to return to Rome in AD 85. The same year, as if to trump Agricola's achievements, Domitian launched an expedition of his own. Decebalus, the ruler of Dacia (modern Romania), had led an army south across the Danube into a Roman province called Moesia. Domitian's forces succeeded in ousting the Dacians from their territory, but suffered significant setbacks as they proceeded westwards.[30] The Romans were left to pay tribute in exchange for peace. They would live to regret Domitian's failure to remove Decebalus there and then.

Pliny, for his part, was less concerned with documenting Domitian's military record than acts of cruelty committed against his own people. He was discernibly shaken by the emperor's decision to bury a Vestal Virgin alive.[31]

The Vestals were priestesses who honoured the Roman goddess of the hearth. There were six of them, plucked predominantly from wealthy families, and charged with keeping the goddess Vesta's flame burning eternally, day and night, for the protection and well-being of Rome itself. The loss of a Vestal's virginity had long been regarded as an ill omen, but Domitian decreed that any Vestal who failed to keep her body pure for the thirty years required of her should not merely be flogged, but confined as in ancient times to a suffocating chamber underground.[32] No one in Domitian's Rome had seen a Vestal Virgin buried alive until now.

When the chief Vestal, Cornelia, was accused of having broken her vows of chastity, Domitian acted 'through his powers as Pontifex Maximus [chief priest] – or rather through the heinousness of a tyrant and immunity of a despot' to condemn her to execution.[33] In spite of his disgust, Pliny felt compelled to go and watch. The woman was strapped to a sedan chair and borne in a canopied litter as far as the Colline Gate, at the northernmost reach of Rome. A large crowd was waiting there, but Pliny managed to obtain a good view. The chair was put down, its fastenings unloosed, and the veiled woman raised to her feet. As Pliny watched her being led towards an underground vault he heard her cry out, over and over again: 'Caesar thinks I'm unchaste, but it's because of my sacred acts that he is victorious and triumphant!'

To Pliny she certainly 'seemed innocent'. As she lowered herself into the dark chamber by way of a ladder, her very reflexes appeared to testify to her chastity. She had just begun the miserable descent when her robe got caught, causing her to pause and turn to gather it. As she did so, a man offered her his hand to help. She looked up and saw her 'executioner', Domitian. Without a moment's thought, Cornelia sprang back and 'pushed his filthy touch away from her pure and innocent body as if in a final act of chastity'. Cornelia descended. As Pliny watched her disappearing to her death he was reminded of the virginal Trojan princess Polyxena, the youngest of King Priam's daughters, who in Euripides' *Hecuba* submits courageously to the sword of Achilles' son Neoptolemus. In the play, Polyxena does not merely give in. She boldly and defiantly yields her breast and neck. She falls, her modesty intact. And then she is gone.

Cornelia disappeared from view, the ladder was pulled up and earth thrown against the chamber door. Inside there would have awaited her a small bed with an oil lamp, a morsel of bread, some milk, olive oil, a vessel of water. It was as if, by providing these meagre provisions, the Romans 'would absolve themselves of the guilt of destroying a body devoted to the holiest rituals', as the Greek-born biographer Plutarch put it.[34] In a short time she suffocated to death.

This portrait of Domitian, made when he was in his mid thirties, escaped destruction by the Roman people who determined to obliterate his face from history. It shows his distinctive upper lip, weak jaw and receding hairline. Domitian is said to have consoled himself over his hair loss by writing a book *On the Care of Hair*.

Pliny the Elder once wrote that, 'for man alone, one's first time is full of regret, which is surely an accurate augury for life' – a description unlikely to entice many readers into accepting his broader views on the damaging effects of sexual desire.[35] In the *Natural History* he compares humans unfavourably with animals on the basis of their sexual habits. While animals have established seasons for mating, he says, humans view every hour as having the potential for sex, and go on doing it throughout the year, never sated. Animals get satisfaction from intercourse but humans, 'almost none'. One of the gravest impediments to their satisfaction, he conjectured, is the seasonal incompatibility of the sexes. As early as the seventh century BC it was believed that women were lustiest in the summer, just as men were at their feeblest, and women so indifferent to sex in the colder months that, like an octopus gnawing its own foot (as one poet put it), a man must resort to masturbating alone in his passionless house.[36] Lack of satisfaction breeds 'sexual deviation', which is, according to Pliny the Elder, 'a crime against Nature'. Sexual deviation could take many forms, but Pliny the Elder's immediate point of reference was the promiscuity of Messalina, third wife of Emperor Claudius, who was alleged to have engaged in a contest with a prostitute to sleep with as many men as possible within a twenty-four-hour window, and promptly achieved a score of twenty-five. The charge of sexual deviancy was more often applied to men, however, for women's sexuality tended to be held in check by the limits placed on their freedom outside the home. As far as Pliny the Elder was concerned, the most serious sexual crime a woman could commit was to terminate a pregnancy.

The imperial household was rumoured to be guilty on both fronts. Domitian was married to Domitia Longina, the daughter of Corbulo (under whose command Pliny the Elder had battled trees in AD 47) but was rumoured to have had an incestuous affair with his niece Julia. No stranger to the exercise he called 'bed-wrestling' – his preferred term for sex – Domitian allegedly impregnated the girl and forced her into a termination that killed her. Julia's abortion was frowned upon by men in Rome almost as severely as Domitian's perversion. It inspired some of the foulest verse imaginable: 'Julia freed her fertile uterus by many/ an abortion and shed clots which resembled their uncle.'[37] The behaviour of Domitian, meanwhile, only lent credence to Pliny the Elder's exclamation of 'how much more criminal we are in this area [of sex] than wild beasts!'

When Domitian heard that people were now speaking of his iniquity he 'was blazing'.[38] For all the rumours of his misdemeanours, he was said to have been a man of justice. He was even known to overturn decisions made in the Court of One Hundred – Pliny's court – if he believed them to have been influenced by the ambition of the jurors.[39] Anxious that his reputation should not be blemished, Domitian diverted blame for the Virgin's death on to a senator named Valerius Licinianus, whom he had arrested on accusation of having concealed one of the Virgin's freedwomen on his estate.[40] According to Pliny, the senator confessed, 'but it was unclear whether he confessed because it was true or because he feared worse if he denied it'.[41] The defendant did not attend his own trial. In his absence, his lawyer, a man named Herennius Senecio, came before the court and gave him what Pliny called the 'Patroclus is dead' treatment.[42] With a direct and serviceable 'Licinianus *recessit*' ('Licinianus has withdrawn his defence'), Senecio saw his client free to gather up his belongings and leave Rome in a lenient exile. Licinianus eventually became a rhetoric teacher in Sicily – a not altogether unpleasant ending, though in Pliny's eyes a sorry one: 'Such is his demise: from a senator to an exile, from an orator to a rhetoric teacher.'

As for the lawyer, Senecio, it soon transpired that he had diverted his attentions elsewhere. While Pliny proceeded in AD

93 to the prestigious magistracy of praetor, Senecio steadily withdrew from public life.[43] He and a fellow senator named Arulenus Rusticus had undertaken to write biographies of two 'most sacred men': Thrasea Paetus and his son-in-law Helvidius Priscus.[44] Pliny knew who they were. They were famous Stoics.

Stoicism was the most prominent philosophy in Rome, far outshining Epicureanism and Pythagoreanism as a school of thought. Cicero, Virgil, Seneca the Younger, Pliny the Elder and, later, the emperor Marcus Aurelius, did much to elevate and perpetuate its teachings through their work. Introduced to Rome from Greece in the second century BC by a philosopher from Rhodes named Panaetius and his pupil Poseidonius, Stoicism encouraged reverence towards Nature. 'Nature, which is to say, Life,' wrote Pliny the Elder, 'is my subject.' She was the only divinity he believed in as such.[45] The traditional pantheon of Roman gods was indeed for many Stoics little more than a collection of allegories for aspects of the universe such as the sun and moon.

Pliny the Elder followed the oldest Stoics in believing that the universe existed in a cycle without beginning or end, subject only to *ekpyrosis* – the sudden destruction by conflagration – after which it would recover its force and proceed on a fresh cycle. Although the word 'encyclopaedia' only gained currency in the fifteenth century, Pliny the Elder presented his *Natural History* as the Latin equivalent to what the Greeks had called *enkyklios paideia*, 'all-round education' – education that surrounds the pupil in a circle.[46] He was concerned neither with what lay above the earth's sphere nor with what might be lurking in 'Hades'. What point is there in seeking what exists outside our world, he wondered, when we are yet to discover everything within it?[47] The *Natural History*, a work that the younger Pliny described as 'wide-ranging and erudite and no less varied than Nature herself', was an attempt to lay down all that had been found on earth to date so that it would forever encircle us in its beauty.[48]

The Stoics rarely went as far as the Cynic philosophers of Greece in their rejection of wealth and comfort, but they shared with them their ability to maintain perspective in moments of perceived crisis. Zeno, the man credited with founding the Stoic school of thought, was said to have learned the art of keeping his cool after scalding himself with soup. Arriving in Athens from his native Cyprus in around 312 BC, he encountered the Cynic philosopher Crates, who playfully challenged him to carry a steaming bowl of lentil soup through the potters' quarters of the Kerameikos. Zeno accepted and, to maintain a semblance of propriety, did his best to conceal it as he started. Crates smashed the bowl with his walking stick. When the soup began to dribble down his legs, Zeno turned red and scurried off to hide his shame. As he hastened away, Crates calmly told him, 'You have suffered nothing terrible.'[49]

Stoicism was at heart a philosophy for achieving equilibrium in a frantic world, through which you learned to become master of yourself and your emotions, and it was in the spring of his youth, a few years after he escaped the confounding disaster of Vesuvius, that Pliny had the opportunity to learn it first-hand. Dispatched to Syria on military service, he spent his days going over the account books of the Roman cavalry and cohorts stationed in the province, and his leisure hours becoming acquainted with at least three Stoic philosophers.[50]

Of the Stoics he met in Syria, there were some who preached their way of life and others who knew better. Musonius Rufus was firmly in the first camp. A philosopher of Etruscan extraction, he was something of a 'Roman Socrates'.[51] In the civil war that followed the death of Nero, he was dispatched as an envoy to negotiate a peace settlement, but ended up philosophising so intensely with the opposing army on the ugliness of conflict that he incurred only ridicule for his 'untimely wisdom'.[52] On another occasion, he told the Athenians that they should cease hosting gladiatorial shows under the walls of the Acropolis lest they spatter with blood the seats occupied by the priests of Dionysus.[53] The Greeks would have struggled, at the best of times, to take lessons from a man who believed as fervently as Musonius Rufus did (on moral rather than specifically Stoic grounds) that one should abstain from homosexual practices, and from sex alto- gether except in cases of determined procreation.

In the second camp was Musonius Rufus' pupil, Euphrates, a philosopher who developed more convincing methods of bringing people round to the Stoic way of life. If Musonius Rufus was Socrates, then Euphrates was Plato.[54] He was clever and subtle, but had a way of speaking that captivated even the most reluctant learners: 'you would not shudder upon meeting him'. He 'pursued crimes, not individuals' because he understood that it was more effective to correct the way a man lived than punish him for it. Pliny came to know him particularly well during his service. He visited him at his home and found him to be open and approachable and 'full of the humanity which he teaches', which was very different from the portrait of him that emerged over a century later. According to an author of the early third century AD, Euphrates came into bitter conflict with a Pythagorean philosopher and professed miracle man named Apollonius. Originally from Tyana (modern Kemerhisar), a city in a Roman province in what is now Turkey, Apollonius travelled the world – India, Ethiopia, Egypt, Rome – issuing advice and predictions, and performing such improbable feats as releasing the city of Ephesus from plague. He met several Roman emperors, including Vespasian, Titus, and Domitian, the last of whom had him locked up after hearing Euphrates' complaints. Allegedly, Euphrates devised 'false letters' about the wondrous Apollonius and spoke out against his philosophy.[55] Apollonius was said to have vanished magically during his ensuing trial after describing Euphrates as lingering in the doorways of powerful men in the manner of 'greedy dogs' and clinging to his 'fountains of wealth'.[56] These may have been empty rumours but they hinted at the hypocrisy of Euphrates' philosophy. The Stoics were often wealthy men endowed with the kind of extravagant possessions their philosophy taught them to eschew. The line between necessity and luxury was a highly subjective one.

Pliny did not acknowledge these stories in his letters. In his eyes, Euphrates was entirely admirable. Although he could not have looked more like a philosopher when Pliny first met him – he was 'tall and becoming, with long hair and a huge white beard' – when he later moved to Rome he did his utmost to be seen as a philosopher for the way he ate and drank, slept and helped others, rather than for how he looked.[57] Euphrates was afraid that the philosopher's traditional cloak and beard might give the impression that everything he did was for show.[58] Stoics were discouraged from vaunting their philosophy, for it was intended as an improvement of the self. As Seneca the Younger used to say, 'one can be wise without ceremony, and without inviting ill-will'.[59] This was where Euphrates' teacher Musonius Rufus had failed. He broadcast his views too widely. His fame as a philosopher and as a philosophy teacher had brought him to the attention of Nero, who exiled him in the belief that he had been involved in the conspiracy against his life in AD 65.

Musonius Rufus was on his third exile when Pliny met him in Syria (it was just as well that he thought 'Exile is Not a Bad Thing') and soon earned his affection.[60] Although Pliny grew closer to his son-in-law, Artemidorus, a man he admired for 'the endurance of his body in winter and summer alike', he came to love the elder man 'as much as one can across an age gap'.[61] Musonius Rufus' sanctimonious attitudes towards luxury and concern for protecting the environment from human greed might well have made Pliny think of his uncle: 'But for that briefest of moments when we feel pleasure,' wrote Musonius, 'innumerable fish courses are prepared, the sea is sailed to its furthest limits; cooks are far more sought after than farmers; some prioritise their meals over spending on their estates, though our bodies are in no way aided by extravagant food.'[62]

Musonius Rufus objected to the mining of Nature on both environmental and moral grounds. Since every jewel acquired or oyster cracked open only whetted the appetite for something rarer and more refined, he advocated a diet that satisfied need not want: vegetables, raw foods, a little cheese, no meat.[63] Musonius Rufus disapproved of sweeping the oceans for oysters as much as Pliny the Elder did of probing (like surgeons with their tools) the 'bowels' of the earth for gold and silver, amber, bronze, iron, and gems, 'as if the ground we tread were not generous or fertile enough'.[64]

Stoicism taught them that Nature was a god to be revered, not dominated, assisted, not ignored, and as proof of this, Pliny the Elder had pointed to the lowly bramble bush. It is so wild and resilient in its growth, he said, that it would overwhelm the earth if man did not prune it. From this we should accept that Nature does not exist for the pleasure of man, but rather, 'man can seem to be born for the sake of the earth'.[65] His appetite for luxury may sooner lead him to plunder than prune, but even the fattest, idlest, most ignorant individual is obliged to attend Nature from time to time. Man would do well to understand that, while the sweeping of oceans and ploughing of rich landscapes is ruinous to the earth, it is positively deadly to his own true interests. 'We all reach into the bowels of the earth while living on top of it,' he wrote, 'but are amazed when occasionally it splits open or quakes, as if it were possible that this wasn't an expression of disapproval by our sacred parent.'[66]

This was not simply a question of morality after all. Rejecting oysters and amber and gold may prevent you from falling down a rabbit hole of obsession, but more importantly, it offered you some protection against earth's fury. Pliny and his uncle had grown up in living memory of the earth splitting open as Vesuvius began to stir. Their experience could only have fortified their beliefs about the perils of disrupting the earth's layers. Both Plinys had learned that Nature, while predominantly kind, had evils lurking deep inside it. Man had no one but himself to blame if he unleashed them by prodding at its bowels.

It had occurred to Pliny the Elder that there had to be a reason why Nature, otherwise so generous and nurturing of life, produced the poisons she did. Was it possible that humans are simply too vulnerable to the world around them? Oysters have their shells, boars their fur, birds their feathers.[67] Trees hide behind their bark, but man – man is hideously exposed. Plunged naked onto the earth with a pulsating fontanelle, he does what no other creature does at birth. He cries. This is the only thing he knows how to do instinctively. Everything else he must learn for himself. According to the *Natural History* it will be at least forty days before the infant manages so much as a laugh.

The image of a baby writhing helplessly in his cot persuaded Pliny the Elder of Nature's potential to be a tricky stepmother, but the image of an elderly man struggling in his bed made him think of her rather as a kindly mother. Nature, he decided, has given us two main gifts. One is brevity of life. The other is the means of ending life. Mortality should not be seen as a curse, for it is the one thing we have that the gods do not.[68] If life becomes too much then we have a way out. Zeus had no choice but to carry on when he saw his son Sarpedon die and be carried from the battlefield in the arms of Sleep and Death. The elderly man can escape his bed of pain by ending his life there and then. The earth will cover him over, embracing his body like a mother. The simplest explanation Pliny the Elder could find for why Nature had sowed poisons in the earth was to provide us with a means of committing suicide. We need only learn which mushrooms, leaves, or berries to pick.*

His was in many ways an age marked by reasoned acceptance of death. Seneca the Younger encapsulated a popular Stoic view when, around the time of Pliny's birth, he said that it was foolish to prolong life for the sake of enduring pain, but cowardly to seek death because of pain alone.[69] As Pliny the Elder recalled, the admirable Seneca, who had written richly Stoic works on clemency, mutual kindness and 'the tranquillity of the mind', was 'the foremost of intellectuals whose power ultimately overcame him'.[70] Forced to commit suicide by Nero following the conspiracy that landed Musonius Rufus in exile, he died a long, suffering and determinedly theatrical death. He cut into his veins, and then took poison when he failed to bleed out sufficiently. When the poison did not work he got into a hot bath and died 'by its vapour'.[71] Decades after leaving Syria for Rome, Pliny's Stoic friend Euphrates committed suicide by hemlock to avert the pains of illness and old age.[72]

Pliny understood the logic of the arguments for suicide but, even after his time with the philosophers in Syria, struggled to see it put into practice. He had a friend called Titius Aristo

---

* Pliny the Elder was critical of suicides by drowning and sword. He was also critical of antidotes to poison. In the first century BC, Pompey the Great had conquered the kingdom of Pontus on the south coast of the Black Sea and carried home with him new knowledge of the nature of poisons. The vanquished King of Pontus, Mithridates VI Eupator, had discovered that, by ingesting a little poison every day, you can build up an immunity to it. He allegedly became so resistant that he found himself unable to commit suicide by poison following his defeat. According to Pliny the Elder, Mithridates had also developed an antidote against poison that consisted of fifty-four ingredients. The recipe for the 'mithridate' was tweaked over the years at Rome and became steadily more opiate in its composition. The supposed antidote of the foreign king remained popular in medieval times, when it was optimistically employed as protection against plague. Pliny the Elder derided the ostentation of the science.

with whom he used to spend time deliberating matters of constitutional law. If, for argument's sake, there was a defendant who might be acquitted, left to go into exile, or put to death, Pliny might ask him whether it was right that senators who supported the death penalty should consult with those who favoured banishment. Might not such collusion ensure that acquittal was impossible? Titius Aristo would have the answer, for he was a 'treasury [of knowledge]' and 'there was nothing you might want to learn that he could not teach'.[73] When Pliny heard that he had fallen ill and resolved to die he hastened to his bedside.

Pliny found his bedchamber sparse and cold and adorned solely 'with the greatness of his mind'. Titius Aristo lay sweating beneath his covers, which he insisted remained on in spite of his raging fever. As Pliny approached, his friend leaned in to him and bade him ask the doctors whether his illness was fatal. If it was, he said, he was indeed resolved to die. But if the doctors believed it was merely a long and painful sickness then he would endure it, for he could not contemplate suicide against the wishes of his wife, daughter and friends.

The Stoics, too, were obliged to weigh their own discomfort against the agony their relatives would feel as a result of their deaths. Pliny considered the ability to understand the arguments on both sides the mark of a great mind. He did as Titius Aristo asked him and discovered that the doctors were optimistic for his friend's health. This was the perfect opportunity for Pliny to adopt a Stoic resolve.

Pliny confessed that he struggled to grasp the tenets of Stoicism. On returning to Rome from Syria and reuniting with Euphrates years later, he admitted that he could not fully understand his philosophical virtues 'even now; for just as one cannot judge painting, sculpture or modelling unless one is an artist, so only a wise man can recognise wisdom'.[74] Pliny's disavowal was not a rejection of Stoicism but rather a test. Like a Stoic who refused to wear a beard, Pliny's modest statement was an invitation to others to look beneath his facade for signs of his wisdom. A new acquaintance who sought hints of Stoicism in Pliny might begin by watching how he conducted himself in court. The benches of the Court of One Hundred provided a good vantage point. Was he flustered, or did he look as though anxiety was clouding his thoughts? The ideal Stoic never ceded to his emotions or fears. Was Pliny hesitant? The Stoic did not act on impulse. When pressure was applied, was he rational? The Stoic had a deep sense of security and inner confidence; he knew that it was in his power to make the right choice.

And when Pliny was at a sick friend's bedside, how was he then? Was he calm and accepting of the ill man's desire for death? He was not. When Pliny was sitting with the ailing Titius Aristo he described himself as *attonitus*, 'struck by terror', a word he used on only one other occasion in his letters, which was when he recalled the state of the crowd which tried to flee the eruption of Vesuvius.[75] This time he was too panicked to read, let alone to make notes. Over the course of his life Pliny witnessed the suicides of a large number of his friends. His efforts to save them were almost always in vain. Pliny did not record whether his friend Aristo lived or died, but the moments he spent by his bedside would have reinforced the challenges of Stoicism.

Seeing how difficult it was to maintain calm in the face of uncertainty might have provided Pliny with some incentive to lead a Stoic life. Despite appreciating the *humanitas* and *sanctitas* of the philosophy, however, he chose not to define himself by it. In the years following his encounter with the Stoics in Syria, he came to know a network of Stoic philosophers in Rome. His associations with them would serve him well as he proceeded in his legal career, but disastrously as he came up against the tyranny of Domitian's rule. Pliny's decision not to immerse himself too deeply in the precepts of any particular school of thought might even have saved him.

If the impassioned, wholehearted reverence for Nature that Pliny the Elder inspired in his readers was the least contentious aspect of his philosophy, then it was also the feature of Stoicism that Pliny observed most closely. It was in spring that he had the chance to appreciate the gifts of Nature anew after the long, studious days of winter.

PART THREE

SPRING

SIX

Pliniana

Harsh winter makes way for the welcome return of spring
And its breezes, and machines lug dry hulls to sea
And cows cease caring for their stables, farmers for their
   fires,
The meadows are no longer white with alabaster frost.

From Horace, Odes, 1.4

Spring came in February, turning the ground from white to green and, in Laurentum, to purple, as Pliny's terrace became 'fragrant with violets' and his kitchen garden burst into life. There is an old saying, still cherished in Italy, that 'out of bad, comes good' – '*Dal male nasce il bene*', or, *ex malo bonum*.[1] Nature will make amends for the losses it inflicts. The sun will thaw the frost. The bald soil will recover its tendrils. The elements may always be in battle, but in spring one begins to realise that what they really seek is balance.

Pliny the Elder knew that nothing ever stayed still. 'Rain falls,' he wrote, 'clouds draw in, rivers dry up, hail plummets down . . . steam rises from the heights and sinks to the depths again . . . so Nature goes to and fro of its own accord.'[2] Spring exemplified better than any other season the changeability of Nature. 'Don't be deceived,' advised Ovid on the first day of spring, 'cold days lie ahead of you yet;/ Winter leaves prominent signs of itself behind as it departs.'[3] The unpredictability of the seasons may have been a source of frustration to the landowner but it was also what made him feel alive. As Pliny the Elder explained, we experience life best through vicissitudes, 'for what real joys does Fortune bestow except those which follow disaster, or what true disasters except those which follow great joy?'[4]

About twenty years after Pliny the Elder died in the ash that blanketed Campania like snow, spring returned foliage to the fields and blossom to the cherry trees, the most glorious of which was known locally as the 'Pliniana'.[5] The elder Pliny had observed in his *Natural History* that flowers wither as quickly as they bloom for the sake of warning men of the evanescence of life.[6] Nature may not 'exist for the pleasure of man', but it does well to remind him of his limitations. No flower could have prompted Pliny the Elder to muse more deeply on his ephemerality than the cherry blossom. One pictures him almost as a young A. E. Housman, pondering his mortality beneath the 'Loveliest of trees, the cherry'.[7]

The cherry tree originated in the East and displayed its other-worldliness in its blossom, the clusters so light that they blew open in the wind, so taken with their own gravity that they bowed from their branches, as though snow was still weighing them down. The first cherry to grow in Italy had been carried all the way from Pontus in Asia Minor by the Roman general Lucullus in the mid first century BC.[8] Many different genera had since been cultivated across the countryside, but Pliny the Elder had deemed the *Pliniana* to be the best of the hardy varieties to grow in Italy. He might well have assumed that one of his ancestors had introduced it from overseas.[9] Traditionally planted at the same time as lettuce, upon the winter solstice, it was each spring 'among the first of the fruit to pay back its annual thanks to the farmer'.[10]

After the cherry blossom came the beginnings of the figs. Pliny grew his own in the grounds of his villa at Laurentum. The *gestatio* or driveway to his house was circular with a central island edged with box and, in the gaps, with rosemary, which was more tolerant than the hedge of the sea's spray. In the middle of the island was an ornamental vine and around that was a melee of mulberry and fig trees, 'of which the soil there is particularly supportive, though it is rather harsher to other trees'.[11] Pliny would have to wait until late summer before his figs were ready to harvest (they might even fruit twice in a warm year), but to see the green fruit begin to set against the new leaves was nonetheless an important moment in spring.[12]

The appearance of the first fig leaves had been long taken as a sign that the new season was afoot and the sea ready to navigate after the storms of winter. Although he recommended waiting until summer to embark, the Greek poet Hesiod, a near contemporary of Homer and important source for Pliny the Elder, described spring as the first sailing season in his *Works and Days*, a seventh-century BC poem on the farmer's year:

> When first man sees at the crown of the fig-tree
> A leaf as big as the footprint a crow makes
> As it goes, the sea may then be navigated.
> This is the spring sailing season. I for my part
> Could not enjoy it, for to my mind it gives no pleasure;
> It is snatched. You would struggle to avoid danger, but
> Even so men proceed with it in their idiocy
> For trade in goods means life for wretched mortals
> Though it is terrible to die beneath the waves.[13]

For Pliny, too, spring was snatched: a season 'where nothing is lost from the day and very little taken from the night'.[14] While he fretted over the night-time writing hours he lost as the days grew steadily longer, sailors recommenced the voyages which had provoked his uncle's no less than Hesiod's ambivalence towards the season.[15] The 'wretched mortals' who sailed for 'trade in goods' in Hesiod's age were still risking their lives at sea. As Pliny's uncle complained, the expansion of empire had led men to become only more degenerate since Hesiod's time, as thirst for knowledge ceded to avarice.

The fig itself had represented to Pliny the Elder the folly of expansion and slight grounds upon which Romans were prepared to initiate war. By the time he was writing his encyclopaedia it had become folklore that Rome had sacked Carthage for the sake of a single fruit. The First and Second Punic Wars were waged between Rome and Carthage in the third century BC and resulted in Rome fortifying its control over the western Mediterranean. Hannibal had been defeated at Zama, and Sicily, Corsica, Sardinia and the Iberian Peninsula were now theirs. The Romans resolved to destroy Carthage once and for all by declaring war again in 149 BC. In his determination to see Carthage fall, the senator and historian Cato the Elder was said to have brought a fresh north African fig with him to the senate house and asked his fellow senators to guess when it had been picked. When he told them that it had still been on its tree two days previously they were alarmed at Carthage being so close – and, 'at once', said Pliny the Elder, the Third Punic War began.[16]

Although native to the Near East, figs had been cultivated by the Romans for hundreds of years and looked upon with such pride that, after the Gauls migrated into Italy in the second and first centuries BC, it was supposed that they had done so out of greed for dried figs (as well as Italian wine, olives, and grapes).[17] Pliny the Elder provided 111 observations on figs in one section of his *Natural History* alone.[18] Pliny may have struggled to remember them all, but whether he needed a laxative or a throat lozenge, a balm to soothe a wasp sting or a feed to fatten goose and sow livers to make foie gras, he could never have been short of uses for his figs.[19]

Despite owning thousands of acres across Italy, Pliny was convinced that an intelligent man needed little more than a few fruit trees and a modest path to make himself happy. 'Getting to know one's vines and counting one's fruit trees,' he said, is the surest way of 'freeing the mind and refreshing the eyes.'[20] It also roused the ardent gardener in him. His first response upon receiving some dates from a friend one year was that they would 'have to compete with' his own figs and mushrooms.[21] Pliny followed his uncle's advice in growing his own mushrooms (if anyone was capable of identifying the safe ones it was going to be the farmer and picker). He grew not *fungi* but *boleti*, the variety a Roman served with oysters or turbot, or two-pound mullet if he wanted to impress his guests.[22]

The first fruits of spring appealed to Pliny's mind as they did to his stomach. The chief pleasure lay in their variety. When Pliny advised alternating business and leisure like 'savoury and spicy foods with sweet', he was thinking of how 'our creative mind is replenished by switching from one study to the next' like soil 'refreshed by various changes of seed'.[23] Unlike the vicissitudes his uncle discerned in Nature, the changes of seed and study Pliny envisaged were perfectly controllable. We sow the seeds of our own creativity, he suggested, by favouring variety over uniformity. Just as man stimulates Nature by varying the seeds he sows, so the fruits those seeds grow into stimulate man when applied variously to his palate. Man and Nature benefit from each other, as Pliny the Elder well knew. The promise of inspiration provided Pliny with an incentive to deviate from his winter routine of work, work, and more work, to vary the vegetables he grew as well as the foods he ate. It was in spring, a season of long waits and short rewards, that he finally took the chance to refresh his mind and palate through welcoming a change in course.

The first fruits of spring made Pliny ravenous for poetry. As soon as it was warm enough to sit outside he made his way to Rome, where 'there was barely a day in the whole month of April when someone was not giving a recital'.[24] Pliny sometimes found himself alone in his enthusiasm for the latest compositions. He would arrive at a reading and look around and notice how fidgety the other listeners were. Some arrived late and others slipped out early. Some sat down to gossip and others demanded to know how long each poem would be. The generous Emperor Titus was said to have sighed 'I have wasted a day' when he realised it was evening and he had not yet bestowed a gift upon his people.[25] Pliny felt the same about days which passed without poetry. 'Today,' he observed, 'he who has all the time in the world is invited [to a recital] with good notice and reminded repeatedly, but still either fails to turn up or turns up but complains that he has wasted a day – because he has not *wasted* it!'[26]

Pliny did not go to poetry readings because he thought he ought to or because he believed they were good for him. He appreciated the skill and wit and indeed the courage that were required to compose poetry for popular consumption. An amateur poet himself, he was known to give readings at small gatherings, fending off the critics who accused him of pride in order to use the opportunity to gain distance from his work. He was often amending speeches after reading them aloud to friends, and hoped that the process of reciting his poems would help similarly with their editing – for an audience would indicate how they felt about one line or another through 'their facial expressions, their eyes, the nodding of their heads, their hands, the murmurs or the silence'.[27] A writer can always distinguish between what is genuine appreciation, and what feigned 'out of humanity'.

There was a large part of him that yearned to be a famous poet – a Callimachus, perhaps, or someone like Calvus, who had distinguished himself as both a lawyer and a poet in the circle of Catullus in the previous century. His only worry was that if he moonlighted as a poet, he might no longer be taken seriously as a senator and lawyer. Ever the pragmatist, Pliny therefore resolved to justify his poetic ambitions by drawing up a list of the most respectable men in history who had expressed themselves in the kind of literature that proclaimed 'I'm human': Cicero and Calvus, Asinius Pollio, Messala, Hortensius, Brutus, Sulla, the politician Catulus, Scaevola, Sulpicius, Varro, Torquatus (in fact, several Torquati), Memmius, Lentulus Gaetulicus, Seneca the Younger, Verginius Rufus, Julius Caesar – and that was not to mention the emperors.[28]

The reputations of these men had suffered less for what they wrote than for what others had written about them. Julius Caesar had been furious when, in the fifties BC, Catullus had branded him 'a shameless, grasping gambler', an 'adulterer', and lover of 'little girls' in his poems, but forgave him.[29] Pliny would never have gone so far. He heroised Catullus but struggled to write as uninhibitedly, 'not because I am more serious, but because I am more timid'.[30] As the Veronese always remembered, Pliny's uncle had invoked Catullus as his 'fellow countryman'; his native Comum and Catullus' Verona both having formed part of Cisalpine Gaul. Pliny the Elder had even given his encyclopaedia an unexpectedly playful preface by addressing Titus as *iucundissime* ('most pleasant chap'), a thoroughly Catullan term of endearment. Catullus was the romantic and expressive poet that the younger Pliny most dreamed of emulating.

Pliny's friends knew where his aspirations lay. Good ones were willing to humour him. He might have seen through their flattery (he suspected even booksellers of exaggerating when they told him his work was popular), but he could only smile when one compared him to his idols Catullus and Calvus in a fawning poem:[31]

> I sing songs in verse concise
> As once my dear Catullus, Calvus too.
> All the poets of old. But what are these to me?
> Pliny is the only precedent, I say,
> Preferring his poems short on departing the forum,
> Seeking something to love and supposing he's loved
>   back.
> Come now, ye who love, love no more.
> What a man, that Pliny, how many Catos he is worth![32]

In reality Pliny was more Cato than Catullus. He could not write of affairs with other men's wives or of 'nine consecutive fucks' at midday. Nor, as a lawyer, was he about to threaten fellow citizens with rape – *pedicabo . . . et irrumabo* – or to jest about having pockets full of cobwebs. The sight of a joke or rude graffito scrawled across a voting tablet would have delighted Catullus; it incensed Pliny.[33]

If poetry is a 'secretion', as the cherry-loving A. E. Housman famously said, then it was for Pliny 'a morbid secretion, like the pearl in the oyster', not 'a natural secretion, like turpentine in the fir'.[34] (Housman had read Pliny's letters closely and offered suggestions on an edition of the text prepared by a classics don in 1906.[35] He seems to have found little inspiration in Pliny's literary style, however.) But while poetry did not come to Pliny as naturally as seven-hour declamations or competitive vegetable growing, he persevered. He wrote his first major work, a Greek tragedy, when he was just fourteen.[36] Five years later, his journey home from Syria inspired an elegy on the sea and the Aegean island of Icaria after he was detained there by bad weather. Sporadically throughout his adulthood – whether over dinner, in the bath or on sleepless nights or in the carriage – Pliny turned his hand to writing poetry. He even completed a volume of hendecasyllables, energetic, eleven-syllable lines of verse first made famous in Rome by Catullus.[37] In his efforts to emulate the style of the earlier poet, Pliny steadily began to find the confidence to display something of his candour in his own lines, as he explained in a letter to a friend:

> In these poems I jest and play and love and grieve and moan and rage. I go from describing something simply to elaborately and aim at variety so as to please some people with some things and everyone with a few. If some bits seem a bit too ripe to you, then it will be a sign of your learning that you can appreciate how men of utmost standing and severity who wrote such verses in the past did not only not abstain from lasciviousness – they went as far as to express it in the plainest vocabulary.[38]

This was Pliny at his most defensive. Would people laugh to read a lawyer's woes and erotic dreams? Did a serious man debase himself by sharing his private thoughts? How 'ripe' was too ripe? You cannot help but wonder what – or whom – he could possibly have been writing about to be so nervous.

Pliny married at least twice, and while he never mentions so much as his first wife's name in his surviving letters, he proved himself quite the romantic in his letters to his second.[39] He married Calpurnia within perhaps a year of the death of his first wife in about AD 97.[40] Orphaned as a child, Calpurnia had been raised by her aunt, whom Pliny had known since he was a boy because she was an old friend of his mother. 'We thank you,' he wrote to her after she arranged the match: 'I because

117

you gave her to me, she because you gave me to her, as if we were chosen for each other.'[41] Pliny was in his mid to late thirties at the time of the wedding and more understanding than many of his contemporaries of a young woman's desires. He was always being asked to find husbands for his friends' daughters and would consider a man eligible only if he were rich, accomplished, handsome – specifically 'rosy-cheeked' – 'for some sort of reward ought to be given in exchange for a girl's virginity'.[42] Under no illusion as to what he could offer his own bride, he confessed to her aunt that 'it is not my age or body that she loves, which gradually declines and decays, but my renown'.[43]

Once, when work kept him from seeing her, Pliny presented himself to Calpurnia as an *exclusus amator*. In the love poetry of Ovid and others, the 'locked-out lover' weeps on the doorstep of his beloved in the hope that she will let him in. He is young and idealistic while Pliny was level-headed and nearing middle age, but the passionate trope appealed to him in his loneliness as no doubt it did to Calpurnia in hers.[44] For all his expressions of love and longing, the letter was not, however, in the least sense 'ripe'. None of the surviving letters to Calpurnia are. The lascivious poems over which Pliny felt such unease were apparently not intended for her.

Only once in his letters did Pliny quote from one of his fruitier poems. He was suffering from insomnia when he wrote it, restless and fuddled from having heard a poem, supposedly by Cicero, in which the orator bemoaned his male secretary Tiro's refusal to kiss him. The poem was probably spurious, but this did not seem to trouble or even to occur to Pliny, who welcomed it as proof that 'the minds of great men rejoice/ in natural wit and charm of variety rich'.[45] Hearing Cicero's sorry complaints roused something deep inside him. In his wakefulness, Pliny found himself able to express what he had bottled up for some

time. Through the example of 'Cicero', he discovered an inner
confidence to 'plough out in verse that very thing that had trig-
gered me to write':

> 'Why after this,' I ask, 'Should I conceal my affairs
> And be afraid to bring some light to my Tiro's wiles and
> confess
> That I have known the alluring refusals of a Tiro
> Which furtively heap flame on new flame?'[46]

They were not the lightest or freest or most elegant of words (he
admitted that he was out of practice), but Pliny had at last found
a voice in which to express his private feelings – 'to love and
grieve and moan and rage'. In his rather overladen hexameters
he gave up the fight to conceal his experience of sexual frustration. This frustration was brought on not by his wife, the
mild-mannered Calpurnia, but by a fickle and teasing youth.
Was he a boy? Or was he, like Tiro, a former slave of similar
age to his master? Pliny was playing a poetic game in likening
himself to Cicero, but he was also revealing something of his
own struggle as an ordinarily buttoned-up, self-regarding man of
responsibilities in thrall to a frivolous male 'tease'.[47] Pliny would
never write with the confidence and elegance of Catullus or
Calvus, but he had taken a leap, and in doing so satisfied his
literary if not his sexual appetite.

When Pliny wasn't confessing his secret desires he was seeking
to capture the beauty of art and Nature in his verses. His contemporaries even sang some of his poems before an audience
– though few of the lines have survived the course of history. In
one poem Pliny attempted to describe the malleability of the
human mind:

Praise is like wax, it softens, yields and obeys
The skilled fingers which press it into art;
Now shaping Mars or chaste Minerva,
Now resembling Venus, now Venus' child;
And as sacred springs not only quench fires
But succour flowers and spring meadows, too,
So the mind of man ought to learn the flexibility
Of change; to be altered and influenced by malleable
    art.[48]

It was rather overwrought and scientific, but Pliny's poem was at least inspired by life. The first 'flowers and spring meadows' were not to be found in Rome's poetry schools but in the landscapes surrounding his Tuscan and Laurentine villas. At the coming of spring, the sheep and cattle and horses would be driven from the hills of Laurentum and 'develop glossy coats from the grass and spring temperatures' of the meadowland.[49] Pliny had observed how his flowers responded to water, changing shape in accordance with their thirst. In his poem he compares them to the human mind in the mind's ability to alter its form through absorbing the beauty of art.

The mind and the meadow are associated through Pliny's allusion to wax, the product of the bees which pollenate the flowers. The most industrious of all the creatures to feature in the Elder's *Natural History*, the bee had an important role to play in Pliny's life, too, flitting through his fields as soon as she stirred from hibernation with the flowering of the bean plant.[50] The urgency of her work is missing from most men's lives. The bee draws pollen from the meadows while she still can, knowing that the opportunity will soon pass. Pliny was already as diligent as a honey bee, but in his poem he proposed to display something of her flexibility. Heeding his own advice to refresh his mind by altering the seeds he sowed, he determined to move with the seasons.

For the 'sacred springs' of his poem, Pliny needed to look no further than his home town of Comum (modern Como) and its lake – which was known in ancient times as Larius. On the lake's southern shores, near the modern town of Torno, was a spring beside a waterfall that impressed Leonardo da Vinci no less than Pliny and his uncle with its peculiar motion. Centuries after Pliny the Elder first recorded the water's continuous ebb and flow, Leonardo observed the spring swelling for six hours and then diminishing so far for the next six that it was 'like watching water in a deep well'.[51] In fair weather, Pliny would lie down beside the spring and remove a ring from his finger. Placing the ring on the edge of the rocks, he would observe the 'great phenomenon' of water rising to conceal it, and then falling to reveal it again.[52]

The sight of the water and its curious rise and fall brought Pliny to the minds of Percy Bysshe and Mary Shelley during their visit to Lake Como in April 1818. This was the first lake they had seen since Lake Geneva two years earlier, and for Shelley, who spent much of his life in boats, something of a respite after the Swiss experience. Eighteen sixteen had been the 'Year Without a Summer', the Tambora volcano having erupted in Indonesia and blackened the skies across much of Europe and eastern America. Arriving in Switzerland in the spring of that year only to find it still covered in snow, the couple had resolved to make the most of the cold and murky darkness by exchanging ghost stories over the long nights with Lord Byron and Dr John Polidori. While Shelley found himself sufficiently spooked by the tales to fall into a hallucinatory stupor, Mary suffered a nightmare in which there appeared to her 'the hideous phantasm of a man', still at first, then awakened 'on the working of some powerful engine'.[53] Her dream spawned *Frankenstein*, which was published anonymously two years later.

The Shelleys travelled to Como a few months after the book

came out in search of better weather and health. 'This lone lake, in this far land,' as Shelley described it in his *Rosalind and Helen*, struck them as the perfect retreat for the coming summer.[54] The volcanic gloom had cleared by the time they arrived in April, and it was in the course of seeking a villa to rent that they found themselves thinking of Pliny. Having made their way from Como they came to 'a villa called the Pliniana, from its being built on the site of a fountain, whose periodical ebb and flow is described by the younger Pliny in his letters', which Mary had recently been reading.[55] The fountain and its spring must also have been familiar to Shelley, who had translated almost half the *Natural History* in his youth, including the passage in which Pliny the Elder described their ebbing waters.[56] The Pliniana villa had been built in 1573 around the spring. The villa's courtyard overlooked the lake on one side. The other side was occupied by the fountain and, as Mary Shelley recalled, 'bounded by a mountain, from whose stony side gushed, with roar and splash, the celebrated fountain'.

The Shelleys were quite taken with the property but failed to obtain the lease. According to Claire Clairmont, Mary Shelley's stepsister and mother of Byron's daughter Allegra, Percy had the misfortune of being taken into custody after deciding to fire his pistol in 'some solitary place' on the lake. He was released only after Mary gave assurance that he was not intending to kill himself (or presumably anyone else).[57] The episode may have cost him the Villa Pliniana or it may have been a story invented to disguise Shelley's impregnation of a servant during the trip.[58] Whatever it was that prevented the Shelleys from securing the Villa Pliniana, their memories of Pliny's spring stayed with them long after they had left. More than twenty years later, Mary was still thinking of 'the Pliniana, which remained in my recollection as a place adorned by magical beauty'.[59] The influence of Pliny's spring and waterfall (as well as the Swiss Alps) can also be seen in the imagery of Percy Shelley's *Prometheus Unbound*, a story of the ancient counterpart to 'the modern Prometheus' of Mary's *Frankenstein*: 'Like fountain-vapours when the winds are dumb,/ That climb up the ravine in scattered lines./ And, hark! is it the music of the pines?/ Is it the lake? Is it the waterfall?'[60]

Now a luxury hotel, Villa Pliniana – *Pliniana* like Pliny the Elder's favourite cherry – retains its mysterious spring. It runs under the building; open a window on an otherwise unremarkable corridor and it's there, as loud as the flow from a dozen ruptured pipes, a glittering white slide upon a stairwell of rock. The spring continues to flow and tinkle over the moss of the courtyard pool even when, quite without warning, the water ceases to gush down the mountain side. For months at a time the cliff lies dry. Rainfall has no apparent influence upon the proclivities of its flow. On the terrace at dusk, some visitors gamely soak their hands in the mountain-cold waters where Pliny once drank and watched 'with the greatest pleasure' before retrieving his ring from the rocky ledge. As they repair to their rooms the more circumspect guests notice that, just as suddenly as it vanished, the waterfall has begun to play again.

Pliny never stopped wondering how the spring worked. Does it follow the progress of the waves, or is it like a river, forced back as it flows towards the sea by the strength of the wind or tide? Does *spiritus*, Nature's breath, the same force that his uncle believed could trigger earthquakes, pass in and out of hidden apertures? Puzzled by the ebb and flow of the spring in particular, Pliny wrote to a friend, a senator named Licinius Sura, to ask him for an explanation. He was the same friend he wrote to regarding the possible existence of ghosts. Although Pliny did not in general keep practical friends – *sunt enim omnes togati et urbani* ('they are all toga-wearers and city men') – Licinius Sura clearly had a keen interest in natural and supernatural phenomena.[61] He is known to have been a wealthy man, who built a gymnasium for the people of Rome, as well as a gifted orator.[62] He later became such a good friend to the emperor Trajan that he hosted him for dinner and was even honoured by him with a public funeral and statue when he died. Pliny clearly considered him a man of great intellect – Sura was 'the most famous of learned men', according to Martial – and the likeliest of his friends to understand the mysteries of Nature.[63] Licinius' response to Pliny's letter does not survive, but perhaps he explained to him that the depth of the water was determined by the displacement of air by a siphon-like mechanism within the spring.[64]

Pliny made use of a similar mechanism in the 'Tuscan villa' he owned in the countryside near modern Perugia. In the shade of four vine-covered Carystian marble columns, he kept a curved bench made of shining white marble, from which would pour forth little jets of water 'as if squeezed out by the weight of the people who sat on it'.[65] The water collected in a delicate basin fitted with a siphon so that it never overflowed. When he wanted to be particularly lavish, Pliny would fill the basin with little models of ships and birds, upon which he would balance his lightest hors d'oeuvres for dinner guests to fish out at their leisure. The starters and heavier courses would be arranged around the basin's edge, like his ring upon the spring's verge. If Pliny had discovered the secret of the rising and falling spring near Comum, then he put this knowledge to imaginative use in his majestic floating dining table.

SEVEN

The Shadow of Verona

Filled as our culture is with the classical spirit, we can
hardly imagine how deeply the human mind was moved,
when, at the Renaissance, in the midst of a frozen world,
the buried fire of ancient art rose up from under the soil.

Walter Pater, *The Renaissance*, 1873[1]

Pliny once visited a lake filled with floating islands, 'all of
them grassy with reeds and sedge and whatever else fertile
marsh at the edge of a lake puts forth'.[2] Lake Vadimon (Lago di
Bassano), situated some eighty kilometres north of Rome, captivated him with its rare beauty. It is small and round, 'very like
a wheel lying on its side'; its water was said to be so healing that
it could mend fractured bones.

Pliny stooped to smell it: sulphuric. And to taste it: medicinal.
While the lake had no boats, for it was 'sacred', the sight of the
islands passing over its surface called to mind a busy harbour.
When the smaller islands weren't attaching themselves to the
larger ones, 'like skiffs to merchant ships', they were brushing
past each other and knocking pieces out of each other's sides.
If not entirely unlike the pumice islands which formed on the
waters off Pompeii in the early stages of the eruption, the floating

masses of Vadimon delighted Pliny as they raced one another over the 'whiter than sky blue' water.

The most extraordinary spectacle of all was of cattle inadvertently stepping onto the islands while they grazed. It was only when the poor cows were some distance from the mainland that they realised that the ground was moving. Though terrified to be surrounded by water, they seemed to Pliny to be oblivious to disembarking onto terra firma once the wind had blown their islands back to the banks. 'There are very many things in our city and near our city which we know neither with our eyes nor with our ears,' Pliny wrote soon after visiting the lake for the first time. He left convinced that people were too quick to go abroad in search of new sights when there were so many wonders 'under their eyes'. He asked himself why this was and considered that it was not necessarily through desire for exoticism, or even avarice, as Pliny the Elder had often supposed, but simply because we put off going to see what we know we can visit at any time.

Pliny could never have been accused of overlooking the places nearest him. Even in his home town of Comum he was forever going in search of new sights. Lake Larius may have lacked the symmetry and cows of Lake Vadimon, but it had its own quirks which he was only too keen to explore. From the mysterious spring where he placed his ring he would wander down to the coast and boat up the lake. Once he was far enough out, he enjoyed looking at the villas on the shoreline and trying to spot the private terraces and gardens which were ordinarily hidden from view.

He was not far now from the main town. Novum Comum, as it was formerly known, was founded by Julius Caesar in 59 BC within a neat, rectangular grid of roads to the south of the lake. Going some way towards compensating for the Romans' defeat of the local tribes in 196 BC, Caesar had conferred first Latin rights then Roman citizenship upon the people of the new town, which entitled them to vote in Rome's elections.[3] A vibrant centre with high walls and low horizons, Comum was accessible from both water and road. Visitors from nearby Mediolanum (Milan) and its environs came by the latter, filing into the town via a large gate flanked by two octagonal towers. There was one entrance for pedestrians and two for horses and carriages; their heavy wheels left grooves in the stone, much of which was quarried from Moltrasio, just across the lake from Torno and its spring.

Limestone from the same quarry was used in the construction of a large set of baths nearby. A maze of rooms – rectangular, octagonal, crescent-shaped – was laid out between barrel-vaulted corridors adorned with richly decorated red walls and rounded archways.[4] Every year during the festivals of Neptune, the bathers and exercisers of Comum would receive free perfumed oil at the bequest of one Lucius Caecilius Cilo, a local magistrate who set aside a generous 40,000 sesterces for this purpose in his will.[5] He has been identified variously as Pliny's father, paternal grand-father, and great-uncle, but could equally have been a more distant relation.[6] Pliny provided in his own will for the construc-tion and decoration of baths in the town. Perhaps his funds went towards developing the existing set, which were expanded and refurbished in the century he died.[7] (Their foundations survive today in the basement of a car park.)

Buildings were being erected in such numbers both within and beyond Comum's town walls that Pliny could only 'rejoice, because my *patria* is going from strength to strength'.[8] There were temples to Jupiter and Mercury, and one to Rome and her emperors which was built by a local magistrate and military engineer named Lucius Caecilius Secundus, another contender for being Pliny's father, and dedicated by his son.[9] A magnificent sculpture of Augustus in the guise of Pontifex Maximus presided over what was probably the forum, at Piazza San Fedele.[10] There was also a theatre and, just beyond the walls, on the very outskirts of the town, a meticulously designed brothel. A labyrinth of small rooms, each with their own heating system, was arranged around a central courtyard and large communal kitchen.[11] The complex extended to perhaps 6,000 square metres. Business must have been thriving.

Pliny never tired of coming back to Comum. It was his *deliciae*, his 'delight', a word he might sooner have used to describe a lover or a pet than a town.[12] Whenever he was away he longed for its fishing (the lake is particularly rich in trout, pike and perch) and hunting 'as an ill man desires wine and baths and springs'.[13] Though never the most dexterous of sportsmen, Pliny boasted of being able to fish and hunt and read while he was here – all at the same time. You appreciate how far he was exaggerating when you see how steeply the mountains rise from the lake. The people of Comum appear to have had rather a habit of magnifying the opportunities of their landscapes. A large relief sculpture exhibited in their town celebrated their prowess at hunting with horses, dogs and spears.[14] One bold hunter is shown grappling with an enormous lion.

Comum was a hunter's paradise but also an Arcadia. Pliny had a friend, a fellow equestrian named Caninius Rufus, who transformed his corner of the town into something out of Virgil's *Eclogues*. His villa had a colonnade where it was 'always spring' with views over a shady grove of plane trees, sun-soaked, open-air baths, and a sparkling green stream that flowed into the lake.[15] Italian archaeologists have been eager to locate it on Via Zezio on the lower slopes of the Colle di Brunate mountain.[16] Built in the late first century AD, possibly over three storeys, the villa they excavated had a long paved walkway, black and white mosaic floors, and extravagantly adorned walls.[17] Some had frescoes inspired by the waves of the sea or lake. Others featured niches mosaicked in blue, turquoise, green, yellow, brown and white glass – a 'new invention' when Pliny the Elder was alive.[18] Pliny made no hesitation in crowning Caninius Rufus' house *suburbanum amoenissimum* after the *locus amoenus* or idealised countryside setting of pastoral poetry. Amorous shepherds may not have been reclining beneath its porch, but the goddess of love was not far away; an exquisite bronze and gilt statuette of the Venus Pudica was discovered in a charred wooden box at the site.[19]

In the sixteenth century, the Como scholar Benedetto Giovio stumbled upon some tesserae of an ancient mosaic which he believed to have come from the villa of Caninius Rufus. The remains lay at Borgo Vico, at the south of the lake, some distance from the town and the Colle di Brunate. When Benedetto's brother Paolo saw this stretch of coast he felt it was so evocative of the plane trees and ancient baths and springtime walks which Pliny had described at Caninius Rufus' villa in his letter, that he determined to establish a villa-museum on top of it.[20]

It was in the brothers' interests to highlight as many Como sites as possible in Pliny's letters to counter the claims of the Veronese. In constructing his museum on the supposed grounds of Caninius Rufus' former estate, Paolo Giovio established a new Plinian landmark. When the building was finished in 1543 its walls were hung with hundreds of portraits of famous poets, scholars, politicians and artists. The portraits of the artists were a particular attraction. Paolo Giovio had read an early draft of Vasari's (ultimately illustrated) *Lives of the Most Excellent Painters, Sculptors, and Architects* and urged its immediate publication before it could be illustrated.[21] While it was not Paolo's intention to divert readers from Vasari's book, anyone who did want to look into the eyes of the most celebrated artists needed only to make their way to his Plinian museum. His magnificent building had views over the lake and a balcony to fish from in homage to one of the villas Pliny described in his letters.[22]

Pliny had 'many villas' near Comum, including an undisclosed number inherited from his parents, but there were two firm favourites.[23] Perched on a high ridge 'overlooking the lake like the villas at Baiae' (in the Bay of Naples) was 'Tragedy'. It was elevated on a rock that divided two bays, and in a marvellous conceit it was said to resemble a pair of *cothurni* – calf-hugging, heavy-soled, lace-up boots worn by actors when they performed Greek tragedies. Then there was 'Comedy', which curved around a single bay and sat low in its plot like a comic actor in his little *socci* slippers. It took some imagination to liken the two villas to footwear, not least because the theatre was not as popular in Pliny's time as it once was, but whoever first named them might have taken his cue from the lake itself. Lake Como is shaped like a pair of splayed legs with two feet – or the thong of a sandal.[24] Pliny extended both houses and endeavoured to make the most of their peculiarities. For once he let loose, indulging his fantasies of a spoiling *otium* ('leisure') and putting on a display worthy of the theatre itself. Throwing a line from a window of his low-rise 'Comedy', he would sit and fish from his bedroom – 'and practically even from the bed'.[25]

Paolo Giovio liked to tell people that his museum stood on the site of one of these villas rather than Caninius Rufus'. His brother Benedetto, however, was anxious not to mislead.[26] If he could only find evidence of where Pliny's villas had really stood then the Veronese would have to concede defeat. Taking Pliny's letters in his hands, Benedetto cast his eye over every 'high ridge dividing two bays' of the lake in the hope that he might still find Pliny's 'Tragedy'. While he had to admit there were rather a lot of bays, he could not help but notice one particularly prominent ridge overlooking the water. Positioned at the groin of the two legs of the lake, some hours from Como town, was Bellagio. Until recently it had been home to the palace of a courtier of Ludovico Sforza of Milan, but a fire had destroyed the building, leaving the expanse now occupied by the handsome gardens of Villa Serbelloni.[27]

Benedetto began the steep ascent from the lakefront to these elevated grounds. This would have been a trying walk for Pliny, who, as Benedetto recalled, had 'a slender frame that could not tolerate much exertion', but he found its inhabitants insistent that the famous 'Tragedy' had once stood here.[28] The steep hills of Bellagio offered an exquisite panoramic view of the three branches of the lake and the Alps beyond. Resting here, Benedetto was high enough up to watch the fishermen without being sprayed by their catch: the site seemed to match Pliny's description. Although the historian could see nothing of the villa itself, he learned of the discovery of some pieces of stone inscribed with the name of one Marcus Plinius.[29] Dated to the first or second century AD, these fragments, made from black Varenna marble, reveal that Marcus Plinius came from the same tribe as Pliny and was involved in the 'administration of justice' as a *quattuorvir* or local magistrate.[30] He may have been no relation of Pliny, but clearly Bellagio was a desirable spot for the wealthy men of Comum to keep a home.

A few decades after Benedetto surveyed the lake, a cartographer named Abraham Ortelius began to prepare what would be the first modern atlas. As he set about creating a map of Lake Como, he turned to the Giovio brothers and their recent scholarship. Depicting each and every mountain peak on the perimeters of the water, every town, village, and monument of interest, Ortelius marked Bellagio as the promontory where Pliny kept his villa called 'Tragedy'.[31] Benedetto's ventures had not been in vain. The town of Torno, meanwhile, was identified merely as 'Fons Plinianus' (Pliny's Spring), and 'Comedy' was situated at the town of Lenno.[32] Looking at the finished map in Ortelius' *Theatrum Orbis Terrarum* it is easy to imagine Pliny rowing leisurely from one to the other across the water. Ortelius' drawing

131

made it clear that, if Tragedy and Comedy were located at Bellagio and Lenno, then they had good views of one another across the lake, which would have been entirely appropriate to Pliny's tastes and humour. Tragedy is the opposite of Comedy. Bellagio is opposite Lenno. As with so many features of his life, Pliny found his two villas all the more pleasant for the contrast between them. The contrast could only have been keener for the two villas being in sight of each other. With his seminal atlas Ortelius reinforced Pliny's connection with Como.

Benedetto Giovio's *Historiae Patriae*, published posthumously the following century, remains one of the most elegant pieces of scholarship on the lives of the Plinys in Comum. Yet to be translated from the Latin and Italian, it is a testament to one man's pride in his native town. In it he demolished the arguments of the Veronese, illuminating the errors of Jerome, Petrarch, Biondo and others, and used his knowledge of former Gaul to explain what Pliny the Elder meant when he called Catullus his 'fellow countryman'. Together with his brother Paolo, he had done everything he could to re-establish the place of the Plinys in Como's history. To this day no trace of Tragedy or Comedy has been found, but Bellagio and Lenno remain for many scholars the most probable locations. Paolo's lakeside museum no longer survives, but many of the antiquities and inscriptions he acquired were transferred to a palazzo formerly owned by his family. This palazzo is now home to Como's Museo Civico. A plaque on the stairway commemorates the two brothers who invested so much in the lives of their ancient forebears.

EIGHT

Portrait of a Man

He peered in front of him and right and left through the
gloom and thought that those must be portraits. It was dark
and silent and his eyes were weak and tired with tears so
that he could not see. But he thought they were the portraits
of the saints and great men of the order who were looking
down on him silently as he passed . . .

James Joyce, A *Portrait of the Artist as a Young Man,*
1916

Pliny bestowed many, many gifts upon Comum in his lifetime
– 1.6 million sesterces' worth in all. But there was one
particular piece, a work of art purchased for the temple of Jupiter,
about which he could not contain his excitement.[1] Made of
Corinthian bronze and cast in the shape of a naked, balding,
sinewy old man, it was far from the most appealing sculpture
ever to have been placed before a god, but that was precisely
why Pliny liked it.* The bronze does not survive but similar art

---

* Like the Romans of the Republic, Pliny favoured verisimilitude over abstraction
in figural art. He once sought for a scholar's library copies of a portrait of
Cornelius Nepos, the historian and patron of Catullus, and one of Titus Catius,
an Epicurean philosopher, and stressed that, though copies of a copy, they ought
to be as accurate as possible.

works do: there is a small terracotta figurine of a fat, middle-aged bald man dressed in a toga from a similar date in the Giovio archaeological museum.

Pliny was full of praise for the honesty of his new acquisition: 'This is a statue that even I can understand. For it is nude, so cannot conceal any imperfections it may have or give too limited a display of its virtues. It represents an old man standing: his bones, muscles, sinews, veins and even his wrinkles are visible as if he were living and breathing. What hair he has is receding, his forehead is broad, his face drawn, his neck slender; his shoulders slope, his chest is slack, his stomach hollowed; from the back it gives the same picture of age.'[2]

Pliny did not presume to know anything about art. In his description he was careful not to emulate the private collectors in Rome who were notorious for 'feigning knowledge . . . so as to separate themselves from the masses, as opposed to having any real understanding of the subject', as Pliny the Elder sharply put it.[3] It had become the particular mark of a pseud to sniff metal in the belief that authentic Corinthian bronze could be identified by scent.[4] Petronius, Nero's former 'arbiter of excellence', had written a satire in which a braggart freedman named Trimalchio claimed to prefer glassware to bronze as 'it certainly does not smell'. The inspiration for F. Scott Fitzgerald's Jay Gatsby, Trimalchio bores his guests with ludicrously inaccurate descriptions of Corinthian bronze having been formed by the melting of statues following 'Hannibal's sack of Troy'.[5]

Pliny the Elder had dedicated practically an entire book of his encyclopaedia to the discussion of metal sculptures. He had described how bronze came to be preferred to wood and clay for representations of men as well as gods, and dated its introduction to Italy to Lucius Scipio's treasure-laden return to Rome after his victory in Asia Minor in the second century BC.[6]

Although these were the triumphal parades which were held responsible for the birth of luxury in Rome, Pliny the Elder's initial disapproval of bronze had steadily been supplanted by an appreciation of its capacity to capture life. As far as he was aware, portraiture originated in Corinth in the seventh century BC when a girl used the light of a lamp to trace the shadow of her lover's face on a wall before he left for overseas.[7] Once she had produced the outline, her father, a potter named Butades, worked it up using clay so as to produce a novel portrait. The model was fired and provided the girl with something to remember her lover's face by. Now that people had taken to casting portraits of their loved ones in the more valuable medium of bronze, Pliny the Elder feared that a time would come when 'no one's true likeness survived'.[8] He claimed that the Romans had already taken to melting down bronze sculptures of their family members and adorning their homes with portraits of strangers instead.

Pliny the Elder's words proved in his own and his nephew's case to be prescient. There is not a contemporary likeness of either Pliny to be found. However, a skull that has long been rumoured to be Pliny the Elder's is currently undergoing investigation and could, potentially, be used to produce a three-dimensional model of his head.[9] The skull, which belonged to a man of the right sort of age to be Pliny the Elder, was excavated near the mouth of the river Sarno in the region of former Stabiae by an amateur archaeologist at the beginning of the twentieth century. During a series of privately funded digs, Gennaro Matrone uncovered a total of seventy-three ancient human skeletons and an assortment of personal belongings, including oil lamps, jewellery, and a Roman *gladius* (dagger) with ivory sheath.[10] The *gladius* is said to have been found beside a skeleton that lay apart from the others, with a skull resting on a nearby pillar; a collection of bracelets, three large rings, and a heavy neck chain formed of seventy-five links, all in gold, was gathered around the torso.[11] Matrone's suggestion that these were the mortal remains of Pliny the Elder was met with ridicule by the archaeological establishment. The *gladius* and skull were bequeathed to the Museo Storico Nazionale dell'Arte Sanitaria in Rome, where they have remained ever since. The Italian press is optimistic that isotope analysis will confirm the identity of the skull, but experts remain rightly sceptical. The mandible that holds the teeth may even have come from another skeleton entirely.[12] If someone did report to Pliny having seen his uncle's body lying as if asleep on the day after the eruption, would he really have left him there without a tomb?

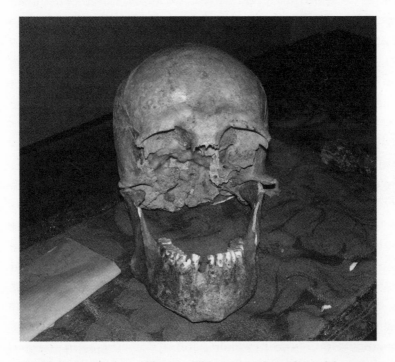

Could this be the face of Pliny the Elder? Scientific analysis of the isotopes in its teeth enamel should determine the geographical origins of the deceased.

Pliny the Elder might sooner have found his portrait reflected in his work and in his nephew than in his 2,000-year-old broken skull. The Romans liked to speak of their descendants inheriting not only their physical characteristics and family traits, but their passions, bad habits, and obsessions, too. As one man complained, 'A fascination with actors and obsession with gladiators and horses . . . almost seem to be conceived in the mother's womb.'[13] Behind this humour lay a genuine belief in the propensity of flaws to be passed down. It is not going too far to see in such ideas an early understanding of the evolutionary basis of inherited characteristics that would later be expounded by Charles Darwin. A keen reader of Pliny the Elder's *Natural History*, of which he owned a 'well skimmed' translation, Darwin had joined the Plinian Society for collectors as a medical student at Edinburgh before eventually developing his theory of the inheritability of tendencies in *The Descent of Man* in 1871.[14] Evoking the Romans, Darwin suggested that humans could inherit not only good habits, such as self-control and virtue, but bad ones such as stealing as well.[15]

The notion of the inheritability of good and bad qualities proved instructive for Pliny, who came to recognise sons in their fathers and even grandmothers in their granddaughters through their personalities more often than their faces. One day, he came by a terrible speech that had been copied out thousands of times and disseminated from Rome for public recital. It described the life of a boy who had died, but to hear it, said Pliny, 'you would believe it was written by a boy, not about one'.[16] Regulus had lost his son and composed an extended eulogy in his honour. Pliny had to admit that this was the one injustice Regulus did not deserve. The death of the boy might have prevented the superstitious lawyer from passing his cruelty on to future generations through his blood, but it was also a tragedy. The poet Martial, who enjoyed Regulus' support, had praised 'little Regulus' for the love he showed his father. Pliny might have shown some humanity by paying a similar tribute. Instead he used the occasion to describe the boy as 'sharp-witted but flaky'.[17] He followed Regulus' mourning with a morbid fascination: the overblown eulogy, the portraits of the deceased cast in wax, bronze, silver, gold, ivory and marble, the funeral pyre piled high with his pet Gallic ponies and dogs, nightingales, parrots, the blackbirds slaughtered around it.[18] 'That was not grief,' offered Pliny, his imagination fired by the scene, 'but a display of grief.' A son was little more than an underdeveloped portrait of his parents. Given time, 'little Regulus' would no doubt have proved himself his father's son.

Pliny's mean-heartedness over Regulus' boy resounds in his letters because it was so at odds with the immense generosity he normally showed the younger generation. A considerable proportion of the 1.6 million sesterces Pliny bestowed upon Comum was directed towards the education of schoolboys and girls. Until a time came for him to have children of his own, he concentrated on instilling his virtues in the sons and daughters of his townspeople. Pliny took the long view, envisaging a time when Comum would be so famous for its scholarship and learning that families from all over Italy would seek to send their children to study there. If he oversaw the education of one generation then he might hope that they would grow up to produce intelligent children of their own.

Pliny knew from experience where Comum fell short. He had received his own education there under a *grammaticus* (private tutor) before leaving for Rome while 'barely a young adolescent' to study under Nicetes Sacerdos, a well-known Greek scholar from Smyrna (Izmir), and Quintilian, a professor of oratory who originally came from Spain.[19] From these men Pliny would have learned how malleable young minds can be. As Quintilian said, children took to learning 'as naturally as birds take to flight, horses to the racecourse, and wild beasts to savagery'.[20] Pliny reasoned that if he could only provide a fuller education for the children of Comum on their home soil then they would be more willing to stay there and enhance its position and reputation within Italy in the future.[21]

Pliny had been left unimpressed, also, by the youths he saw employed by the Court of One Hundred. Writers had in recent years voiced their concerns over a general decline in educational standards. Wistful for the old days, when boys had accompanied their fathers to the courts to learn oratory first hand, they despaired at the increasing irrelevance of the curriculum.[22] Pupils often now engaged in practice debates on topics drawn from Greek tragedy, and while these were often very dynamic, it was sometimes difficult to see what application arguments about tyrannicide or the ethics of Greek burial could have to everyday life in Rome. As a consequence of this kind of training, oratory was said to have lost its force and seriousness. At the beginning of the *Satyricon*, Nero's former 'arbiter of elegance' Petronius has his narrator observe how young men enter the courtroom only to find themselves in a totally different world from the one they had been prepared for:

> And so I believe that young men turn into complete idiots in the rhetoric schools because they neither hear nor see anything that's useful; instead they hear of pirates standing enchained on the shore, of tyrants writing edicts impelling their sons to chop off their fathers' heads, of oracles given in times of plague encouraging three or more virgins to be sacrificed, of little honey-dipped balls of words – all that's said and done as good as sprinkled in poppy and sesame seeds.[23]

Pliny seems to have viewed his wealth and standing as an opportunity to hone a new and improved generation. A chance encounter with a local boy provided him with all the impetus he needed to lay the first foundations in this venture. The unfortunate boy was having to travel all the way to Mediolanum to study because there was such a shortage of teachers in Comum. Since he did 'not yet' have any children of his own, Pliny kindly proposed to pay a third of whatever sum the boy's father could raise to employ a new teacher for the town. He likened his contribution to one he would make 'on behalf of a daughter or mother', by which he meant that it would not be so large that he would miss it were it to be misdirected, 'as I've seen happen in many places in which teachers are paid from public funds'. While he cast around for a suitable candidate – and called upon the ever resourceful Tacitus to help him find one – he arranged for all the parents of Comum to pool their funds with his, 'for those who are, perhaps, forgetful with other people's money are certainly careful with their own'.[24]

It was a source of continual worry to the wealthy men of Comum that their acts of generosity might be abused. Pliny's friend Caninius Rufus, who kept the colonnade where it was 'always spring', sought his advice about how best to protect the money he had set aside in his will for an annual feast in the town.[25] Pliny recommended that he follow his own example, which involved feeding the intended sum through an interest-raising scheme. Pliny pledged 500,000 sesterces to support the education of at least 150 freeborn boys and girls in Comum (Quintilian had also advocated the education of girls, if only to ensure they became good examples to their future sons).[26] To raise the revenue, he released to an agent some of his property, which was valued far higher, at a rent of 30,000 sesterces a year. The process provided him with an annual return of six per cent on his 500,000 and a reliable flow of money to the education fund.[27] And it would appear that Pliny's investments paid off. The people of Comum received such an excellent teacher in the shape of one Publius Atilius Septicianus that they elected to honour him with a statue in their town centre.[28]

Once Pliny had started he found it very difficult to stop: 'My long and deeply pondered love of liberality loosens the bonds that bind me to greed.'[29] He had a library built at Comum and put aside a generous sum for its decoration and maintenance. There survives a set of exquisitely carved marbles which are thought to have adorned the column bases of an important building in the town – possibly the library itself. They feature a master or a muse teaching a pupil, a boxing contest, and mythological scenes including Perseus rescuing Andromeda, Leda and the swan, and Apollo with the Delphic tripod.[30]

To mark the opening of the new library, Pliny delivered a speech to the councillors of Comum. 'A little too vainglorious and lofty' was his verdict upon re-reading it some time later.[31] He knew that good Stoics ought to be generous but not draw attention to their acts of generosity. Torn, however, between his altruism on the one hand and desire for praise on the other, Pliny had also found himself obliged to enlarge upon the kindnesses his own parents had showered upon the town before him. Such obligations rather hindered his ability to present himself as the modest philanthropist.

Despite this difficulty, he knew that Comum was where he stood the best chance of securing his legacy through the next generation. The truest portrait of Pliny ever to have existed was not a bust or a bronze but the vast panorama of people who gathered here to revere and thank him for the buildings he had financed.

NINE

The Death of Principle

The Country Mouse had never seen anything like it, and
sat down to enjoy the luxuries his friend provided: but
before they had well begun, the door of the larder opened
and someone came in.

From Aesop's 'The Town Mouse and the Country Mouse'[1]

Pliny shared in common with his uncle an enquiring mind,
an eye for minutiae, obsessive diligence, and an eagerness
to extend the bounds of mortal existence. He also shared his
love of stories, not only of the natural world, but of extremes of
human behaviour. It is when Pliny digresses on some tale or
other that he sounds most like the elder Pliny. He was probably
conscious of this: the more he sounded like his uncle, the more
he would prove himself worthy of being his adopted son. While
Pliny was not inclined to record observations in the manner of
a naturalist, he did like to share stories which revealed the gulf
between man and Nature to be less yawning than one might
have anticipated it to be. The line between man and animal,
bird and man, creeping insect and bodily affliction grew hazier
with almost every discovery he made.

Nature was never so interesting to Pliny as when it mirrored
what he perceived to be a human characteristic. Perhaps he

thought of his uncle's description of birds with the 'tongues of men' when Regulus piled his son's funeral pyre high with parrots and nightingales. In the *Natural History*, nightingales are said to possess 'a perfect understanding of music', breaking the silence of winter by settling in the trees and 'singing for fifteen days and nights without cease while the buds spring into life'.[2] They display what Pliny the Elder had seen as a kind of expertise in the modulation of their song, drawing out a long note in a single exhalation one moment, quavering and trilling the next. Pliny the Elder had shuddered to recall how an actor once served an exorbitant dish consisting purely of birds whose song emulated human speech, 'seduced to such folly for no other reason than that he might eat an imitation of man'.[3]

Pliny was as aggrieved as his uncle had been by the idea that humans might punish creatures with near-human traits, and developed it further in his letters. In the *Natural History*, the sea-dwelling equivalent to the nightingale is the dolphin, 'the very fastest of all animals, not only of sea creatures, faster than a bird' which has a short, wide tongue – 'not unlike a pig's' – which allows it to sigh in what Pliny the Elder supposed could be mistaken for a human voice.[4] In a letter to his Comum friend Caninius Rufus, Pliny decided to retell a story that had also featured in his uncle's encyclopaedia. In his version of the tale he went beyond comparing the dolphin's sigh to a man's to show that it possessed more humanity and intelligence than humans themselves.

His story is set in the Roman town of Hippo Diarrhytus (Bizerte) on the coast of north Africa, where some boys are holding a competition to swim as far as possible across a lake and towards an estuary leading out to sea. One boy has come into deep water when he sees a dolphin, which proceeds to carry him safely back to shore. Caninius Rufus would have been reminded of a famous Greek story about a musician named Arion, who was said to have been saved by a dolphin after he threw himself into the sea to escape some evil sailors.[5] In Pliny's story, the villain is rather Roman superstition. Having been saved once by the dolphin, the boy returns over several days to play with it, and soon others join in. 'It is incredible,' said Pliny, 'but as true as what I've told already, that the dolphin that carried and sported with the boys would also be dragged out onto the land, dry out in the sand, and be rolled back into the sea when it grew hot.'[6] Through its tameness and tricks the dolphin wins over the residents who initially feared it. But then one of the Roman governors is driven by 'crooked belief' to pour perfume over its back, 'the novelty and smell of which made it retreat into deeper water'.[7] Eventually the dolphin returns, but becomes such an attraction that locals mourn the loss of peace. In a bid to banish the tourists from the town, the dolphin is secretly killed.

This had to be one of the most affecting stories Pliny had heard. 'With what pity you will weep,' he wrote to Caninius, whom he hoped would retell it without embellishment. He had captured perfectly in his version the contrast between the dolphin's intelligence and the humans' lack of instinct. Pliny found stories like these worthy of inclusion in his letters because they demonstrated the ignorance of assuming man's superiority over Nature and highlighted the risks of celebrating its more arcane elements over the things 'under the eyes'. His uncle had displayed a far deeper fascination with wondrous species. In his *Natural History* he described briefly such phenomena as 'scia-pods' – one-legged people in India who allegedly reclined on their backs with their legs in the air and shaded themselves from the sun beneath their enormous feet – and individuals in the Balkans with two pupils in each eye who could kill with a look.[8] While Pliny the Elder wrote with such conviction as to almost be believable, his nephew evidently had less interest in stories of fabulous creatures than in moral tales.

Pliny's friends appreciated his appetite for unusual ones and raced to add their own to his repertoire. Of the 'various miraculous stories from here and there' which found their way into Pliny's letters, there was one that challenged more than any other his way of thinking about the tales we tell each other. Like the story of the dolphin, it was concerned with the unpredictable choices humans make in unusual situations. He heard it while he and an elderly friend were sailing over Lake Larius (Como) and passed by a villa with a bedroom overlooking the water.[9] Gesturing at the house, his companion began, 'From that bedroom there, a woman from our town once threw herself – and her husband – to her death.' The wife, he revealed, had bound herself to her husband with a rope, and together they had toppled over the window sill, sunk deep beneath the water, and drowned. Earlier in the day, her husband had confessed something to her. For some time, he said, he had been suffering from a terrible, ulcerating rash across his genitals. She insisted on taking a look at it to decide whether there was any hope. No sooner had he raised his toga to reveal his sores than his wife had deemed it terminal and decided that they were better off dead.

Pliny offered no comment on the unfortunate condition of the husband or speculation as to what might have been wrong with him. He was fascinated only by the courage and selflessness of the wife. She had not been thinking of her own health when she resolved to throw herself from the window. She had seemingly been imagining the rumours people would spread of her husband's disregard for his family had he committed suicide without her complicity. Her suicide gave his suicide a certain dignity. But was her decision not rather precipitate? Had the couple even attempted to find a cure?

The longest list of remedies for sores and ulcers was to be found in Pliny the Elder's *Natural History*.[10] Drawing, presumably, on what he had learned from the elderly plantsman, Antonius Castor, Pliny the Elder had assembled a sprawling list of natural treatments.

Greater Centaury could be applied to the skin as a powder or lotion, while the leaves of the Lesser were suitable for rubbing into unsightly swellings and sores. Then there was gentian; chelidonia; vervain; potentilla; salt and honey; butter; the ashes of a cremated dog's head; animal dung; millipedes ground up with turpentine and ochre; and smashed snails. There was also a stringent concoction of hemlock, wheat, wine, and white sedum (*aizoum*), which Pliny the Elder prescribed for 'herpetic sores' – a possible diagnosis of the man's rash. The herpes virus had been known to the Greeks since at least the fifth century BC, when Hippocrates, the father of medicine, likened it to a serpent. It crawled beneath the skin, undetected, then lay dormant, waiting to break out. Pliny the Elder recalled that the Greeks had also named a particular animal 'herpes' ('creeper') because they believed it could help to treat the sores.[11] Neither Pliny nor the couple from Comum seemed to realise that the infection was transmitted sexually, however. The wife was perhaps right to deem it terminal in so far as it is incurable, but wrong if she assumed that the sores were fatal. Had her husband waited a few more days, he might have seen his rash disappear, at least for a while.

Their suicides made a deep impression upon Pliny, who found himself less perturbed by the details than by the fact that he had not heard them before now. The story reinforced his suspicion that it is not what you do but who you are that matters. Some of the noblest deeds go unnoticed simply because they are performed by ordinary people. Every little thing a rich and famous man does, by contrast, is broadcast whether it is worthy or not.

This sad realisation sent Pliny on a trail of thoughts about the men and women who were remembered for their self-inflicted deaths – and those who were not. The most startling reports of suicide had reached Rome from the Jewish War in the late sixties and early seventies AD. Pliny would have passed the Arch of Titus with its cluttered scenes of war spoils whenever he walked through the Velia on his way to and from his home on the Esquiline Hill.[12] But Pliny was not thinking of the Jews. The suicides he recalled in his letters were less recent than those of the Jewish War, but distinctly more local. He thought of Caecina Paetus, a former Roman senator who was involved in a rebellion in Claudius' time, accused of treason, and forced to kill himself.[13] And of Caecina Paetus' wife Arria who, on sensing his fear, was said to have taken a dagger, stabbed herself, then handed him the weapon to do the same with the words, 'It does not hurt, Paetus.'

A large menorah was among the objects taken from the Temple of Jerusalem and paraded through Rome when Vespasian and Titus celebrated a triumph for their Jewish War in AD 71. The occasion is commemorated in this relief from the Arch of Titus, which was erected after the emperor's sudden death a decade later. Another panel on the arch shows the much-missed emperor being carried by an eagle in apotheosis.

It was while he reflected on these stories that Pliny began to reconsider his position on suicide itself. He had known Arria and considered her a friend, but after hearing about the suicide of the wife from Comum, he came to realise that Arria had acted when 'glory and immortality were before her eyes', which to his mind made her death perhaps the less honourable of the two.[14] He began to see that suicide was something people could turn to in order to achieve fame. The idea repulsed him. Fame was not necessarily Arria's motivation, but a conversation he had had with her granddaughter encouraged Pliny to believe that Arria ought to be remembered for the acts in her past which were truer testaments to her integrity. He would record these acts in his letters and in so doing rehabilitate her character in his own mind.

Pliny learned that Arria had once tended her husband and son when they were unwell and, when the boy died, concealed his death from her husband. She used to tell him that the boy was improving every day, 'then, when the tears she held in for so long overcame her and began to fall, she would leave the room' and only return when she had dried her eyes and composed herself.[15] This, not the suicide, was surely the most courageous thing she had ever done.

Pliny found Arria's granddaughter Fannia to be equally strong-willed. She had seen her father, Thrasea Paetus, and husband, Helvidius Priscus, put to death under Nero and Vespasian respectively and was determined to honour their memories. Thrasea had been a distinguished senator with a keen interest in Stoicism, and Pliny knew of his many aphorisms, including: 'He who hates vices, hates mankind.'[16]

Some vices, however, were too terrible not to hate. When Nero kicked his pregnant wife Poppaea to death in AD 65, Thrasea chose not to attend her funeral. He had then found himself facing a list of accusations carried by a disgruntled senator he had once prosecuted for extortion. The most serious of them was that he had failed to attend not only Poppaea's funeral but also the past three years' meetings in the senate. On one side there were claims that Thrasea had supporters, which made him a potential threat to Nero's power. On the other, his political secession and purported focus on private legal cases posed the greater risk to national stability, for 'if many dared to do the same, it would be war'.[17] The tense relationship between Thrasea and Nero was likened to that between Cato the Younger and Julius Caesar. When it emerged that Thrasea had been spending his time writing a biography of none other than the Stoic, Cato the Younger, Nero's fears seemed to be confirmed: Thrasea was in bitter opposition to his rule.[18]

Stoics were encouraged to play an active role in public life but might withdraw if they considered the man they were serving to be morally corrupt. While Stoicism was unlikely to turn a man into a demagogue, Thrasea's interests in the philosophy had only made him more suspect.[19] Nero had decreed that the Stoic Seneca commit suicide on grounds of having conspired against him. The Stoics had increasingly come to be seen as troublemakers. Thrasea's son-in-law Helvidius, a senator raised with Stoic beliefs, had campaigned for the senate to exercise authority independently of the emperor's desires and had shown Vespasian little respect. He was deemed a particular threat to the emperor because he behaved 'as if it were the task of his philosophy to besmirch those in power and to stir up the crowds, to confound the established order and foment change'.[20] Neither Nero nor Vespasian had been prepared to wait to see what might happen. Thrasea was condemned to death by Nero in AD 66, while his son-in-law went into exile a number of times before being executed upon Vespasian's orders about a decade later.

Fannia waited until Domitian was emperor before attempting to do something to honour both men. She had secreted away her husband's diaries and now sought a biographer brave enough to commemorate the lives of the men she had loved. Pliny saw two of his friends take up the task. Arulenus Rusticus, a consul who had encouraged him in his youth, agreed to write the life of Fannia's late father.[21] The biography of Fannia's late husband, meanwhile, was to be written by Pliny's colleague in the courts, Herennius Senecio.

If Pliny was uncertain as to why his friend Senecio had failed to climb the senatorial ladder with the same speed as he himself had, he now knew. The orator had withdrawn from political life in order to write. He was treading a perilous line considering the fate of the subject of his biography, and unfortunately seemed destined to go the same way. Compounding his withdrawal from public life with his decidedly Stoic book, Herennius Senecio found himself in hot water. In AD 93, in an uncomfortable echo of the events of Nero's rule, he was summoned before the senate. Here began a series of trials that culminated in Domitian's expulsion of philosophers from Italy.

Of all the crimes committed in the period around Herennius Senecio's arrest, 'none seemed more atrocious than the fact that a senator should have laid his hands . . . on a senator in the senate house'.[22] Pliny was back in Rome with Tacitus in AD 93 to witness the onslaught of senator against senator, *in senatu senator senatori* (Pliny's polyptoton conveyed the dreadfulness of the scene) as their colleagues laid out the case against the Stoic writers.

Senecio spoke in his own defence and confessed that Fannia had approached him to write a biography of her late husband.[23] She was then summoned to stand. The senator prosecuting her was a notorious political informer named Mettius Carus. Did she ask Senecio to write this book, he asked her?

'I did ask him.'

'Did you give Senecio your husband's diaries?'

'I did.'

'Did your mother know?'

'She did not know.'

Truly, the spirit of Fannia's relations was with her as she withstood the force of the prosecution. Behind her 'pleasant and charming' facade she was every bit as tough as her late grandmother who had plunged a dagger in her chest and told her husband it did not hurt.[24]

The questioning was in all cases fierce and relentless. As Mettius Carus proceeded with his case, Regulus, Pliny's fiend from the Centumviral Court, stepped in and began to savage one of the defendants. Assisting in the prosecution, Regulus went so far as to brand Arulenus Rusticus 'Stoicorum simiam' ('the Stoics' Ape') for his authorship of the biography. He was particularly proud of that line. Domitian was said to have dreamed that Rusticus had come upon him with a sword.[25] With his clever turn of phrase, Regulus saw him reduced to an animal.

Pliny did not confess in his letters to having any involvement in these proceedings. From the way he described his horror at watching one senator savage another and his grief at witnessing each Stoic suffer, anyone would think he had been a mere bystander. But the trial was taking place before the senate and at the direction of the senators. Pliny was a senator. At the end of the speeches the senators were required to cast votes on the case. When Tacitus described this moment some decades later he did so with far greater transparency than Pliny, documenting the role that he and his fellow senators played in words which were almost as tearful as they were confessional. Both he and Pliny had risen through the ranks of the senate under Domitian's rule and through his favour ('I would not deny it,' said Tacitus of his own progress under Domitian; Pliny was somewhat quieter on that front[26]). Both he and Pliny were reluctant participants in the philosophers' fall. 'Our hands led Helvidius into prison; the sight of Mauricus and Rusticus shattered us; Senecio drenched us in his innocent blood,' wrote Tacitus.[27]

At the denouement of the trials, the biographers Senecio and Rusticus were condemned to death. Rusticus' brother Mauricus, a recent consul, was exiled. His wife, exiled. Fannia and her mother, also exiled. Though at pains not to make it explicit in his letters, Pliny was complicit in the conviction of the men and women he called friends.[28] Did he feel that an admission of guilt would detract from the difficulty of the predicament he had found himself in? He alone could not have saved the Stoic biographers any more than Tacitus could have done. They were serving an emperor who took sadistic pleasure in watching his senators squirm. 'While Nero averted his eyes and did not watch the crimes he ordered,' Tacitus claimed, 'under Domitian it was the chief part of our miseries to see and be seen; our gasps were recorded and, the pallor of so many men duly noted, that savage face of his was tinged with the redness with which he guarded himself from shame.'[29] The flush Pliny had observed in Domitian's face had deepened.

The senate also passed a decree ordering the destruction of the two Stoic biographies. The books in which Fannia had invested so much hope, 'records of distinguished characters', Tacitus called them, were seized for burning in the forum. 'Certainly,' Tacitus said, 'it was thought that the voice of the Roman people and freedom of the senate and conscience of mankind would be obliterated in that fire.'[30] Somehow, Fannia managed to save the diaries, for Pliny said that she separated them from the other possessions of hers which were confiscated.[31] But still worse was to come.

Fannia had a stepson who was also put on trial. The young man had written a farce in which he was alleged to have mocked Domitian's marriage.[32] To the emperor's shame, his wife had once fallen for a young Egyptian actor named Paris. Her affections for the renowned 'wit of the Nile' of Egypt and 'delight of the city' of Rome had not gone unnoticed, but after a brief separation Domitian had decided to forgive her and take her back.[33] Paris was not seen after that, sparking a rumour that Domitian had had him killed in the street.[34] For embedding a reference to these embarrassing events in his farce, Fannia's stepson was put to death.

'Upon the occasion of the crime' of the biographers, Domitian 'banished all the philosophers from Italy and Rome,' wrote Suetonius.[35] No record was made of how many 'all' constituted, but Senecio and Rusticus were far from the only people to die 'on this same charge against philosophy'.[36] Their Stoicism in fact had very little to do with it.[37] In a bid to assert his influence and maintain a status quo, Domitian was prepared to silence anyone who was too vocal in their opinions or support for men his predecessors had deemed threats to imperial stability. One quip about the influence of the Egyptian actor Paris was sufficient to land the satirist Juvenal into exile in the Egyptian desert.[38] The Christians would later view Domitian as the second emperor to persecute them after Nero.[39] John the Apostle was relegated to Patmos. Domitian's own cousin Flavius Clemens was put to death 'on a very slight suspicion' of atheism, a charge frequently applied to those who had adopted the Jewish or Christian faith (monotheists, who believed in God, were seen as atheists for their failure to worship the Roman gods).[40] Flavius Clemens' wife and Domitian's niece, Flavia Domitilla, left for exile.[41] She would later be canonised.

Domitian's paranoia served the Christians better than it did the philosophers. According to a near-contemporary Christian, Domitian became so fearful of the Second Coming that he sought a meeting with the surviving grandchildren of Jude, who was said to have been a brother or cousin of Christ, to enquire about the kingdom of Christ.[42] Whether it was his new knowledge of the coming Judgement that did it, or what another Christian called his 'humanity', Domitian ceased to pursue the Christians and recalled any he had exiled.[43] The Stoics who were fortunate enough to have survived the death sentence, meanwhile, were left to languish in exile.

Back in Rome, Regulus gloated over what he saw as *his* victory over the philosophers.[44] He gave a public reading of the speech he had made branding Arulenus Rusticus 'the Stoics' Ape', wisely omitting Pliny from the guest list. The Stoic deaths became something for the vultures to pick over. Not content with broadcasting and then publishing his transcript, Regulus proceeded to mock the other biographer, Senecio, despite having played no part in his downfall. He was not only mocking but 'lacerating' him, said Pliny, who had not forgotten the rumour that Regulus had once bitten the head of a corpse. If anyone was an animal it was Regulus, but to have called him *simia* ('ape') would have been a disservice to an animal of 'extraordinary ingenuity'.[45] Reclaiming his spoils, Mettius Carus, the senator who *had* secured Senecio's conviction, tore into Regulus: 'What are my dead men to do with you?'[46]

Pliny had his colleagues in the senate on one side and his surviving 'friends' on the other. He later claimed to have been 'a comfort' to Fannia and her mother in their exile and to have lent them his services 'in good times and bad'.[47] Whatever he did to help them, he understood the danger that could come from associating with the condemned. He felt the risk, the heat, the flame of 'so many thunderbolts' falling around him like showers of molten rock, and was certain 'that the same fate was hanging over me too'.[48] He could not have suspected it at this stage, but Mettius Carus, one of the prosecution lawyers, would soon hand over to Domitian a list of accusations against him. The document would be found on the emperor's desk three years later, but already Pliny feared the impending fire of a thunderbolt.

*

Throughout his life Pliny felt the pull of leisure and the countryside – of Comum and its lake, of Laurentum, of his meadows
in central Italy – against the drama and necessity of work in the
city. The fates of the philosophers who had withdrawn from
public life could only have heightened his anxiety over staying
away from Rome for too long. While Domitian fell 'violently
upon many like a thunderbolt', it would have been natural for
Pliny to seek the spiciness of political life in Domitian's service
with all the more zeal. Instead, he made his way out of Rome.[49]

And where did he go but to the house of a Stoic outside the
city. Among the philosophers Domitian banished from Rome
were two Pliny had first met in Syria: Euphrates and Artemidorus.
A son-in-law of the frugal-eating, sex-despising Musonius Rufus,
Artemidorus had impressed Pliny with his bodily endurance 'in
winter and summer alike' while they were young men. No less
resilient now, the exiled Artemidorus opened his door to Pliny.
How long Pliny stayed here he did not say, but on returning to
Rome later he admitted that the move had been 'rather
dangerous'. This was, nonetheless, the last place anyone would
have expected Pliny to take cover from falling thunderbolts. He
would soon plan a reprisal for the Stoics who had survived.

PART FOUR

SUMMER

TEN

The Imitation of Nature

God, that is Nature superior, interrupted this dispute;
For she separated the land from the sky and the waves from
    the land
And split the blue sky from the misty air.
And having rolled them out and extracted them from their
    grim pile,
Bound them in their separate zones in blissful peace.

Ovid, Metamorphoses, 1.21–5

Pliny did not need a shower of thunderbolts to chase him to
the countryside or a storm to confine him to a study. He
liked to hide himself away. If it was easier to be tucked up in
winter, when there was little to see in the woods of Laurentum,
in summer he found a means of appreciating the natural world
– from indoors. The 'Tuscan' estate he inherited from his uncle
lay amid the plains of the upper Tiber valley in the region of
modern Perugia. The main villa had been built in Augustan
times and boasted a set of baths, a ball court,* and a remarkable

---

* The Romans played a variety of ball games, including one much like Eton Fives
in which they would hit a ball against a wall with their hands and compete to
score. However it is difficult to imagine the portly Pliny the Elder getting much
use out of the ball court at his Tuscan villa.

colonnade which culminated in a dining room – 'the folding doors of which open out onto the end of a terrace and meadow beyond and much countryside besides'.[1] It sat on the lower incline of a hill that rose so gently that one never noticed the climb. Vineyards, fields and agricultural buildings lay around it, and all were girt by the Apennines, the surrounding landscapes together forming a natural bowl.

For all the beauty of the estate, Pliny's friends used to grow anxious when he travelled there in summer. Letters arrived, fraught with warnings of the malarial conditions of the coast. While Pliny insisted that his villa was a good distance from the sea, the marshes of the Tiber posed a latent threat. Not one to be deterred, Pliny hastened here for the new season to cherish the meadows, mountain breeze and sense of freedom afforded by being near a town where wearing a toga, the formal wear of Rome, was only optional. The residents of laid-back Tifernum Tiberinum (Città di Castello) had made him their patron when he was still just a boy – an act, Pliny said, that displayed 'as much enthusiasm as lack of judgement'.[2] They were mostly very elderly, grandfathers, great-grandfathers of grown men, full of stories of their distant ancestors.* If you felt as though you had stepped back in time when you arrived, after a few days here, wrote Pliny, 'you should think you were born in another century'.[3] For all his disavowals, Pliny came to appreciate the honour of his position. Whenever he arrived and whenever he left, the people of the local town would gather to greet or see him off.

Such was Pliny's ardour for his uncle's former estate that his eighteenth-century biographer, the 5th Earl of Orrery, went so far as to describe it as his mistress: 'The lover dwells upon the charms of his mistress; he views in rapture every feature, and

---

* It was Pliny's duty as patron to arbitrate between townsmen wherever a dispute arose. The position must have provided excellent early training for the future lawyer.

seems uneasy, lest she should not appear equally amiable to others, as to himself. That state of love must certainly be happy, where jealousy can find no intrusion.'[4] Pliny was certainly keen to show his estate off. Being the good patron that he was, he wrote to reassure one anxious friend that it was quite safe to visit; even his slaves were at their healthiest when they came to Tifernum: 'Certainly up to now I haven't lost any of those I brought with me here (forgive me).'[5]

If Pliny was half as relaxed as he said he was about the risk of disease in summer, it was because his estate conformed almost perfectly to the best advice available at the time. According to Cato the Elder, whose ideas Pliny the Elder often reproduced in his encyclopaedia, a farm ought to be south-facing and situated at the foot of a mountain.[6] Pliny's main villa faced mostly south. The Apennines, 'healthiest of mountains', rose at its rear, but at some distance, so there was always good movement of air. Cato's dream estate is well watered and near the sea or a river that can be traversed by boat. Tributaries of the Tiber flowed through Pliny's land but dried up in summer, reducing the risk of malarial infection. Perhaps the greatest danger Pliny the Elder had perceived when he was living at the estate came from shrews, whose bites he knew to be venomous.[7] It was easy enough for Pliny to avoid those.

A series of roads connected the estate to Rome. Passing over the Apennines, the Via Flaminia had recently been relaid with black basalt from the volcanic provinces just north of the region, each luscious slab swollen and organic, like a loaf that had burned and spilled over its tin.[8] Approach the mountains from Perugia, and you may still visit the site of Pliny's estate. From the town of Città di Castello, head towards Pitigliano in the comune of San Giustino. Beside the Campo di Santa Fiora lies a plain named Colle Plinio. The area was inhabited as early as the Bronze Age, but rightly belongs to Pliny.[9] In the nineteenth century, a clutch of roof tiles bearing Pliny's full set of initials was discovered beneath the plain. While one man watched the tiles, then pieces of marble, then black-and-white tesserae of mosaic being lifted from the soil, the resident of a neighbouring estate 'lovingly' gathered up whatever fragments he could find.[10]

Pliny had left nothing to chance. He was not the first or the last man to have his name inscribed on his building materials, but he did so with particular pride. His tiles were made of local clay from the surrounding plains and stamped with fat, rounded letters, 'CPCS': Gaius Plinius Caecilius Secundus.[11] It would have been easier to have had his initials printed in relief, but these were raised from the surface, like a scratch freshly applied to the skin. They were designed to be read, but not by anyone visiting in Pliny's lifetime. Hidden away in the roof of an agricultural outbuilding, they were largely obscured from sight.

Guests at Pliny's Tuscan villa would have noticed rather the signature he had created in its grounds. Seven letters, snipped from box hedge, revealed the identity of the estate owner: PLINIUS. If the tiles bearing his initials secured Pliny's place in the history of Perugia (how rare it is to find a house from a description in a Latin letter), then the topiary secured his place in daily conversation. Pliny was so proud of his gardener's skilful manipulation of Nature that he allowed him to cut his own name from another hedge nearby. Their topiary names grew together in the middle of a large garden fashioned out of a former hippodrome.

Visitors to Pliny's hippodrome garden were treated to a display of obelisks and roses, fruit trees and acanthus, and many more topiary names and figures cut out of box. At the head of the garden lay Pliny's marble bench which spurted water whenever someone sat down on it, and the basin he filled with floating hors d'oeuvres. The whole hippodrome was planted round with plane trees, like Plato's Academy in Athens, ivy weaving its way

The most complete set of horse-trappings to survive from ancient Rome happens to feature the name and position of Pliny the Elder. The inscription on this attractive roundel, *Plinio praef(ecto) eq(uitum)*, refers to his command of the cavalry, probably in the 50s AD, when he was in the Rhineland.

Pliny the Elder recorded that the town of Stabiae, where this wall painting was found, was destroyed in the Social War that broke out in 91 BC when Rome's allies in Italy demanded Roman citizenship. To judge by this painting, which probably shows its harbour, and the archaeological remains of luxurious villas, Stabiae had been largely rebuilt by the time Pliny the Elder died there during the eruption.

The eruption of AD 79 is believed to have changed the shape of the volcano from a single cone, like the one depicted in this wall painting from Pompeii, to the famous twin peaks we see today. Vesuvius was formed within the caldera of the older and now inactive Monte Somma.

In the *Iliad*, Zeus' mortal son Sarpedon is speared in the chest by the Greek warrior Patroclus. As he falls he is said to resemble an oak, white poplar, or pine tree felled for ship timber.

In this fifteenth-century manuscript, as in the reliefs on Como Cathedral, Pliny the Elder is closeted in his study. The scene outside encapsulates the breadth of his encyclopedia. The artist has omitted from his painting some of the more outlandish creatures to feature in Pliny the Elder's book, including the tritons and nereids (the equivalent of mermen and mermaids) which many people in his time claimed to have seen.

A cast of a victim of the eruption. Remains of humans and animals continue to be found in the areas surrounding Vesuvius. In late 2018, a particularly rare discovery was made at Pompeii of a horse with harness and saddle.

The two Plinys would have kept on their desks a selection of papyri for formal work, an inkwell, and wax tablets for drafts. Incised with a pen-like tool known as a 'stylus', wax tablets were often joined together by hinges like books and could be warmed, scraped clean and re-used. The English phrase 'clean slate' comes from the Latin for 'smoothed tablet', *tabula rasa*.

Pliny tells the daughter of his mentor Corellius Rufus of his great respect for him and hopes for her son in this letter preserved in a remarkably early manuscript from the late fifth (or possibly early sixth) century. Written in black ink enlivened by the occasional red adornment, the surviving leaves are plain by comparison with Renaissance manuscripts, but precious for their rarity.

In the early second century, Emperor Trajan granted Pliny his request to be made a priest. In the honorary role of 'augur', Pliny was required to study and interpret the movement of birds and other signs which were supposedly issued by the gods.

Readers have been attempting to reconstruct Pliny's villas from the descriptions in his letters for hundreds of years. Clifford Fanshawe Pember, an Oxford graduate and trainee architect, created this 3D model of Pliny's Laurentine villa in the 1940s.

Emperor Constantine established his new capital at Byzantium in AD 324, two centuries after Pliny visited. He credited his victory over his co-emperor Maxentius to the support of the Christian God. Depicted at the right of the mosaic, he holds a model of his city up to the Madonna and Child, while Emperor Justinian, who lived from AD c.482–565 and reformed Roman law, holds a model of Hagia Sophia.

The Romans were forbidden from burying their dead inside the *pomerium* or sacred boundary line that surrounded the city. An exception was made for Emperor Trajan, whose ashes were interred in the base of his Column in the city itself.

Francesco I de'Medici intended his private study in the Palazzo Vecchio in Florence as a celebration of Art and Nature and as a home for his 'rare and precious things'.

Domitian's wife, the Empress Domitia, was more fortunate than her husband with her locks, sporting here the most fashionable hairstyle of the period, the so-called 'Toupetfrisur' beehive.

Pliny was fascinated by the movement of water. In the region of his Tuscan villa he visited the source of a river that honoured a deity called Clitumnus. At Comum he strove to discover what determined the rise and fall of the spring pictured here.

Sculpture of Pliny the
Elder in Como.

Sculpture of Pliny the
Younger in Como.

among the branches and box hedging filling in the spaces between each trunk. Around the box grew laurel, and two rows of shorter plane trees defined the sun-drenched space at the centre of the garden. Pliny was so proud of his plane tree and topiary hippo-drome that he believed that it 'far, far outstripped the design and pleasantness of the buildings'. Millennia after the topiary withered and died, an outline of the hippodrome appears to have been preserved and become part of the landscape. An aerial view of the Colle Plinio reveals a long field with a semi-circular end, like an elongated horseshoe. Looking at it from above it is easy to imagine how majestic it once was, when its centre 'lay open and offered itself up to full view as soon as one entered it'.

That Pliny should have admired a garden fashioned out of a former hippodrome is surprising because he dismissed horse-racing as 'inane'.[12] The sport was as popular as it had ever been at Rome, where Domitian introduced Capitoline Games in honour of Jupiter, with lyre contests, Latin and Greek declama-tion competitions, foot races for girls, and equestrian events.[13] The sight of men behaving like boys as the horses went round and round irritated Pliny, not least because he suspected it was really the racing colours they came to see and that they were engaging in illicit gambling. A few years later, the Circus Maximus in Rome was restored and enlarged to accommodate an unprecedented quarter of a million spectators.[14] Although Pliny insisted that the circus did not interest him either, the driveway at his Tuscan estate was shaped like one. Pliny despised horse-racing and yet he kept a hippodrome garden, a circus drive – and wore a seal ring engraved with a picture of horses and chariot, as if to bring something of his Tuscan estate to the documents which were passed across his desk.[15] Equestrianism as such formed part of his signature. It was a lively vignette of fleeting time.

The location of the 'Tuscan' estate Pliny described in his letters was confirmed by the remarkable discovery of a number of roof tiles stamped with his initials, C.P.C.S, for Gaius Plinius Caecilius Secundus.

Like most equestrians and senators, Pliny owned in addition to his seal ring a gold ring which distinguished him from plebeians. He may not have given much thought to what it symbolised when he twiddled it on his finger or used it as a gauge to measure the water level at Comum, but he could hardly have forgotten his uncle's trenchant views on finger rings in general.[16] Pliny the Elder had not minded the early Romans wearing iron rings as symbols of courage in war. It was gold and gemstone-encrusted rings he despised: gold, mined from the bowels of the earth and pressed over a man's knuckles only to broadcast his status and wealth. Slaves wore merely iron rings (though some now covered the iron in gold). In Germania, too, the Chatti tribesmen whom he had encountered as a young soldier wore iron rings as signs of bravery.[17] Pliny the Elder deemed even seal rings to be super-fluous to human needs on the basis that the otherwise flamboyant Egyptians were content to sign their letters by hand.[18] 'The man who first adorned his fingers,' he concluded, 'committed the worst crime against life.'[19]

Gold rings, like oysters and pearls, earned a prominent place in the *Natural History* because they represented to Pliny the Elder the kind of luxury that was most damaging to the earth and human morality. When his encyclopaedia was read in the Renaissance it was the passages on extravagances such as these which often attracted the most interest. Pliny the Elder's discussion of rings was particularly influential, inspiring the central ceiling panel in one of the most important cabinets of curiosity of the sixteenth century. Francesco I de'Medici, Grand Duke of Tuscany from 1574, commissioned the cabinet as a private study – accessible by secret passage – in the Palazzo Vecchio in Florence. His passion was alchemy, and his secret study-gallery housed the products of his experiments.[20] Thirty-four compartments were concealed behind paintings inspired by antiquity and Nature. Designed by Giorgio Vasari, author of the *Lives*, and Vincenzo Borghini, a humanist and Benedictine prelate, Francesco's *Studiolo* was less a room than an oversized jewellery box. It is perhaps the closest anyone has ever come to rendering Pliny the Elder's *Natural History* in three dimensions.[21]

The printing of the first edition of the *Natural History* in 1469 had roused considerable interest in Pliny the Elder as both a naturalist and art historian. Fourteen further editions were produced before the end of the century as his reputation spread through Italy.[22] Leonardo da Vinci acquired a copy. Christopher Columbus owned an Italian translation from 1489.[23] Vasari seems to have consulted the earliest Italian translation of the text when writing his *Lives*.[24] Each man found his own area of interest in the work, from the engineering of ancient buildings to the geography of the Roman empire and creative possibilities for combining artifice with Nature. The text inspired artistic studies of the natural world, some of which were incorporated into the work itself. A page of an exquisitely illuminated fifteenth-century manuscript of the encyclopaedia, now in the British Library in

London, is adorned with a scene of Pliny the Elder hard at work in his study. His desk overlooks a beautiful landscape with sun and moon, sea and mountains, rivers and woods, and fields full of animals and birds.[25] When Francesco de'Medici and his designers set about creating his *Studiolo* the following century, they divided Nature similarly into groups according to the elements, after the manner of Aristotle.

Paintings for the walls of Francesco's grand study include the fall of Icarus to denote air, the primordial flood from Ovid's *Metamorphoses* to evoke water, and scenes of gold miners, jewellery makers and glass blowers for earth and fire. In one panel, pearl fishers pour into boats and tumble out of them in their eagerness to scoop oysters from a bay. The nymphs and tritons in the scene are all but naked, their sashes drenched from their underwater forays. Pearls pile up in foreign shells – conches, roomier than the oyster's own. Another of the paintings is inspired by the story in the *Natural History* of Cleopatra's pearls. According to Pliny the Elder, a sculpture of Venus in the Pantheon at Rome wore enormous earrings formed of two halves of a single pearl formerly owned by Cleopatra. The 'courtesan queen' had originally had a pair of pearls, but having wagered with Mark Antony that she could consume 10 million sesterces at a single banquet, she dissolved one in a cup of vinegar and drank it.[26] In Francesco's painting she is shown removing the enormous pearl from her ear and resting it in a cup. Her fellow banqueters lean in to witness her consume its wealth in a single sitting.

Francesco de'Medici had a keen interest in pearls and gems. He established with his brother a pietra dura industry, where pieces of mother-of-pearl, coloured marble, and other precious stones were cut and smoothed and slotted together to create seamless decorative panels. The central ceiling painting commissioned for his private study encapsulated the process. An artist named Francesco Morandini was instructed to paint within its frame the titan Prometheus as 'first inventor of precious stones and rings, as testified by Pliny [the Elder]'.[27] In the Greek myth, Zeus punishes Prometheus for stealing fire from the gods and giving it to men by chaining him to a rock in the Caucasus for 30,000 years. While so enchained, Prometheus is said to have enclosed a fragment of rock in his shackles and worn it on his finger. Although Pliny the Elder called this story 'wholly fiction' in his encyclopaedia, the mere fact that he mentioned it, if only to reject it, persuaded Francesco de'Medici and his designers of its worthiness as inspiration for the centrepiece of the *Studiolo*. In the finished painting, Prometheus is depicted alongside Nature, who nurtures a baby, rabbit, snake, and unicorn. While still enchained he receives from Nature a rough stone to transform into something more beautiful. Nature's rock will yield a glittering gem for the ring Prometheus has formed from his chains.

The Renaissance portrait of Prometheus in the guise of an artist was a development of the ancient poets' depiction of him as a creator of men from clay. In the late fourteenth century, a Florentine chronicler likened the work of the painter and poet to that of Prometheus in fashioning life.[28] Among the artists he considered most divine in their talents were Praxiteles and Apelles. Both had flourished in classical Greece and were well known to Renaissance humanists from the elder Pliny's *Natural History*. Praxiteles was the Athenian sculptor of the celebrated *Aphrodite of Knidos*, a work so beautiful and lifelike that one man was said to have made love to it then killed himself out of shame. Apelles was a painter from Kos who, according to Pliny the Elder, surpassed 'all [the artists] born before him and yet to be born'.[29] Pliny the Elder had admired both men for their ability to capture their subjects with such accuracy – despite, in Apelles' case, using a palette of only white, yellow ochre, red, and black – as to give the illusion of having created something entirely tangible. Pliny the Elder's passages on the close imitation of life in ancient art were so esteemed in the Renaissance that they helped to inspire a new appetite for naturalism in art.

Artists and art theorists of the fifteenth and sixteenth centuries were particularly interested in an anecdote told in the thirty-fifth book of the *Natural History*. Here Pliny the Elder described how two artists of fourth-century BC Greece had once challenged each other to a contest.[30] The first painter, Zeuxis of Heraclea, painted grapes so lifelike that the birds were tempted to eat them. Meanwhile his rival, Parrhasius of Ephesus, the artist credited with discovering the use of proportion, painted a curtain that looked so real that Zeuxis, 'gasconading over the judgement of his birds, urged that the curtain be pulled back and the picture revealed'. As soon as Zeuxis realised his error he conceded the prize. He, after all, had deceived only birds, but Parrhasius had fooled him, an artist.

These stories helped to awake in Renaissance artists an ambition to imitate Nature – or even to surpass it, forging life from their paints and marbles as Prometheus had from clay. Pliny the Elder's *Natural History* taught them to aspire to the standards of naturalism achieved by the artists of antiquity. Painters now strove to be hailed 'Apelles' for their skills of representation. They had no way of knowing how real Apelles' paintings looked, or of gauging how well they measured up to him, but they had it on Pliny the Elder's authority that Apelles was the best, and it was as the best that they sought to be hailed in turn. Titian, Mantegna and Pisanello were among the artists who succeeded in earning the sobriquet 'Apelles' for their genius.[31] All three studied Nature closely and excelled in recreating it in paint. The emphasis that Pliny the Elder had placed on art as the imitation of Nature was perpetuated further by the leading theorists of the day. Vasari, Leon Battista Alberti, Lodovico Dolce and, earlier, Lorenzo Ghiberti, stressed its importance in their works of criticism. In Dolce's *Aretino*, an influential dialogue on art from 1557, the protagonist proclaims, in true Pliny the Elder fashion, 'Painting . . . is nothing other than the imitation of Nature.'[32] Pliny the Elder's descriptions of the perfection achieved by Apelles, Parrhasius and Praxiteles shaped a new competition between the artists of modernity and the artists of antiquity, between object and paint. It was a competition that no one had the authority to judge but everyone the opportunity to form an opinion on. Artists and viewers would now scrutinise art and Nature side by side. The *Natural History* steadily inculcated their ways of seeing.

It is tempting to see the influence of Pliny the Elder's passages on art in the design of the Tuscan estate itself. Outside, in the hippodrome garden, Nature was shaped by artifice. Inside, in the rooms used for entertaining, artifice was shaped by Nature. Pliny described a bedroom painted with a fresco of birds sitting on branches.[33] Fragments discovered at the site of his villa provide further clues to its decoration. Leaves and vines were painted in stylised columns and framed by theatrical trompe l'oeil panels on walls of red, white, azzurro and yellow.[34] Carvings depicted scenes from theatre and myth as though they derived from Nature. A deceptively friendly-faced gorgon poked out from a frieze; a griffin – resembling a cat with wings – posed in profile; a theatre mask carved in deep relief had eyebrows raised so high that they consumed the actor's entire forehead.[35] Pliny the Elder wrote in his encyclopaedia of a species of people from Scythia (the Russian Steppe) with a single eye in the centre of their foreheads who warred against griffins for gold.[36] It is uncertain whether he would have known the surviving designs from the villa or whether they were introduced later by his nephew, but they point to a man whose tastes were for the lively and cheering.

The carvings and wall paintings, many of which are charac-

169

teristic of the first century AD, provided a suitably dramatic backdrop for the entertainers who came to perform at the villa after Pliny inherited it. Forgoing his evening entertainments throughout the winter to retreat to his soundproof study, Pliny liked to invite lyre players and comedians to strum and jest away the long light nights of the summer. On some evenings at the Tuscan estate he was joined by his wife, Calpurnia, who had been known to adapt his poems to the cithara and sing to them. Whenever Pliny gave readings from his own work to groups of male guests, she would 'sit behind a veil' and wait eagerly for the applause. Her aunt, Pliny said, had 'often predicted that I would seem to my wife to be such a man as I am now'.[37] He prided himself on being as good a husband to her as she was a wife to him.

ELEVEN

A Difficult, Arduous, Fastidious Thing

But when the blissful summer is summoned by the West
  Wind
To send each flock out to pasture in the glades,
Let us lose ourselves in the chill fields at first light
While the morning is fresh, while the grass is white
And the dew on the delicate blades most delicious to graze.

Virgil, Georgics, 3.322–6

Even in the relaxed setting of his Tuscan villa, Pliny endeavoured to keep a strict routine. He had set hours for seeing Calpurnia – in the middle of the day, over dinner and at recitals – and set hours for exercising, bathing, writing and dictating.[1] Anyone who did not know him would have said he got off to a slow start in the summer months, waking around sunrise only to lie in bed like a laggard. But Pliny rested, his shutters closed, to make the most of the darkness. He liked the way his thoughts flowed unimpeded when there was nothing for his eyes to fix upon except the pictures in his head.

My mind does not follow my eyes, but my eyes my mind. They see what my mind sees, since they cannot see anything else. If I have something current to work on, I'll think it through in much the same way I would if I were writing and editing it. Sometimes I'll do more, sometimes less, depending on how easily it can be composed or retained in my head.[2]

This was Pliny lengthening the day from the moment he awoke. Ignoring any instinct to spring from his bed to his desk, he indulged in a protracted levee in order to settle his ideas. In these quiet moments, he might write an entire letter or edit a flight of speech before he had so much as picked up his stylus. It was only when he had something worth remembering that he would summon his secretary, throw open his windows, and dictate what he had formed in his head. The process must have taken time to perfect. Was it born in necessity, when his eyes became inflamed and red and sensitive to light? Did he learn to 'see' more clearly with his mind once his vision had begun to fail? Whatever the circumstances surrounding his routine, nothing seemed to diminish the pleasure Pliny took in thinking in the dark.

Sometimes he was just relieved to be able to complete something. Writing did not always come as easily to him at his Tuscan villa as it did in Rome or at his 'seat of the Muses', Laurentum. 'I have revised the odd little speech,' he confessed to Tacitus one summer, 'though it's the kind of work that's toilsome and devoid of pleasure, resembling more the burdens of the countryside than its pleasures.'[3] He was always anxious to update Tacitus on his progress. He was overcome by excitement whenever Tacitus told him that their names were being uttered in the same conversations about literature. Pliny seldom believed common hearsay, but he gathered hard evidence that proved that he was really catching up with Tacitus – or even level-pegging him: 'You ought to have noticed it even as far as wills are concerned: unless someone happens to be a very close friend of one of us, we receive the same legacies which are equal in worth.'[4] Tacitus, who appears to have been more flattered than offended by Pliny's tireless efforts to tie his own name up with his, advised him to take a break, and mix a little 'Diana with his Minerva' by picking up his hunting nets as well as his books. 'I wish I could obey your orders,' Pliny replied, 'but there is such a shortage of boars that . . . I cannot. It simply isn't possible.'[5]

After a morning's work Pliny usually went for a walk or ride across his grounds. Assuaging his guilt at being away from his desk by reminding himself 'how the mind is roused by exercise and the movement of the body', he would be outside again in the afternoon for further exertion before his bath and dinner.[6] But if Tacitus wanted him to hunt, then he would go. With his hunting nets trailing behind him, he padded up and down his plains with all the enthusiasm of a field mouse on a hot day. It is estimated that his land extended to some 5,000 hectares (twenty square miles).[7] It could be hours before he heard the rustling of a boar in the undergrowth. The landscapes surrounding his villa formed an amphitheatre, but it was an amphitheatre such as 'only Nature can create'. The Colosseum at Rome was enviably enclosed and confined, its eighty entrances and vomitoria (passages designed to 'spew forth' spectators on their way in and out of the auditorium) servicing the humans, not the beasts, which had nowhere to hide during the emperor's staged hunts.[8] Pliny's estate felt limitless by comparison. Hunting here was a real sport, where man stalked beast over grasslands which stretched on forever.

Nor was it merely animals Pliny was attempting to hunt. In Tacitus' plea for him to worship Diana scholars have detected a hidden request for poetry.[9] *Aper*, the Latin for 'boar', was the name of the protagonist of an imaginary debate Tacitus composed between a group of men on the status of modern oratory. Tacitus and Pliny were playing a literary game. Tacitus' Aper argued that rhetoric was more important than poetry but praised the 'woods and groves' as a setting for writing verse.[10] In his own woods and groves Pliny set his hunting nets and lance to one side, his books to the other, and did his very best to entwine the arts of Diana with the arts of Minerva. In the end, he found that the poems Tacitus assumed 'could be finished off so easily among the woods and groves came to a standstill'.[11] Aper the Boar's swift dismissal of poetry as almost a folly one could roll out in the peace of the countryside, unencumbered by other concerns, could not have been more irritating. Literature, said Pliny, is 'a difficult, arduous, fastidious thing' that 'has contempt for those who have contempt for it'.[12]

Pliny was more eloquent in his letters from the countryside than he realised. While he struggled to complete a poem, his prose swam with observations which might readily have inspired a dozen lines of verse. He described the flowering of trefoil; the way bristly acanthus looks so peculiarly soft from a distance that 'I would almost say it looked like water'; the blurring of time that the city-dweller does not notice. In the letters, City Pliny has no trouble in recollecting what he has done with his day. Country Pliny cannot account for how he has spent the last few weeks: all the weddings and engagement parties and errands which usually filled his time between work seeped away into nothing.[13] Being away from Rome made Pliny alert to many of the things which ordinarily passed him by. Above all, it showed him how similar one day in the city was to another. Upon leaving Rome behind it became a joy rather than a frustration for him to exclaim, 'How many days I have wasted on trivial things!'

The difficulty came when mixing his two worlds. The Court of One Hundred was his arena, the Tuscan estate his amphi-theatre. They were the same shape as one another – and also the same size. To have fitted them together would have required the genius of the engineers who designed Curio's theatre in Rome – the famous double theatre constructed in the late Republic out of two half-circles which could be arranged back-to-back to provide two separate performances, then pushed together to create a single amphitheatre.[14] The mechanics of the building eluded scholars and architects for centuries until finally Leonardo da Vinci discovered a solution. Using the description he found in Pliny the Elder's *Natural History*, he imagined the theatres propped up on wheels and connected via two chain-like devices which could be pulled to bring the two halves together almost seamlessly.[15] It was not for want of trying that Pliny found himself unable to position his arena alongside his amphitheatre in quite the same way. He might scatter the seeds of his barley, beans and other legumes in the courtroom and reap whichever happened to take, but he seemed incapable of making his speeches take root in his fields.

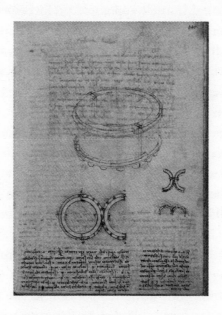

Leonardo da Vinci's drawing of Curio's Revolving Double Theatre

Attempts to bring the legal arena into the Tuscan amphitheatre only seemed to illuminate the shortcomings of both. The glories of the trefoil and acanthus would pale as Pliny's labourers set about filling his ears with their worries. *Querelae rusticorum* mounted upon *agrestes querelae* – complaints of a kind only a peasant could contrive. Pliny's farm manager and probably also some of his labourers lived in a villa in the agricultural quarters of his estate, some distance from the main house. Although Pliny gave them time to discuss their work with him before bed, it was never enough. He would dread coming back to Tifernum when they thought it was 'their right to exhaust my ears after a lengthy absence'.[16] And it was stressful when their grievances piled on top of his urgent legal work. The situation was even worse when 'city business' followed him to the countryside as well.

Pliny's urban responsibilities increased significantly after AD 98 when he found himself appointed prefect of the Treasury of Saturn at Rome. Based in the god's temple at the foot of the Capitoline Hill, the treasury was the store for money and civil documents, which the prefect was responsible for preserving. Important payments were weighed out in a large pair of scales inside the temple.[17] Pliny already had some experience of handling finances; although he never mentioned it in his letters, he had previously worked in the *aerarium militare* (military treasury) that existed to organise the pensions of army veterans.[18] This work, and the fact that he was stepping into a role previously occupied by the stepfather of his first wife, meant that he was far from ignorant of what the treasury prefecture would entail. Neither of which stopped him from complaining about the book-balancing and 'very many very unliterary letters' he was required to write.[19] But while his position in the treasury made it even harder for him to escape to the countryside in peace, Pliny had little choice but to embrace it: the promotion had come about as a direct consequence of the death of the emperor he most despised.

Domitian was assassinated in AD 96 after ruling for fifteen years. He had grown increasingly paranoid in the three years since the trials of the philosophers and eventually fell victim to his own superstition. In his youth, said Suetonius, Domitian had received a prediction of the day, year and time at which his death would occur – and even an explanation of how it would happen.[20] He had become so fixated by this prediction that his father, Vespasian, teased him for forgetting his coming fate when he refused mushrooms at dinner (he had sooner fear death by iron, he was told, than by poison). Domitian was on his guard as the fatal moment approached. He watched for a blood-red moon in Aquarius. The following day, he asked the time and was tricked into believing that the hour he most feared had passed. As he began to celebrate cheating death, his chamberlain announced that someone had arrived to see him and would not go away. The visitor turned out to be Stephanus, the private secretary of Flavia Domitilla, the niece Domitian had exiled after executing her husband Flavius Clemens for adopting the Jewish or Christian faith. Stephanus claimed to have evidence of a plot.

Making the fateful mistake of dismissing his slaves, Domitian entered his bedchamber to meet with Stephanus. To avert suspicion over the previous days, the scribe had feigned injury and worn his arm in a bandage.[21] With his available hand he now passed the emperor a document. While Domitian was absorbed in his reading, Stephanus retrieved from his bandages a dagger and inflicted a blow to the emperor's groin. Stephanus had recently been accused of embezzling money. With nothing to lose, he had agreed to lend his support to a plot to murder Domitian who was now 'feared and hated by all'.[22] The conspiracy was said to have been hatched by Domitian's 'friends and closest freedmen in conjunction with his wife [Domitia]'.[23]

Reeling from the attack, Domitian ordered a boy who was attending the household gods to fetch the dagger he kept under his pillow and summon his slaves. The boy did as he was told but found that the blade had been removed and all exits closed. Domitian had no choice but to wrestle Stephanus. As he tried desperately to gouge the scribe's eyes, the emperor was set upon by a throng of men from the imperial household, including his chief chamberlain and a gladiator. Domitian was stabbed seven more times. Injured but still breathing, he struggled on but to no avail. He died from his injuries, aged forty-four.[24]

Pliny looked back on Domitian's rule as a period of intense secrecy and political chicanery. It was clear to him that the age of political informing had not died with Nero. Believing that it could be more calamitous to hound men from the senate on suspicion of being informers than to let sleeping rogues lie, the Flavian emperors had required senators merely to swear on oath that they had not backed any activity that could endanger another's safety, or benefited at the expense of others.[25] Meanwhile, Pliny saw informers everywhere – in temples, at the treasury, across the forum – despite their determined efforts to conceal themselves from view.[26] He was convinced that Regulus was as active a spy under Domitian as he had been in his youth.[27] And he had good reason. Discovered on the late emperor's desk was a petition that the lawyer-turned-informer Mettius Carus had lodged against Pliny following the trial of the Stoics.

Pliny might have panicked, had he heard of the document while Domitian was still alive, and had he not been reassured by the fact that two members of his household happened to have the same 'dream'. One of his slave boys told him that he had been sleeping when he witnessed two people in white tunics enter his room through a window, cut his hair, and leave by the way they came. The next morning the slave claimed to have discovered his hair on the floor and a bald patch on the crown of his head.[28] Either Pliny's slaves had very inventive ways for accounting for the sudden onset of age, or something else was adrift, for one of his 'not uneducated' freedmen reported a similar attack. This time, a lone man had entered the room where he was sleeping beside his brother, sat on the bed, and cut a circle of hair from his head. Again, daylight revealed the scatterings of hair across the floor. In Rome, men accused of crimes were accustomed to grow their hair long. The fact that these men claimed to have had their hair shorn off was a sign to Pliny that all was well. He no longer stood accused. The danger had passed before Pliny had so much as been summoned to trial. Mettius Carus' attempt to incriminate him through his informing had come to nothing.

Pliny had risen through the ranks of the senate during Domitian's rule. Although one cannot help but suspect that he had been in less danger from Domitian than he claimed, at least until Mettius Carus lodged his allegations against him, he had escaped the emperor's thunderbolts and outlived him. During his refuge outside Rome he had done his best to support the Stoic Artemidorus, paying off debts he had incurred 'through the most glorious causes' (causes too glorious for Pliny to have troubled recording). Now that Domitian was dead, Pliny proposed to do whatever he could to help some of the other philosophers who had suffered. Domitian's death was never anything more to Pliny than 'a great and glorious opportunity to pursue the guilty, avenge the maligned, and put oneself forward'.[29] He ached for such a case and perhaps more so for atonement for his complicity in the condemnation of the Stoics. He might have ached also for distraction. It was in this period that he was overcome by 'very great sadness' at the death of his first wife.

For all the talk of his relentless libido, Domitian had failed to produce an heir. The one son he conceived with his wife had died in childhood, leaving his conspirators free to engineer the rise of Nerva, an apparently benign sixty-six-year-old former advisor to Nero. Pliny had reason to be optimistic for the new government when he saw Nerva recall the surviving philosophers from exile, among them his Stoic 'friends'. Pliny now acted as quickly as he could. Ordinarily he would have sought the advice of Corellius Rufus, his old mentor, the man he 'always referred everything to'.[30] But Corellius was rather cautious, and besides, Pliny had learned from experience that 'You should not consult those whose advice you ought to take on a matter you have already decided on.' Proceeding therefore alone, he approached the returning philosophers to discuss his plans for exacting justice for their plight.

His first thought was to punish Regulus, who was so apprehensive in this period of uncertainty that he even attempted a reconciliation. He and Pliny communicated first through intermediaries and then face to face. Pliny left their brief meeting without giving him so much as a guarantee of his future safety. He longed to prosecute him – to exact revenge for his vile treatment of the philosophers, to conquer him once and for all. But Regulus was rich and, for reasons which had long eluded Pliny, influential.[31] He was too slippery a character to take on with any confidence of success. Pliny therefore turned his attention to the other lawyers who had served the prosecution. He alighted upon Publicius Certus, who had helped condemn Fannia's stepson for his risqué farce about Domitian's marriage. Although he was a senator and treasury official he seemed to Pliny like a safer target.

It was never going to be easy to secure a trial of a senator. To stab a fellow senator in the back was one thing, to turn him over to the law, quite another. As a preliminary, Pliny voiced his intentions in the senate without so much as mentioning Publicius

Certus' name. As he predicted, the reaction of his fellow senators was broadly hostile. 'What are you trying to do?' one cried: 'Where are you going with this? What of the dangers you'll encounter?' They knew perfectly well whom Pliny intended to bring down. They would not endorse it. Even the stepfather of Pliny's late wife spoke out in Certus' defence.

But then they were reminded of what Fannia and her mother had suffered at his hands. Any empathy these reminiscences stirred among the senators was Pliny's to exploit as he rose to make his speech. This was his moment, his chance to vent whatever feelings of fear and anger he had had upon witnessing Domitian's treatment of the philosophers of Rome. It was also his opportunity to make his name, to do something more than use his riches to pay off the debts of impoverished Stoics. And he triumphed. By Pliny's own account, his speech garnered such admiration, such applause, that by the time he had finished delivering it, he had won the approval of almost the entire house for speaking out: 'There was barely anyone in the senate who did not embrace me, kiss me, and verily lavish me with praise.'[32]

It was to no avail, however. Nerva decided not to take Pliny's motion any further. He could remember the chaos into which the senate had descended when senator turned against senator in the direst age of political informing. If Pliny condemned Publicius Certus, he would give fresh wind to the informers, initiate a frenzied witch hunt, perhaps trigger the downfall of the senate itself. If at first Pliny shared Tacitus' belief that the accession of Nerva marked 'the dawn of a most blissful age', he soon realised that the new emperor was weak.[33] In one of his letters, he records part of a conversation one of the returning Stoics had with Nerva over dinner. What would happen to the cruellest of Domitian's political informers, Nerva asks, if he were still alive? 'He would be dining with us,' the Stoic replies.[34]

Disenchanted and increasingly angered by Nerva's passivity and reluctance to hand over the men responsible for Domitian's assassination, the Praetorian Guard responded more aggressively still, seizing two of the suspected killers and putting them to death; according to one late source, they removed his chamberlain's genitals and stuffed them in his mouth.[35] Humiliated and weakened by the Guard's display of power, Nerva had little choice but to succumb to the pressure they now placed on him to adopt a son and successor. The emperor had put off making a decision until now, and given his advancing years, it was only natural that his people should have become anxious. If there was no plan for the succession, then who knew who might attempt to seize power?[36]

There were many men who might have made a worthy successor, but some of the most powerful senators favoured one candidate in particular. The man they wanted was hundreds of miles away, commanding one of the provinces of Germania; a soldier from Italica in Baetica (modern Andalusia), and son of a senator who had commanded formidably in the Jewish War: Marcus Ulpius Traianus – Trajan.

Pliny described Nerva taking the advice 'of men and gods' in his decision to adopt the young governor. It is uncertain what role Trajan played in these plans, but he was surely aware of the manoeuvring of both the senate and the Praetorian Guard at Rome.[37] News of his adoption was proclaimed at Rome in October, AD 97. Pliny celebrated the fact that 'the adoption was enacted not in the bedroom but in a temple, not before the marriage bed but before the couch of Jupiter Best and Greatest'.[38] Rome had just received news of a victory in the region of the Danube. As Nerva laid the victory laurels before Jupiter, he used the occasion to rejoice in his new 'son'. Nerva and Trajan would share power by serving as joint consuls or heads of the senate. It would not be long before Trajan was sole emperor of Rome.

Nerva's adoption of Trajan settled the Guard but did little for Pliny in his immediate plans. Masking his disappointment over the emperor's prevarication and his reluctance to bring Publicius Certus to trial, Pliny satisfied himself with believing that he had won on principle. He had 'revived the long-lapsed tradition' of raising matters which concerned the public in the senate house while risking the hostility of his fellow senators, and had an excellent speech to show for it.[39] If this was insufficient to assuage his guilt, Pliny also did what he could privately to support the relatives of the philosophers who had died. He found a tutor for the children of one of the Stoic biographers. He continued to be a source of comfort to Fannia until she fell gravely ill while nursing a Vestal Virgin. As her fever and cough worsened, Pliny said that she maintained a spirit worthy of her late husband and father. 'I grieve that so great-hearted a woman is being seized from our very eyes,' he wrote, 'and doubt whether the likes of her will ever be seen again.'[40]

Although there was no trial, Publicius Certus was robbed of the consulship he had hoped for and dismissed from his post as prefect of the Treasury of Saturn. Then Pliny heard that, 'by coincidence, though it was as if it was no coincidence', he had become very ill and died. 'I have heard people say that he had seen a sort of vision of me in his mind's eye, threatening him with a sword. Whether this is true, I would not dare to say, but it would set an example if it did appear to be so.'[41] For all Pliny complained of the writing of 'very many very unliterary letters' and infringement of the treasury responsibilities upon his time, the promotion was a symbolic victory after his efforts to bring Publicius Certus to trial were scuppered. As his Stoic friend Euphrates told him when he complained about the duties of his new post, a man who performs a public service and administers the justice that philosophers can only talk about, has the most beautiful share in the philosophic life.[42] It was a line to repeat like a creed whenever the city impinged upon his contemplation amidst the meadows and watery acanthus.

TWELVE

Head, Heart, Womb

[6 June] Then I was shown that after the sacred Ides of
    June
Is a good time for brides and their husbands,
And the first part of the month found to be unfavourable
To their marriage bed. For the holy wife of the high priest
    said:
'Until the gentle Tiber has swept the cut hair
From Vesta's shrine on its yellow waters out to sea,
I may not brush my hair with a wooden comb
Or cut my nails with iron, or touch my husband,
Even though he is Jupiter's priest
Even though he was given to me to be with forever.'

Ovid, *Fasti*, 6.223–32

Every year the people of Tifernum and the surrounding towns
would make their way to Pliny's Tuscan estate before the
harvest. Within its grounds stood a temple to Ceres, the goddess
credited with introducing men to corn when, in their primordial
savagery, they feasted only on acorns.[1] While the crowds who
came to feast in her honour grew over the years, the temple only
crumbled. There came a point when anyone who saw it might
have supposed it had been caught up in a cyclone it was so

184

battered. The walls were weathered. The old wooden statue of the goddess was missing limbs. It was a wonder Ceres could protect the crops at all, given the state that she was in.

Pliny summoned the soothsayers, who told him what he already knew: the temple needed to be larger and grander.[2] With no shelter to be found beyond the temple walls, it was a case of worshippers either getting wet in the autumn rain or being blinded by the sun as it dipped ever lower in the sky. Reluctant to see another harvest slip by without proper provision, Pliny resolved to build as beautiful a temple as he could imagine. He employed an architect to draw up plans for a sizeable monument with marble statue, tetrastyle porch and – so as to 'seem to be generous as well as pious' – porticoes. 'The [temple] for the use of the goddess, and [the porticoes] for the mortals,' Pliny clarified for the benefit of the builders. He was first to admit that he was unused to liaising with tradesmen.[3]

Pliny also planned to remove some statues from the main house. Positioned where they were, these busts stood as relics of a period he would sooner have forgotten. The original owner of his estate, Marcus Granius Marcellus, seems to have left them behind when he was forced to give up his property.[4] A magistrate from Hispellum (Spello in Umbria), Granius Marcellus had been brought to trial by a political informer in AD 15.[5] The accusations against him included the spreading of wicked rumours about Tiberius' personal habits, which carried particular weight, noted Tacitus, because the rumours happened to be true.[6] Although he was cleared of every accusation the informers had made against him, Granius survived only to see his son charged with treason and forced to commit suicide, and his estate seized and pressed into imperial hands.[7]

How Pliny came to live at the Tuscan estate at all after it was requisitioned is a mystery. It has been proposed that his uncle received the estate back in Vespasian's gift on the basis that he

185

was a relation of this Granius Marcellus.[8] In the seventeenth century, a French scholar adduced two fragmentary inscriptions which he believed revealed that Pliny the Elder's mother was called Grania Marcella, daughter of Granius, which would make Pliny Granius' great-grandson.[9] However it was that Pliny the Elder came to own the estate to pass down to Pliny, its tumultuous history could have made them more sensitive to the threat posed by political informers. The fate of the Granii might have been Pliny's own had Domitian not died before he could act on the charges lodged against him.

Among the accusations brought against Granius Marcellus earlier in the century was that he had displayed a statue of himself on a higher podium in his home than those of the Caesars, and replaced the face on a statue of Augustus with that of Tiberius. The act was dangerously redolent of *damnatio memoriae*, the process of scrubbing out one face so as to erase it from history and re-carving it into another, which was what Romans did to portraits of detested emperors, not deified ones such as Augustus. Pliny recalled the zeal with which the Roman people took to demolishing portraits of Domitian in the wake of his death.[10] Domitian had commissioned and restored so many buildings that, years later, Pliny could still remember the feeling of walls trembling and roofs shaking as each block of stone was transported and laid down.[11] An enormous fire had broken out in AD 80 and savaged the temples of Isis and Serapis, Neptune and Capitoline Jupiter, the Pantheon, baths, theatres, and the voting buildings of the Campus Martius.[12] Domitian had continued Titus' work in rebuilding the city, and the new architectural landscape proffered more than a few opportunities for the crowds to obliterate his memory. Pliny witnessed the carnage from close quarters. He even went so far as to cast himself as one of the axe-wielding desecrators:

As admiral of the fleet, Pliny the Elder was alert to the dangers of quails. The quail (Latin: *coturnix*), he wrote, prefers the ground to the sky – one is shown in the claws of a cat in this mosaic from Pompeii – but can also settle on sail cloth at night, causing ships to sink.

It was a pleasure to dash those proud, proud faces to the ground, to strike them with swords, to savage them with axes, as if blood and pain would follow from each and every blow. No one was so measured in his joy and late-found happiness as not to appear to see the lacerated limbs and truncated bodies as a kind of revenge. Those fearsome, horrid portraits were thrown down and cooked in the flames so that they might be transformed from a source of terror and threat for the pleasure and use of men.[13]

Pliny the Elder had mourned the loss of faces from history. The melting of Domitian's busts into liquid bronze satisfied his nephew's desire that something good should come from evil. If any sculptures of Augustus with offensively edited faces remained in his own house, Pliny would have been careful to remove them before transferring the rest of the collection to the local town for public display. Pliny was planning to construct a new temple for the statues when he fell sick.

In about AD 97, when he was in his mid-thirties, Pliny had the misfortune to contract 'a very serious' illness that put him 'in danger of [his] life'.[14] The worst of his symptoms was a raging fever which not even a rigorous rub down with oil could quell. His household called a doctor. Pliny had often told his slaves that if ever he was to become very unwell and lose his senses, they were not to give him anything other than what the doctor prescribed – 'And know that if you did give me something . . . I would punish you in the same way other people would for being denied something.'[15] When the doctor arrived Pliny was no less resolute. Arpocras, an Egyptian whose particular expertise lay in massage, exercise, and nutrition, made him up a preparation. Pliny refused to swallow it.

Many Romans were innately distrustful of doctors, who were notorious for their exorbitant fees and questionable remedies. Tombstones bore outrageous epitaphs which testified to their right to kill with impunity: 'A team of doctors caused his death', they proclaimed with a healthy dose of black humour.[16] Pliny the Elder had taken it upon himself to speak out against the entire profession 'on behalf of the senate and Roman people and 600 years of Rome'.[17] He had railed against the quackery and the thievery, the arrogance and stupidity, the greed and incompetence: only a doctor could charge a fortune for his services, confuse cinnabar with red lead and get away with poisoning his patients.[18] Bring a team of them together and all they would do was argue.

Like Pliny's specialist Arpocras, doctors commonly came to Italy from overseas, a fact that had done little to endear them to Pliny the Elder, who scorned the enervating influence their prescriptions seemed to have upon the population at large: 'there is no greater cause for the loosening of morals than medicine'.[19] Even the healthy had taken to languishing in boiling hot baths, vomiting their food in order to consume more potions, smothering themselves in resins to remove hair from their bodies to expose their pudenda to view.[20] One of the most famous doctors of the past few centuries had recommended baths and music as a means of rebalancing the atoms in the body, and wine as an efficacious medicine for sundry complaints. Asclepiades was said to have left his native Bithynia in the late second century BC and established his surgery in Rome only after failing to make enough money as an orator.[21] Nonetheless, Pliny the Elder was so anxious to promote natural remedies over foreign potions that he was prepared to share some of Asclepiades' more appealing ideas. In his *Natural History* he noted that 'the school of Asclepiades' prescribed onions to improve colour and strength, soften the bowels and relieve haemorrhoids after bathing; and that suspended beds or hammocks, which Asclepiades allegedly invented, could be used to rock the sick gently to sleep.[22]

While Pliny refused to take Arpocras' medicine, he allowed him to be on hand when, on the twentieth day of his illness, he decided that he would finally take a bath. A magnificent suite had been constructed at his Tuscan estate when it passed into imperial hands earlier in the century, with black and white geometric mosaic floors, an undressing room, a *frigidarium* (cold bath) and hot room.[23] Two of the three baths were positioned in direct sunlight. The ailing Pliny was on the verge of being plunged into one of them when he overheard Arpocras talking with his team of doctors. The whole, delicate operation ground to a halt as Pliny insisted on knowing what they were saying. Arpocras had no choice but to admit that, while they supposed a bath would be safe, they could not be absolutely certain. Abandoning his bath without so much as a hesitation, Pliny returned to his bedchamber and 'composed [his] mind and face'.[24]

Pliny later looked back on this moment with enormous pride. In a time of uncertainty, he had proven his capacity for temperance. Like a good Stoic, he had compensated for the weakness of his body with the strength of his mind – and eventually recovered. The fact that Arpocras had done very little to save his patient was what made him so admirable. He had not forced Pliny to take his medicine. He had not expressed a strong opinion either way as to whether Pliny ought to bathe. He had allowed him to remain master of his own body and mind. Later, when he was better, Pliny lobbied the emperor to bestow the citizenship of Alexandria and Rome upon his doctor as a reward for his services, and gave one of his nurses a farm.[25]

Pliny's experience of sickness, both his own and that of his friends, taught him two lessons. The first was that 'we are at our best when we are ill'.[26] When we are suffering, we dream not of extravagant dinner parties or sex or other forms of pleasure, but of water, baths, fresh springs – perhaps, at most, a little wine to dull the pain.[27] Our thoughts vacillate between simple and higher things. Just as the Christians would speak of trials which 'test your faith to see whether or not it is strong and pure', Pliny saw illness as an opportunity for reckoning.[28] He understood that when mortality is weighing upon us, our thoughts turn naturally to the gods and to the end. If there is anything we can do in our final moments to be looked upon more kindly by those on earth and those above, we do it.

Out of his first observations Pliny forged a second adage: 'When we are well, we should strive to be the sort of men we vowed to be in future when we were unwell.'[29] With this, Pliny believed that he had captured in a single line what philosophers had dedicated hundreds of volumes of text in trying to teach. It was presumptuous of him, for although his phrase captured the frustrations and regrets and promises of the sick, it did not explain how we might hold on to them. We may 'strive' to be better, but what is to stop our ambitions from fading when we are returned to full health? Pliny ought to have explained that the hardest part comes in remembering the depth of fear that drives us to bargain with god in the first place. It is only when fear and self-knowledge remain, after all, that we can use them as forces for self-improvement.

There was little chance of Pliny's thoughts of illness fading when Calpurnia came 'in very great danger' of her life as well. She did not realise she was pregnant. She missed the early signs, the 'headaches, dizziness and impaired vision, loss of appetite and vomiting' that Pliny the Elder's *Natural History* taught women to expect on the tenth day after conception.[30] She missed, too, the symptoms of exhaustion which occur 'when the embryo is growing hair and at full moon, a time that is particularly disturbing to unborn babies'. Calpurnia might have been forgiven for her initial oversight had she been expecting a boy, for male foetuses were said to cause their mothers less trouble than girl foetuses, which make their mothers' legs and groin swell and their weight soar to 'unbearable' heights. Even if she was pregnant with a girl, however, Pliny's uncle would have expected her to have realised by the ninetieth day, for this was when female babies began to move in the womb.[31]

Pliny the Elder had consulted the work of female obstetricians, midwives, and what we might call 'sex workers' when he was preparing his passages on gynaecological health. Salpe and Sotira were Greek *obstetrices*. Elephantis was the author of an illustrated manual of sexual positions, Olympias was a female doctor from Thebes, and Lais, who shared her name with a famous Greek courtesan, something between the two. Pliny the Elder spoke of obstetricians and prostitutes in the same breath, convinced there was little to separate them when their work required an equal familiarity with genitalia.[32] Despite using their work as sources, Pliny the Elder remained largely ignorant of female anatomy. The gynaecological sections of his encyclopaedia are peculiarly steeped in superstition. In the fourth century BC, Aristotle had considered menstruating women capable of turning mirrors cloudy just by looking at them. Pliny the Elder developed the idea further, explaining that, when a woman is bleeding: 'Must grows sour at her approach, at her touch, the crops become sterile, grafts die, shoots in the garden are frazzled, fruit falls from trees beneath which she sits; the shine of mirrors is dulled by her reflection, steel becomes less sharp, ivory less gleaming, bees die in the hive, bronze and even iron immediately grow rusty and develop a foul smell, and dogs develop rabies by tasting the blood, and their bite is utterly poisonous.'[33]

These sections of the encyclopaedia could not have been of much use to Calpurnia who, 'like a girl', discovered she was pregnant only when it was too late. Her miscarriage was a devastating shock. Although Pliny did not blame her for losing the child, he did blame her inexperience. Owing to her youth and failure to notice that she was pregnant she 'omitted to do the things one ought to protect one's pregnancy, and did the things she ought not to have done'. The things she ought not to have done might have filled an encyclopaedia of their own, so precarious was the condition of pregnancy. Sneezing, even opening one's mouth too strenuously were deemed sufficient to induce miscarriage. 'The gait and everything that could possibly be spoken about is so significant to pregnant women,' wrote Pliny the Elder, 'that if they eat salty foods, they will give birth to a child without fingernails.'

When Pliny learned what had happened, he wrote to Calpurnia's aunt to ask her whether she might explain the situation to her father, for such understanding 'came more easily to women'.[34] But he also felt he ought to write to Calpurnia's grandfather himself. Calpurnius Fabatus was a powerful equestrian from Comum who had once narrowly escaped Nero's wrath when he was falsely accused of being privy to acts of incest and dark arts.[35] Perhaps hardened by the experience, he was rather an intimidating figure, but as Pliny knew only too well, yearned for great-grandchildren.[36] After torturing himself with thoughts of the easy route to power a potential son would have through both his great-grandfather's connections and his own, Pliny tried to be pragmatic. The one hope to take from this tragedy was that there would be healthy children born soon. 'For her mistake,' Calpurnia had paid a heavy price and endangered her own life. She would be more careful next time. Her miscarriage was proof of her fertility. It could only be so long before she conceived again.

Weak and thin, Calpurnia travelled to Campania 'for the sake of [her] health'.[37] She could have gone to the west coast, or to Comum, or to the Alps, but instead headed for the very region where Vesuvius had spread its virulence not two decades earlier. The return of life and relative normality to Campania had apparently helped to restore its reputation as a place of fertile abundance. On returning to his native Neapolis after the eruption, a poet named Statius had asked whether future generations would believe what was buried beneath the regions near Vesuvius, 'when the crops and these abandoned soils grow green again'.[38] By the time Calpurnia arrived, vegetation had even returned to the worst-affected areas, emerging through the rubble of Pompeii.[39] Already new buildings had begun to encroach upon the zone where no one in AD 79 could have imagined they would ever rise again.

Calpurnia might have stayed at the villa owned by her grand-father.[40] His Villa Camilliana in Campania was old and dilapidated, but on visiting it one day Pliny found that its 'more valuable aspects are either still intact or only very mildly damaged' and proposed to have it restored. Although business prevented Pliny from accompanying his wife this time, he suffered no apparent anxiety about returning to the region where his uncle had died when he did go to stay there on other occasions.[41] As for Calpurnia, he was overcome by anxiety for her general well-being the moment she left.

He wrote her many letters while she was away. They were often shorter than those he sent his colleagues and friends, but what they lacked in length they made up for in feeling. The letters left her in no doubt of how difficult he found it to be separated from her when she was at her weakest:

> Never have I complained more about the responsibilities of my work, which have not allowed me to accompany or even follow you on to Campania ... I was particularly anxious to be with you now, so that I might judge with my own eyes the strength and weight you gain, and whether you are borne safely through the pleasures of your sojourn and the abundance of the region.[42]

In her absence, he admitted, 'I fear everything, imagine everything.'[43] He begged her to write to him once, even twice, a day, 'to delight and to torture me'.[44] Calpurnia agreed and told him that her one consolation while they were apart was to hold his books and gather them beside her where he usually lay. In place of his blood and bones was his scholarship. A valid substitute for the tireless scholar. Pliny in turn wandered to her rooms as he usually did in the middle hours of the day and despaired upon finding them empty. He took her letters in his hands, read them, re-read them as he did his legal speeches, and left as sullen as he came.

Seldom did Pliny lay himself so bare. He wrote with such affection, such concern for the happiness and health of his wife, that it is perhaps not surprising that he was upheld as a model husband still hundreds of years after his death. In the early eighteenth century, the editor of *The Tatler*, Sir Richard Steele, a bachelor with 'no other notions of conjugal tenderness but what I learn from books', was so taken with Pliny's letters to Calpurnia that he felt inspired to reproduce three of them in translation in an essay for the journal.[45] Despite being written by a 'heathen', the missives seemed to promote the kind of concordance and affection that he imagined was still desirable between husband and wife. In particular, Pliny's tender words to the ailing Calpurnia reminded Steele of the saying of one of his married friends: 'Sickness itself is pleasant to a man that is attended in it by one whom he dearly loves.' Pliny gave the impression of suffering as acutely as his wife. His letters revealed to Steele not only the agonies of separation and anxiety, but the solution to tempering their effects. If struck down with lovesick-ness, Pliny showed that a man could do worse than attempt to lose himself in scholarship: 'You can imagine what my life is like when I find relief in work, and comfort in anxiety and worries.'[46] While his mind was occupied by his legal cases it was unable to torment him. Nights, however, were more difficult. Nights he spent alone with his old companion, insomnia. He could lightproof his rooms to achieve perfect darkness, but still he lay awake, thinking of Calpurnia.

If Pliny assumed life would be easier after Domitian, he was ill-prepared for the spate of personal tragedies that followed the emperor's assassination. From the death of his first wife to his own close encounter with the spirits of Hades, he seemed to be on a downward trajectory from which he could only escape. The possibility of happiness was rendered only more remote by news that his friend and former mentor, Corellius Rufus, the man he 'always referred everything to', had resolved to starve himself to death to relieve himself of the agony of gout. Corellius had developed the ailment in his feet when he was in his early thirties. It had now spread through his limbs. Pliny assumed gout was a hereditary disease (Corellius' father had also suffered from it) but might also have viewed it as a modern complaint. Pliny the Elder, who observed that gout was becoming increasingly common, believed that it must be 'a foreign illness' because the word the Romans used to for it, *podagra*, was Greek.[47] While the Hellenes recommended treating it by limiting the intake of meat and wine, Pliny the Elder, as often, prescribed a plant-based treatment: pickled wild cucumber root, cabbage, barley, and vervain.[48]

None of these treatments was likely to appeal to a man on hunger strike. Pliny hurried to his old friend's bedside on the pleas of Corellius' wife to find that he had weighed up his reasons for living (his conscience and reputation, his family and friends) against his reasons for dying (the persistence and severity of his affliction, which he had tried but failed to control through his mind and temperance) and already come out firmly in favour of death.[49] Pliny was devastated but understood why Corellius had chosen the path he had. 'Why do you think I endure so much pain for so long?' Corellius had once asked him. 'So that I might outlive that brigand, if only by a day.'[50] He had outlived Domitian by many, many days, but still there was a possibility that his self-inflicted death might be viewed as an act of political defiance. Cato the Younger's gruesome suicide by self-disembowelment in the late Republic was still remembered as the ultimate act of rebellion against Julius Caesar's tyranny.

Corellius Rufus' death had a profound effect upon the way

Pliny thought about his own life. As he struggled to take comfort from stock phrases about Corellius having being old and sick and fortunate to have lived as good a life as he had, he sought an alternative cure for his grief. Soon after Corellius died, Pliny confessed, 'I fear I shall live more neglectfully.'[51] This was very different from the optimism he displayed for living more mindfully after his own brush with death. His quest to live 'less carefully' came from the realisation that the end could come so suddenly that there was little point in trying to avoid it.

If there was a part of him that felt that Corellius' life was more of a loss to the world than his own could ever be, it was because he could see how much Corellius had left behind. His old mentor would have died sooner had he not had the needs of his family to consider. But what about him? Had Calpurnia died and his own illness been terminal, who would have dissuaded him from death? For all Pliny protested otherwise, there was little sense in living a reckless life until he had established a family to protect him or to mourn his loss. When news came that Calpurnia was out of danger, in good spirits, and well enough to return, he had new reason to hope that, after such an unpropitious start, he might yet have a family of his own.

THIRTEEN

After the Solstice

Threshed corn lay piled like grit of ivory
Or solid as cement in two-lugged sacks
The musty dark hoarded an armoury
Of farmyard implements, harness, plough-socks.
From 'The Barn' by Seamus Heaney,
Death of a Naturalist, 1966

According to the *Natural History*, you could tell the summer solstice was near when you first heard the 'rattle' of the cicada. It was, in fact, less a rattle than an accelerando of little creaks, their pitch heightening with every vibration of the insect's tiny abdomen. It sounded from the tree tops after dusk, when the grape vines glowed white with the flowers of midsummer.[1] The cicada would still be strumming when the blackbird's voice gave out, a phenomenon Pliny the Elder deemed peculiar to the solstice itself.[2] The cicada's strum and the blackbird's silence, the flowering of thyme and the bees' discovery of its pollen were signs that the days would now grow shorter, cooler and, for the landowner, fuller, as the race against 'savage, wild winter' began.[3]

The solstice was an important moment in the year at the Tuscan estate, its coming and going Nature's siren for the labourers to take up the tasks of late summer. The soil was to be turned and the tree roots tidied, the seedbeds hoed and prepared for next planting, the produce of summer gathered and stored.[4] Pliny the Elder cautioned against commencing these tasks too soon. 'Beware of believing the summer solstice has passed,' he said, 'until you've seen the pigeon sitting on her eggs.'[5] The first sighting of an expectant pigeon would in theory set the labourers in motion after the enervating days of May and early June. To be sure of completing their work in time they ought to have been as methodical as hedgehogs, when they 'ready food for winter and attach fallen apples to their spines by rolling over them and, holding another one in their mouth, carry them to the hollows of trees'.[6]

Pliny grew a rich variety of crops in the fields surrounding his villa: grapes and beans and 'other legumes', wheat and spelt, and barley – 'the very oldest food', with which Greeks tradition-ally made their bread.[7] Before they harvested the cereals his farmhands had to prepare the threshing floor. In the summer, they would sprinkle it with olive dregs and level it with a layer of animal dung to provide a base for treading the grain ears.[8] The Etrurians of central Italy used serrated hand mills to crush their spelt, while the Gauls had beasts of burden drag long, tooth-edged poles on wheels through their fields to tear and gather the ears in preparation for threshing later.[9] With poles or horses or a mixture of both, Pliny's labourers threshed his grain and stored it in the agricultural quarters of the estate, which were based some distance from the main house. Next to his granary Pliny constructed a shelter to protect his towering piles of produce. He also formed a new square in which his men could complete their tasks. It was framed by a pair of new outbuildings, probably a stables or further grain store.[10] When the grain was ready it was poured into the vast ceramic jars which still survive, half-submerged, in the storage room floor of the estate.

Pliny liked to say that at Laurentum he could show off a desk, but at his Tuscan estate, a full granary.[11] That was when everything went according to plan. Although the harvest traditionally began with the rising of the Pleiades in May, there was no guarantee the barn would be even half full by the end of the summer solstice. Pliny found it 'troublesome' but necessary to rent out some of his farmland: necessary because he depended on his crops for income, troublesome because it was rare his tenants could be trusted not to gobble them up.[12] In hard times they found it more economical to consume the produce than conserve it for sale. The few crops which reached maturity before autumn had a habit of landing on their plates. Pliny could follow his uncle's advice and employ a farm manager who was 'as close to his master in intelligence as possible without appearing to regard himself as such'.[13] But the manager who seemed bright on first acquaintance was not always so adept at disciplining his juniors. There was no room for the work-shy on a commercial estate. *Pecunia*, the Latin for money, came from *pecus*, the word for 'flock' or 'herd'.[14] Money-making was and always had been closely tied to agriculture. As the poet Hesiod explained in his poem on the farmer's year:

> Both gods and men are rightly indignant at those who live
> Work-shy lives, like the stingless drones in temperament,
> Eating up the products of the honeybees' toil: work-shy.
> You should make a priority of arranging your jobs
> So your barns may brim with life season-round.
> It is from work that men grow wealthy and flock-rich;
> By working that a man becomes much dearer to the gods.[15]

In a good year, Pliny's Tuscan estate could bring in more than 400,000 sesterces – the sum required to qualify as an equestrian.[16]

'Depending as it does on the condition of my farms,' Pliny said, 'my income can be rather small or unpredictable.'[17] Given that almost all his capital was in land, he had little choice but to persevere with his more dependable tenants.[18] Like Hesiod before him he appreciated the moral as well as the financial rewards which could come from investing one's energies in the land. If it was 'from work that men grow wealthy and flock-rich', then it was by attending to the land that he grew much nearer to Nature.

It was only unfortunate that the soil of his estate was so difficult to work. The higher slopes of the Apennines, which Pliny the Elder called 'the most extensive' of the mountains in Italy, were wooded and covered with rich hillocks of fertile soil, the lower were covered in vineyards; but beneath these lay meadows and plains which proved stubborn to go over. The soil of the plains was so unyielding that, on receiving its first plough, it would throw up enormous clods which only the largest oxen and strongest harrows could break up. Even then, it could take many attempts. Pliny the Elder remembered well how the soil in this part of Italy demanded 'nine plough-ings'.[19]

Keeping land as difficult and plentiful as this struck some Romans as akin to self-punishment. In the first century BC, a modest plot with garden, spring and some woodland had satisfied the poet Horace's prayers: 'I ask for nothing more, except, Mercury, that you might make these gifts of mine last.'[20] Horace had known what it felt like to be torn between town and country. He had known what it was like to be snatched away to Rome, where not even snow dispersed the crowds from the busy Esquiline Hill. Horace's modest farm spoke of an earlier, happier time, when, as Pliny the Elder put it, 'the most generous gift one could bestow upon generals and brave citizens was the largest piece of land one could finish ploughing in a single day'.[21] The size of this ideal plot was one *iugerum* (the word was subsequently used to define a Roman 'acre', the equivalent of roughly two-thirds of a modern acre), and it was precisely this that Pliny the Elder remained wistful for. With thousands of *iugera* to plough at the Tuscan estate each year, there was little chance that either he or his nephew could have fulfilled the age-old dream of doing enough work 'in a single day to last him a year without any more work'.[22]

Pliny relinquished that dream the moment he decided to buy up the estate adjoining his own. Thoughts of the money he could save and income he could raise by having his gardeners and workers and even hunting equipment in one place overcame any other reservations. His farm manager would oversee both estates and spread his workforce over the fields and vineyards and woods of each. Pliny needed to maintain only one of the houses on his freshly enlarged estate. Although he was conscious that 'it might be imprudent to subject so large a plot to the same weather and uncertainties', the benefits seemed to outweigh the risks, and after a brief deliberation, he resolved to go ahead with the purchase. Reduced by 2 million sesterces 'through lack of tenants and in generally bad times', the estate was a steal at 3 million sesterces. Pliny looked forward to a steady if moderate return on his investment.[23] If the venture was unsuccessful, then he could at least fall back upon the funds of his late wife's mother, Pompeia Celerina, which he boasted of being able to use 'no differently than if they were my own'.[24] Even after his marriage to Calpurnia he continued to call upon the four or more properties Pompeia Celerina owned near his Tuscan villa and to refer to her as his 'mother-in-law' and part of his 'household'.[25] He was wise to maintain such connections in the region when the income from his property was so precarious.

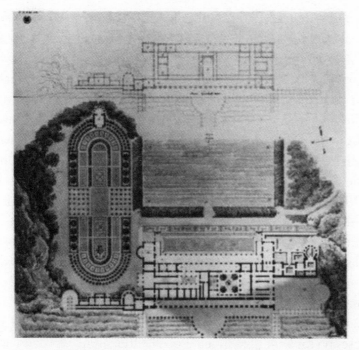

In the nineteenth century, the Prussian designer Karl Friedrich Schinkel drew up plans of Pliny's Tuscan villa from the description in his letter. The architectural historian Pierre de la Ruffinière du Prey criticised Schinkel's reconstruction as 'more like a sanatorium in the high Alps than a villa in the Apennine foothills', but the ground plan is not entirely fanciful. Schinkel also recreated Pliny's hippodrome garden at Charlottenhof Castle in modern Potsdam for Crown Prince Friedrich Wilhelm.

The soil of his landscapes proved to be fertile but irritatingly disobedient to his commands. Pliny planted myrtle. It would not grow. He longed to farm olives, but any trees which chanced to take were scorched by the winter frost.[26] This was particularly frustrating because, elsewhere in Italy, considerable advances had been made in their cultivation. While, centuries earlier, in Greece, Hesiod had lamented the fact that no one who planted an olive tree ever lived to savour its fruit, the invention of nurseries had since encouraged the production of a harvest after only one year's growth.[27] The saplings would be pruned with the vines and their fruit gathered after the grapes each autumn. For all his many *iugera*, Pliny was resigned to purchasing his olive oil from more sheltered estates elsewhere. Pliny the Elder described Italy as holding 'first place in the world' for its olives, and was particularly complimentary of a variety that grew in the shady groves of Venafro, some way north of Naples.[28] Pliny, for his part, preferred something more exotic and artisan. The olive-oil bottles he left behind at his estate came principally from north Africa and Baetica, in southern Spain.[29] Baetica was less famous for its oil than it was for its fine fish products. During the Republic it had become home to the first ever fish-processing plant, from which Romans imported a range of luxury fish sauces. Pliny was rather partial to these, particularly *garum*, which he purchased from all over Spain but most notably from Cadiz.[30] More than a few of Pliny's comestibles came from overseas – a habit his uncle would undoubtedly have scolded him for.

Pliny at least had the means to produce his own, thoroughly Italian, vintage. He grew so many vines at his estate that they encroached upon the villa itself. The summer walkway seemed 'not to look over the vineyards, but in fact to touch them'.[31] One of the bedrooms was constructed almost entirely from marble and contained a cabinet-like alcove for a bed. There were windows on every facet, but in summer the vines shrouded them in shade. Being in the bed then, as flickers of light fought through the foliage, was 'like lying in a wood, but without feeling the rain'. The vines could not be forgotten. They pushed up against Pliny's windows as if to remind him that they were holding the villa up. The grapes were the most valuable crop on the entire plot. Without them, the house would collapse.

A vine could either be trained to a trellis or left to develop 'without any prop, binding itself with its own limbs and feeding its thickness through its shortness'.[32] Roman writers liked to imagine vines as lovers, twining around each other or their supports like husband and wife on their wedding night. Pliny the Elder described the vines of Campania as married to poplars. He had watched them grow and realised that it was 'while embracing their spouses and climbing through their branches with wanton arms' that they reached their full height.[33] Pliny married his vines to props. His uncle was quite right to speak of the laboriousness of growing grapevines. When the grapes at the estate were finally ripe, they would need one labourer per seven Roman acres of vineyard to have the full crop picked before it spoiled.[34]

According to one tradition, the fruit changed hue in a display of honour towards Vertumnus, the Roman god of the seasons.[35] In August, on the cusp of the new season, the beginning of the grape harvest was heralded by a festival called the Vinalia rustica. Pliny took a keen, if theoretical, interest in the process of harvesting his vineyards. One year, he was telling a friend how busy he was gathering in the grapes when he stopped himself short: 'If "to gather in" is to pick the odd grape, visit the wine press, sample the must from the vat, creep up on the city slaves, who are now supervising the rustic ones, leaving me to my secretaries and readers . . .'[36] He looked in at all the important moments. 'Is he checking up on us?' you imagine his slaves wondering, or was he just curious to feel the firmness of the fruit, taste the must, smell the juices forming in the *calcatarium*, the new treading vat that he introduced to the estate so that his grapes could be processed on site?[37] If there was an art to applying pressure by stealth, Pliny had mastered it. Amused by how 'urban' he felt when he tiptoed into the sticky, noisy world of grape-treading, he was relieved to have his secretaries waiting for him at his desk. There were many more drinkers of his wine than there were readers of his work, but Pliny at least professed to prioritise the fruits of his intellect.

While he believed that no harm could come from drinking wine in moderation, Pliny understood the repercussions of drinking too much. Drunkenness had been a cause of some concern in Rome over the past century, Seneca the Younger documenting with particular passion the ill effects that excessive alcohol had had upon otherwise able men such as Mark Antony.[38] It is unlikely the Romans were drinking any more than the Greeks, or indeed the Macedonians (Alexander the Great famously died after a bout of heavy drinking), but the loss of inhibition caused by alcohol jarred with Roman ideals of decorum. For Pliny the Elder, drunkenness was the price man paid for availing himself of wine rather than 'the liquid Nature provided' – water.[39]

Worse than the 'thousands of crimes' its consumption inspired was the kind of life it bestowed upon those who drank it. Pliny the Elder had felt less contempt than pity for the pale-faced, trembling-handed drunks who 'do not see the sun rising and therefore live shorter lives'.[40] He stayed true to his belief that being alive meant being awake, and remained wary of becoming loose-tongued through drink: *veritas . . . vino est*. At the same time, the scholarly encyclopaedist could not help but marvel at the most celebrated wines of the world – the Maronean of Thrace and Pramnian of Smyrna, the dazzling vintages of Pucinum, Setia, and Alba, and the hangover-inducing produce of Pompeii. Pliny the Elder concluded that Italy was so blessed with her vines that 'with these alone she could be seen to have surpassed all the treasures of the world – even the perfumes'.[41]

The desire to celebrate Italian wines became only more urgent in the decades after Pliny the Elder wrote his encyclopaedia. Concerned that the attention lavished on grapes was causing the dearth of other crops, Domitian had banned the planting of vines in Italy and ordered the destruction of at least half of all existing vineyards in the provinces.[42] Although he never officially enforced his ruling (the circulation of threatening, hands-off-my-vine notes allegedly deterred him), the ban remained in place at least nominally for another 188 years. Pliny was among those who decided to ignore it in favour of working to meet the demands of the growing population of Rome. Once a drink for wealthy men, wine was now enjoyed by women and the lower orders, too. The poor man needed his wine as much as the rich one, and in Pliny, he found his ideal supplier.

When Pliny inherited the Tuscan estate its wine seems to have been stored in large amphorae. His uncle had recommended preserving 'weak wines' in large jars in the ground so as to prevent them from spoiling.[43] For all the excitement he felt at watching his grapes being processed, Pliny's vintage turned out to be similarly low in alcohol content. He might have tried to prolong its shelf life by adding certain ingredients to the jars: 'Immediately after the rising of the Dog Star,' his uncle advised, 'wine jars should be coated with pitch, then rinsed with sea water or water mixed with salt, and then sprinkled with ash from wood or white clay, cleaned, and fumigated with myrrh together with the storage rooms.'[44] The addition of oil or seepage of resin from the amphorae could help to slow the processes of spoilage and oxidation. In practice, however, the effects were slight. Pliny decided instead to accept his produce for what it was, a table wine, to be drunk as quickly as possible.[45] Revolutionising his business without so much as getting his feet dirty, he decided not to store his wines, as his predecessor had done, but to arrange instead for the purchase of small, narrow-necked jars, capable of holding no more than fifteen or twenty litres each.[46] Made with flat bottoms, these vessels could be filled with the bright, watery-rimmed produce and put aboard boats to Rome. In autumn, the Tiber streams which passed through the estate would begin to flow again after the drought of summer. His wine could be on Roman tables in time for supper the following evening.

Pliny was not above keeping the odd bottle for himself. He knew men who served their most important guests the finest dinners, and the poorest ones, the cheapest.[47] The sight of wine being distributed 'in tiny flasks in three categories' only made him uncomfortable. Cato the Elder was famously said to have drunk only the wine his sailors drank on his journey to Spain, whence he later returned in triumph.[48] Reviving his example, Pliny made a point of drinking the same wine as his freedmen.[49] The addition of a few herbs or a dash of honey might have made his own vintage at least slightly more potable. It provided the highlight of many a poor man's feast: 'a dry little ham and a jar of young tuna fish, old onions (rations of the Moors) or five bottles of wine, carried down from the Tiber'.[50]

Wines from the upper Tiber valley constituted around a quarter of all wine consumed in Rome in this period – and Pliny was making it by the gallon.[51] Amphorae recovered from his estate and datable to the period of his ownership make up half the production so far accounted for in the region.[52] Many of the vineyards in southern and central Italy had failed in recent years after being ravaged by volcanic activity. Until Vesuvius erupted, the chief supplier of wine to Rome had been Campania.[53] But after everything he had been through, there was no shame in Pliny's striving to fill the gap in the market with his own, seize-the-day vintage.

PART FIVE

-UMN

FOURTEEN

Life in Concrete

There is even a kind of dust that by nature creates awe-inspiring things. It is native to the regions of Baiae and the countryside of the towns surrounding Mount Vesuvius. It is mixed with lime and stones and not only strengthens other buildings, but even causes fortifications constructed in the sea to grow harder under the water.

Vitruvius, *De Architectura*, 2.6.1

Pliny the Elder called the Tiber 'the gentlest merchant of goods in the whole world'.[1] He had followed its route from the Apennines past Tifernum and Oriculum and down to Rome and watched as it rose from a mere trickle to become *aspera et confragosa*, wild and uneven, as it met other rivers and streams. The Tiber could rise very suddenly as it passed through Rome. Pliny the Elder had interpreted its swell as 'always more holy than savage' because it reminded people of the importance of revering Nature. For all the respect he felt towards his uncle, Pliny could not share in his optimism. He knew only too well how quickly this gentle merchant could transform itself into a torrent. The Tiber, said Pliny, 'sheds its name as a great river' in summer.[2] It shed its reputation as a gentle merchant when the rain came. One year, Pliny saw it burst its lower banks,

211

submerge the surrounding valleys and skim the land of its cara-
pace. Whole woods were swept away as the water rushed into
the adjoining River Aniene, swelled, and carried herds, trees and
roof beams away with it.[3]

Autumn was in many ways the most testing time for Pliny. It
was the season when he discovered how much he had to gain
– and to lose – by entrusting his produce to the Tiber as his
streams began to flow again. He might gather in a full harvest
and put the farms to bed, only for the river to dry up or flood
and render all his work in vain. Or he might find that he had
little to entrust to the Tiber at all. When one year his vines
failed, he was reduced to sending a friend some of his poems
instead of his usual gift of wine. When they failed again, he
jested that he would be unable even to do that for want of money
to purchase papyrus.[4] Although Pliny had known his crops to be
struck by both hail and drought, there was one period of 'continuous barrenness' that brought him almost to despair.[5] With a
view to reducing his tenants' rents, he sought leave from his post
at the treasury to reorganise his Tuscan estate. 'I cannot calculate
[the new rents] unless I'm there,' he explained in a letter. Thirty
days were duly granted him by Trajan, who succeeded Nerva as
Emperor of Rome in AD 98.

Nerva had been in power for only sixteen months when he
collapsed and died after what was said to have been a heated
debate with one Regulus.[6] Pliny would not have kept quiet had
it been his old enemy Regulus who dispatched the emperor to
his grave but, whoever he was, he was irksome enough to be
blamed for inducing a sweat in the aged emperor, followed by
a shivering, and finally death. Pliny did not display any grief in
his letters at Nerva's passing. Nerva had feared instability too
much to seek justice for the philosophers. He had failed to
reverse the damage Domitian had caused. But there was still
time. As Tacitus said, 'remedies work more slowly than diseases'.[7]

Pliny therefore proceeded to embrace Trajan with all the warmth and fervour he had withheld from Nerva. 'The immortal gods have hastened to bring your virtues to the helm of the state,' he declared in his gushing letter of congratulation.[8] Seizing the opportunity to ingratiate himself further, Pliny obtained the new emperor's permission to display his portrait in the temple he was building near his villa at Tifernum. Trajan was a tall, handsome man with a wide face and fine head of hair (its premature greying, said Pliny, only made him look more majestic).[9] His portrait would make a welcome addition to the collection.

Pliny would stay in the town for September, the month he knew he would be least missed at the treasury owing to the number of public holidays. The day known as the Ides fell at the middle of each month and was normally celebrated with a festival. In September, the Ides coincided with the Ludi Romani, two weeks of games held at Rome in honour of Jupiter, and was marked with a feast in honour of the god. In Tusculum, meanwhile, the local people would make their way to Pliny's Tuscan estate to participate in a smaller regional celebration of Ceres, the goddess of the harvest. Her new temple, replacing the weather-beaten monument that had been nearing collapse, was now complete and featured porticoes 'for the mortals' as Pliny had requested. The worshippers had no longer to endure the elements.

In spite of his own poor harvests, Pliny later looked back on this period as one of plenty across the Italian countryside. In previous generations, Rome had relied upon Egypt and Sicily for grain, importing more than 130,000 tonnes a year from Egypt alone under Augustus.[10] While Trajan helped to increase the grain supply from the provinces further by reducing levies on produce, Pliny expressed greater enthusiasm for Italian self-sufficiency. In the second year of Trajan's rule, the Nile faltered, its water levels plummeting as 'half-heartedly and languidly it raised itself from its bed'.[11] The vision of haughty Egyptians receiving back what they ordinarily dispatched as the Italians made up the shortfall tickled Pliny pink.

About a year after he had reorganised his estate Pliny was back in Rome rejoicing that crops were no longer being 'seized as if from an enemy only to perish in the granaries . . . but deliver of themselves what the earth begets, what the stars nourish, what the seasons bring forth'.[12] His words formed part of a speech he gave in the senate house on 1 September, AD 100 on the occasion of his appointment to the consulship. This was the most senior executive magistracy in the senate. While Pliny was delighted to have attained it, he was elated to have done so at a 'much younger' age than Cicero.[13] He was thirty-eight or thirty-nine when he achieved the honour; Cicero had been an elderly forty-three. Pliny's was a less powerful consulship than Cicero's. In the late Republic, two consuls served for most of the year but would often then make way for two 'suffect' consuls to complete their term. While Cicero had served as consul for 63 BC (and at the youngest possible age at that time), Pliny would be suffect consul from September to October, AD 100. That his was a less prestigious post did not trouble Pliny in the least. Pliny the Elder had lavished so much praise on Cicero as a setter of precedents – first of all men to be hailed 'father of the country', first man in a toga to win a triumph and laurel for his speeches, father of Latin letters – that Pliny was only too pleased to have anticipated him at something.[14] A few years later, Trajan granted Pliny his wish to be elected to a priesthood. He became Augur or Interpreter of Bird Signs, an honorary office that Cicero had held at the age of fifty-three. The people of Comum celebrated Pliny's first promotion by erecting a statue of him in the town with 'COS' for 'consul' engraved in large letters upon its base.[15] Pliny meanwhile poured all his energies into delivering the best inaugural speech he possibly could in thanksgiving to the emperor on behalf of the state.[16]

Trajan had been emperor for only seventeen months when Pliny set about praising his wisdom, humility and moderation and the transformative effect he had had on the crops. For much of the time, Trajan had been on command outside Rome. Following his governorship in Germania in the time of Nerva, he had proceeded in the direction of the Danube to confront the continuing threat from Dacia (modern Romania). Domitian had expelled the Dacians from the neighbouring Roman province of Moesia after they invaded, but they were once again intent on disrupting Roman control over these territories. With Trajan so often away and only returning to Rome in the autumn of AD 99, Pliny could hardly have known what kind of man he was, but he did know who he wanted him to be, and saw his speech as an opportunity to commend him to virtue and establish a paradigm for his successors to live up to. He believed that if he could only encourage Trajan to rouse Rome's future leaders from their laziness and pleasure-seeking 'for a little while', then it would have been a job well done.[17] Tacitus later professed to write his *Annals* of the emperors *sine ira et studio* ('without bitterness or an agenda'), and Pliny now similarly claimed to be speaking free from the constraints of fear.[18] In one of the most successful moments in his speech, he described Trajan rounding up Rome's political informers, putting them aboard ships, and entrusting them to the uncertainty of the waves: 'It was a memorable sight, a fleet of informers released to every wind, forced to open sails to the storms and to follow the angry waves onto the rocks in their path.'[19]

This was Pliny in epic mode – in full flight. It was as if he was describing the evil suitors undergoing Odysseus' journey in reverse. In the poem, the suitors are slaughtered. For the informers, execution would have been too easy a death. As he

215

stood in front of Trajan in the senate house, Pliny relived the experience of watching them embark upon a journey into exile that he knew they might never complete.

Pliny was conscious that expressions of thanksgiving had proven soporific in the past and strove for a more exalted 'optimistic' tone than he normally used.[20] To modern ears his chosen style is somewhat grating and turgid. In places his speech even sounds fulsome.[21] Its sheer joyfulness, spread over ninety-five chapters, can be difficult to stomach: 'If another man had excelled in just one of these areas, he would long since have worn a halo around his head, had a seat of gold or ivory among the gods, and been invoked with the meatiest sacrifices on high altars,' Pliny flattered.[22]

There are a few moments of unintended comic relief as Pliny compares the courteous Trajan with the uncouth Domitian: Trajan is to be praised for eating his dinner in the company of other men without having already gorged himself earlier in the day; he is to be praised for not throwing – or throwing up – his food in the presence of his hungry guests.[23] And then more obsequy. It was unfortunate for Pliny that a ban imposed upon performances by actors of mime shows known as 'pantomimes' ('an effeminate art-form and pursuit unworthy of our age') lapsed in Trajan's rule.[24] In his desperation to portray Trajan as an eschewer of all luxuries, Pliny was reduced to making the desperate suggestion that his morality was so contagious, that the Roman people had begged for pantomimes to be outlawed all over again.[25]

Pliny was on safer ground when he enlarged on Trajan's military feats. In his final years Trajan would declare war on the Parthian empire (in ancient Iran) that had always eluded Roman conquest. His campaign would lead to the capture of the Parthian capital and annexation of Armenia, and by the time of his death in the East in AD 117, the Roman empire would have reached its largest extent to date. In the early second century, Trajan was still establishing his credentials. He celebrated his most glorious victory over Dacia after a series of difficult campaigns which culminated in the establishment of a new Roman province and the suicide of the Dacian king Decabalus. 'I see tables . . . weighed down under the huge barbarian spoils,' Pliny exclaimed in his speech, 'and the enemy himself, enchained at the wrist, following in parade behind his own accomplishments.'[26]

Pliny's words were later echoed in the carvings applied to Trajan's Column in Rome. Completed thirteen years after Pliny delivered his speech in the senate, the thirty-metre monument was placed at the centre of Trajan's new forum complex, which was funded from spoils from the Dacian Wars. It features the emperor fifty-nine times across its spiralling surface and in as many guises as Pliny described him. He is a military counsellor and a soldier; a pious performer of sacrifice and a stern-faced assessor of men. He stands among his soldiers, his sweat mingling with theirs; elsewhere he floats above them like a god.[27] While the Dacians are depicted preparing to commit mass suicide in defeat, the Roman soldiers lay waste to their villages, administer first aid to injured legionaries, and process towards the Danube.

The construction of Trajan's column and forum was overseen by Apollodorus of Damascus, an architect who had accomplished the unprecedented feat of bridging the lower Danube in the course of the Dacian Wars. Trajan had been anxious to span the river because he feared what would happen if it froze over and war broke out against the Romans on the far bank.[28] Pliny could only marvel at Apollodorus' expertise. His finished bridge was said to have had as many as twenty stone piers. When Pliny heard that his friend Caninius Rufus was planning to write about the wars, he thrilled with excitement at the descriptions he might give of 'new rivers established on land, new bridges thrown up over rivers, mountain edges broken by camps'.[29]

Reports of Apollodorus' success in bridging the Danube led Pliny to ponder man's potential to overcome the challenges of Nature. Whether the Danube froze over in midwinter or dried up in late spring, the man-made structure enabled the Romans to cross it as if it were midsummer. As he wrote in his speech, 'it was just as if the seasons had been changed'.[30]

Pliny's continuing fascination with the rise and fall of water – of the Danube, of the Nile, of the spring at Comum – did not go unnoticed by Trajan who, three years after hearing his long inaugural speech, appointed him *curator alvei Tiberis et riparum et cloacarum urbis* – Curator of the Bed and Banks of the River Tiber and of the City's Sewers.[31] Tasked with monitoring the river levels and making provisions to protect against flooding and drought, Pliny stepped into a role that was reserved for senators, but decidedly better suited to engineers.

He was fortunate to receive a lesson in water-based engineering from Apollodorus of Damascus himself. Between his work bridging the Danube and planning the new forum with its column at Rome, Apollodorus oversaw the construction of a magnificent new harbour at Centum Cellae (Civitavecchia), to the north-west of the city. It would be less famous than the great hexagonal harbour Trajan established at Portus, near Ostia, but for Pliny it was a work of art. He had the opportunity to watch it being built when he went to stay with Trajan at his 'stunning' villa near the shore. He had developed, if not a friendship, then a closeness and familiarity with Trajan, which would deepen over the years. He was invited to Centum Cellae in the first instance to help the emperor assess some civil cases – one involving a charge of adultery against the wife of a military tribune, another, allegations of forgery in a man's will – but his visit would also be a sociable one. 'You will recognise how serious our days were,' Pliny wrote to a friend, 'but the breaks which followed them were very pleasant.' In the evenings he dined with Trajan – not on anything too lavish 'if you consider he is an emperor' – and enjoyed whatever entertainments he laid on.[32]

In breaks during the day, Pliny made his way through 'the greenest fields' to the coast to examine the foundations of his harbour. He gazed in wonder at the 'artistry with which it rises' as he watched enormous stones being hauled into place to form the harbour arms. With his eye cast firmly on the reinforcements laid to tame the sea, Pliny described each new layer as it was applied: 'There is already a towering stone ridge, which breaks the waves as they hit it and throws them up into the air.' You can almost hear in his description the proud voice of Trajan pointing things out, telling him what will go where: 'Then piers will be built on the rocks and soon enough it will resemble an island that has always been there' (the island would serve as an additional breakwater); 'it will be a great source of safety, for it will provide a refuge on this very long, harbourless coastline.'[33] These were the barriers of a river curator's dreams.

Parts of the harbour still survive – a testament to the strength of Roman concrete. An ingenious recipe had been devised for a material that the architectural historian Vitruvius (quoted also by Pliny the Elder) claimed grew only stronger and more impregnable when placed in seawater.[34] The secret was to mix volcanic rock and ash – specifically the 'dust' of Puteoli in the Bay of Naples – with lime and water, which together formed 'a single stone when submerged' in the sea. Vitruvius accounted for the phenomenon by the existence of sulphur, alum, bitumen and flames beneath the ground in these regions: so dry are the natural products of the Bay of Naples that they will swiftly absorb any water they come into contact with and use it to cohere and become hard. In 2017, an international team of scientists put the theory to the test and discovered that, when volcanic ash is combined with water, a series of 'water–rock interactions' takes place which indeed lead to the strengthening of the concrete over time.[35] Volcanic matter, so quick to destroy buildings, was also the ingredient needed to protect them against Nature's battering.

The dichotomy between the destructive and preservative properties of stone fascinated Pliny because he saw it at play in his own life. The experience of delivering his speech to Trajan led him to ponder how quickly words turned to dust. A marble column might stand forever provided it was not felled by an earthquake or an enemy, but a senator's speech tended to be 'contained by the walls of the senate house'.[36] One had the permanence of stone; the other, stone rendered impermanent. Although important speeches were now preserved in bronze alongside proclamations of the emperor, Pliny was sorry that so many had already perished within the house itself.

In the early years of Trajan's rule, Pliny was thinking particularly deeply about his legacy. For all he boasted of being 'much younger' than Cicero at the same stage in his career, Pliny the Younger was beginning to feel decidedly old. The depressing thought that he had lived the best part of his life came to him suddenly when he heard that the last of Nero's consuls had died. Silius Italicus, poet of the *Punic War*, had starved himself to death at the age of seventy-five after developing an incurable tumour. Pliny had never much cared for his poetry ('more diligent than inspired'), or for his habit of buying up properties, lavishing them with treasures, and leaving his old ones to moulder.[37] But his death prompted him to think about the fleetingness of his own life. To Pliny it felt like only yesterday that Nero was on the throne. Now the last surviving consul of Nero's senate had perished. 'Grief for the frailty of human life comes over me as I remember this,' Pliny wrote. He had been a child in Nero's time. Now he was in middle age, a consul himself, with no child of his own.

Pliny had always been conscious of time slipping by, but there was a new urgency to his thinking, a fresh desperation. He began to take a graver view of the necessity of prolonging each moment. There is a famous passage in Herodotus' *Histories* that describes Xerxes, King of Persia, weeping as he surveys his great army because he knows that death will soon come to thousands of his men. As Pliny read it, not for the first time in his life, he now found himself in sympathy with the despised Persian king. 'So narrow are the limits that contain the lives of so many people,' he explained, 'that it seems to me that those royal tears of his ought not merely to be forgiven, but indeed to be praised.'[38] In the aftermath of Silius Italicus' suicide, Pliny renewed his call for his contemporaries to fulfil something in the short time they had: 'Let us leave behind something by which we can prove we have lived!'[39]

But if ephemerality frightened Pliny, the prospect of spending his whole life working, only to die before completing something, was more nightmarish still. 'The deaths of those who are in the process of producing some immortal work,' he said, 'always seem to me to be cruel and premature. For those who live from day to day immersed in pleasures see their reasons for living completed every day; whereas those who think of posterity and prolong the period for which they will be remembered through their work, for them death is always sudden since it interrupts something before it's finished.'[40]

Death, whenever it came, would come too soon for Pliny. To achieve immortality, he believed that he needed to complete a magnum opus, but in order to do that he needed to know when to stop. When he did not allow even his days to reach their natural conclusion, extending his work far into the night, what hope did he have of ever feeling that he had done all he needed to do?

Perhaps this is one reason why he resisted the pressure his

friends put on him to write a work of history. Knowing how important it was to him to leave something behind, they urged him to turn his hand to past events. A chronicle of Rome would have more longevity than any speech delivered in the Court of One Hundred or senate. But it would also require more time, and Pliny had no way of knowing how much of that he had left. If he were to dedicate five years to writing a history of Rome, only to die before completing it, then he would have wasted five years. What would have happened to his uncle's *Natural History* had Vesuvius erupted a few years earlier? Pliny did feel the impulse to write history – ancient rather than modern, he fancied – but he had to revise his speeches for publication first. He promised his friends that he would write something historical – but only when he was too old to write oratory. He perhaps also feared being compared unfavourably to his uncle and to Tacitus.

Pliny had a long list of reasons for putting it off: history-writing and speech-writing are incompatible. Each discipline had its own rhythm, its own vocabulary, its own tone. History was concerned with great events but oratory merely with *sordida* – the lowly things in life. In his view there was no viable method of writing both side by side. This was not what Pliny's uncle had said. Pliny the Elder had described his *Natural History* as a record not of 'expeditions or speeches or conversations or any manner of exotic events', but rather 'of the nature of things, which is life, and often within this, the very basest of matters – *sordidissima*'.[41] Pliny the Elder dealt in *sordidissima*, not speeches. Pliny composed speeches on *sordida*. Their two worlds were far closer than Pliny was prepared to accept. His letters were in themselves a form of history.

It was only some time after Pliny had delivered his speech for Trajan that he realised that speeches were not so very different from history after all. The solution to his stalemate came when he resolved to rewrite and extend the speech. Once he had this in hand he could treat it just as he would a work of history. There was no need for his speech to die within the walls of the senate house or to be swept away on the Tiber. He would do all he could to give it the permanence of stone.

He began by giving a full-length reading of it to his friends at Rome.[42] He may have regretted telling them to come only 'if it's convenient' or 'if you're really free (though it's never convenient and no one is really free to listen to a recital at Rome . . .)' when he awoke to 'the foulest storms' over the city, but not even the inclement weather could keep them away. If the appeal of the *Panegyricus* is often lost on modern ears, it was not on its early audiences, who forced Pliny to continue into a third day when 'modesty' led him to bring his two-day reading to an end. The long speech was written down in its entirety and copied out with such enthusiasm and commitment down the centuries that it flourished far beyond the confines of human memory to become the earliest Latin speech since Cicero's *Philippics* to survive antiquity.[43]

FIFTEEN

Depraved Belief

Whatsoever hath no fins nor scales in the waters, that shall
be an abomination unto you.

Leviticus 11:12

The most important journey Pliny ever made was to Bithynia,
the sprawling Roman province on the north coast of what
is now Turkey. Dispatched there one autumn between AD 109
and 111 as an 'imperial legate', Pliny was to serve as a personal
representative of Trajan himself.[1] He boarded a galley, crossed
the seas towards Greece, rounded Cape Malea in the Peloponnese,
and finally put in at Ephesus.[2] Despite the chill and perils of
traversing what his uncle had considered 'the most savage section
of Nature', the sea, Pliny managed to stay well enough during
the long voyage from Italy to Asia Minor. It was only when he
reached terra firma that he became unwell.[3] He had planned to
proceed from Ephesus to Bithynia by both coastal boat and land,
but after developing a fever in the sudden heat, was forced to
pause at Pergamum.[4]

He was fortunate not to be travelling alone. There were his
crew and attendants. There was also Calpurnia. Senators used
to object to women accompanying their husbands to postings
overseas, believing them to be weak, susceptible to befriending

the worst kind of people, and a liability to the smooth running of things.[5] The provinces, however, were by and large less hostile than they used to be, and over time most senators had come to the conclusion that they should not suffer for the sake of their predecessors' failures to keep their women 'in line'. Some took their wives abroad with a mind to protecting them from the temptations of adultery at home. Pliny presumably took Calpurnia because he could not bear to be parted from her.

Shortly before Pliny and Calpurnia set out, Trajan bestowed upon them the rights ordinarily reserved for parents of three or more children. There was little Pliny could do with the *ius trium liberorum*, which entitled fathers of three to stand for political office before the usual age requirements and their wives to inherit property with greater ease than their childless counterparts, but he accepted the honour.[6] His friend Martial had received the same rights after composing a series of epigrams on the Colosseum.[7] And after thanking the gods for not having granted him children in the 'most lamentable age' of Domitian, and praying that Calpurnia might now be more fortunate and conceive again, Pliny asked Trajan whether he might consider extending the honour to some of his other friends as well.[8] Suetonius had experienced Pliny's kindness in the past when he was a young man embarking upon his career. Now around forty years old, he had found himself suffering a childless marriage of his own.[9] Trajan wrote back to Pliny to say that, though he only rarely conferred such honours upon anyone, he would do so upon Suetonius at his request.

The crew waited until Pliny had recovered from his fever before resuming their journey by coastal boat. They finally reached the province on 17 September. Bithynia (or 'Bithynia-Pontus') dominated the southern coast of the Black Sea. The province had been founded in the first century BC after the King of Bithynia bequeathed his land to Rome and Pompey the Great merged it with territory he had conquered to its east. Deeply forested with oak, beech, pine, and plane, it was desolate by comparison with the landscapes Pliny was used to. From its westernmost towns, Pliny could at least look out across the gulf towards Byzantium, which, he observed, had 'crowds of travellers flowing into it from all sides'.[10] He would examine the finances here as well. It would be almost two centuries before the emperor Diocletian chose Nicomedia (modern Izmit) as the site for his chief residence, and still decades later that Emperor Constantine relocated the Roman capital to Byzantium, but Pliny had come to a part of the world that was becoming steadily more influential.[11]

Pliny's first impressions of the place were not altogether encouraging. He found it a chaotic province, full of unfinished building projects, riddled with debt. His previous involvement in extortion cases arising from the region had convinced him that the Bithynian people were litigious but unpredictable.[12] They spoke mainly Greek and suffered from an unfortunate habit of unleashing torrents of words when two would do. Initial meetings with Bithynians on their home soil did little to challenge his views. His uncle had praised the region's cheese but Pliny struggled to do so much as that.[13] Catullus had travelled to these 'udder-rich' plains a century and a half earlier and complained of making no profit while he set to work on the Bithynians' account books. By the time Pliny arrived, the accounts were once again in considerable disarray. Taxes were owed to Rome, excruciating sums had been wasted on projects which had been undertaken without the completion of adequate plans and subsequently abandoned. Only the contractors had reason to smile as they filled their pockets with the proceeds of the projects which had been left behind.[14] Pliny had his experience in the Roman treasuries to draw on as he inspected the finances, but his responsibilities exceeded the correction of logbooks, covering the administration of the province and its laws more widely.

'Ensure it is clear to [the Bithynian people],' Trajan instructed him, 'that you were selected to be sent to them in my place.'[15] Roman governors had been posted to the provinces during the Republic and early Empire and would continue to be dispatched for years to come. A year or two after Pliny arrived in Bithynia, Tacitus was appointed governor of Asia, the Roman province to its south-west. Pliny, however, presented himself as being as authoritative as the emperor himself. For as long as he was in this post he was to cut as stately a figure as he could imagine. If the need arose for a faster horse or stronger chariot he had only to requisition those he liked best from the local people.[16] It was his duty to command the respect and obedience of everyone he came into contact with. Behind his imperious facade, however, Pliny was still obliged to seek Trajan's approval when it came to making key decisions. He would exchange more than a hundred letters with the emperor over the two or so years he spent in the province. The letters would become less frequent as Pliny grew more familiar with the territory and parameters of his post, but they continued to arrive – concise, business-like, and quickly dashed off though they often were.

In Rome it had been easy for Pliny to establish which messengers were the most efficient and reliable.[17] Sending letters between Rome and Bithynia was far more complicated. It would take at least two months for a letter to arrive, usually much longer, especially as Pliny was frequently on the move.[18] He had to endure the endless frustration of waiting for a response to arrive from Trajan even when the solution to a problem was perfectly obvious. On reaching Prusa (Bursa), a city in the west of the province, for example, Pliny found the public buildings to be in an even worse state than the finances. The baths were 'dirty and old' and in dire need of replacing. A perusal of the account books was all he needed to conceive a plan for constructing new baths by calling in money from those who owed it, and redirecting funds normally reserved for the public distribution of olive oil.[19] Pliny waited and waited until finally a letter from Trajan arrived giving him the go-ahead – on the proviso that his plan did not burden the ordinary functioning of the city or involve additional taxation.

Trajan did not have to reply personally to every letter Pliny sent his way. His private secretary could compose a response following a brief conversation. But several of the letters in Pliny's collection resound with the voice of authority. It is easiest to detect Trajan's tone in the most sharply phrased of his letters. Time and again, Pliny wrote to ask Trajan whether architects and land surveyors might be sent from Rome to assist him in his work. Time and again, Trajan wrote back to remind him that the best men did not always come from Rome: 'no province lacks in skilled and trained men'.[20] There were hardly enough architects in the city as it was, Trajan curtly told him, which was not surprising, given his grand visions for the harbour at Centum Cellae: 'You shouldn't think it would be quicker to have them sent from the city when in fact they usually come to us from Greece!'[21]

Whether more through reluctance to trust the skills of the locals or determination to develop his own, Pliny decided to take on some of the technical work himself. North-east of Prusa lay Nicomedia, the former home of the kings of Bithynia, and its splendid lake. Realising that the people of Nicomedia might export their produce more efficiently if their lake could be connected to the Sea of Marmara, Pliny called in the local people to assess whether doing so would risk draining the lake, as Trajan feared. While the Bithynians attempted to measure its depths, Pliny composed another letter to Trajan requesting an engineer or architect to travel from Rome to assess whether or not it lay above sea level. While he waited for a reply, he carried out an investigation of his own. On noticing an unfinished canal he conceived the idea of connecting the lake to the sea by means of a similar structure.[22] He went no further in his plans until the experts arrived. This time Trajan agreed to send a specialist from Rome.

Pliny had moved on from Nicomedia to another part of the province when he heard news that an enormous fire had broken out and destroyed dozens of the city's buildings. Rerouting the lake could no longer be a priority when houses had been reduced to ashes, the headquarters of the city's elders levelled, and the temple of Isis gutted by flames.[23] The fire had been spread by strong winds and 'the inertia of the people', who had stood by watching helplessly because they lacked the means to put it out. When Pliny heard what happened he gave orders to supply Nicomedia with fire-fighting equipment. At Rome people fought fires with woollen blankets dipped in water and vinegar and ingenious hydraulic water pumps powered by siphons. Pliny also drew up plans to appoint a body of 150 fire marshals to guard against future disasters. He was even prepared to oversee the marshals himself, he told Trajan, assuring him that 'it will not be difficult to keep guard over so few'. Trajan was not convinced. It would be sufficient to issue the townsmen with equipment and teach the Bithynians how to use it. They could fight fires themselves and call upon the crowds to assist if they needed to. For when people come together in common purpose, Trajan explained, they can form *hetaeriae* – political clubs.[24] Trajan did more than just quell Pliny's plans to establish a band of fire marshals. He instructed Pliny to issue an edict on his behalf banning the formation of such groups altogether.

It was only when Pliny proceeded eastwards into the heartlands of old Pontus that he witnessed the dangers of *hetaeriae* for himself.[25] In these remote parts of the province he became used to locals approaching him with their grievances. He handled financial disputes and addressed the problems left behind by errant builders. But nothing he had experienced so far, either here or in Rome, could have prepared him for what he heard next. As if from nowhere, a number of Bithynians were now led before him under accusation of being 'Christian'.

Pliny had heard of Jews who had been banished and taxed throughout his lifetime, but this was his first personal experience of Christians. After Tiberius expelled Jews from Rome in AD 19, Emperor Claudius had felt compelled to exile 'the Jews who were continually causing disturbance at the instigation of Chrestus', by whom Suetonius surely meant Christ.[26] In their bemusement Romans conflated Christianity and Judaism. Peter, after all, would tell the Gentiles to abide by Jewish law. Christianity was still young and remained mysterious to the Romans, even after their engagement in the Jewish War. Pliny was only a child when Titus besieged Jerusalem, but he was in his early thirties when Domitian put his own cousin to death in Rome on suspicions of 'atheism' – for adopting the Jewish or Christian faith.

This was not a passing phenomenon Pliny had stumbled upon. Christianity was well established in the province when he arrived. It was the Christians of Bithynia and Pontus, Galatia, Cappadocia, and Asia whom Peter addressed in his First Epistle. And there were people who were brought before Pliny who professed to have been Christian up to twenty years earlier and who had since renounced their faith. But what was Pliny to do with them? He knew that trials of Christians had taken place in the past by *cognitio* – an investigation led by a senior senator.[27] However there seems to have been no formal law against Christianity specifically and no protocol for dealing with religious perpetrators in such numbers. Pliny did not know how and 'to what extent it is usual to punish or cross-examine [Christians]'.[28] Should distinctions be made depending on age? Should those who repented of being Christian be pardoned?

For other matters he was uncertain about, Pliny was prepared to await a response from Trajan. This time, however, he decided to act at once, apparently too unsettled by what he had seen to risk delay. Without so much as a pause to seek the emperor's advice, he devised his own procedure for trialling the accused. When so-called Christians were brought before him, he would ask them in the first instance whether or not they were Christian. If they said they were, then he would ask them again, and again a third time, threatening them as he did so with punishment. He would have been too young to remember the terrible punishments Nero had inflicted upon the Christians at Rome, but he must have heard of the crucifixions and human torches and allegations of their responsibility for the great fire that burned across the city for seven nights. If these were the sorts of punishment Pliny had in mind, then he would have been wise to recall how they had been viewed in Nero's time. The sight of Christians hanging from crosses had inspired not only fear among the Roman people but also pity and compassion for, as Tacitus said, it was as if their punishments were being received 'not for the public good, but to feed the savagery of one man'.[29]

Pliny believed that any Roman citizen who was brought before him under suspicion of being Christian deserved to be sent to Rome for trial. The accused who were not Roman citizens and who persisted in saying they were Christian, however, were to be executed. 'For I had no doubt that, whatever it was they were confessing to, such obstinacy and obdurate perseverance ought to be punished.'[30] But that was just it: what were they to be punished for? Pliny did not know. Domitian had exiled Christians but he had also exiled Stoic philosophers. Pliny had no reason to view Domitian's treatment of Christians as anything other than part of a broader plan to crush anyone who might have challenged him. When finally Pliny wrote to Trajan to tell him what procedure he had put in place in his province, he asked him explicitly whether it was the name 'Christian' itself that was punishable, even if the 'Christian' had committed no crime, or whether it was 'the crimes associated with the name' which he ought to be punishing.[31]

It was only from interrogating the Christians that he learned what these 'crimes' were. According to Pliny, the Christians believed their own gravest crimes to be that they held meetings on an established day of the week before first light, during which they hymned to Christ as if he were a god; that they bound themselves by oath not to commit sins such as theft or adultery, not to break trust, nor to deny a deposit when it was called upon.[32] Pliny discovered that, before he issued the edict banning *hetaeriae*, the Christians had also held meetings later in the day over food. Although they had ceased these meetings in compliance with his orders, their morning meetings were truly a cause for concern. The Christians called their meetings *ekklesiai* but for Pliny they were still *hetaeriae* and therefore potentially dangerous.[33] Emperor Claudius had initially allowed Jews to live as they wished in Rome provided they refrained from holding meetings.[34] Even among Romans private meetings were treated with suspicion. Throughout history various 'sumptuary' laws had been passed imposing limits on the size of dinner parties in a bid to prevent them from being used for political ends. The very earliest Roman laws had prohibited night-time meetings altogether. The fact that Christians were holding meetings in the dark rendered them all the more threatening. The Romans would come to see them as 'a secretive and light-evading species' and spread rumours of them being incestuous cannibals.[35] The Christians would describe the Romans in turn as 'light-evading' for their refusal to engage with Holy Scripture.[36]

Pliny did not want simply to dismiss or punish the Christians he met. He was curious about what they believed. The cases brought before him became increasingly varied. Some were carried by informers and others arose from an anonymous book 'containing the names of many Christians' which was brought to his attention. When Pliny obtained this private list of alleged Christians he determined to use it. He would test every suspected Christian regardless of the source from which the accusation came. He would place statues of Trajan and the Roman gods in front of the accused, perhaps recalling how Caligula had offended the Jews by planning to have a statue of himself erected in the Temple of Jerusalem. And he would then ask the alleged Christians to invoke the Roman gods, honour the emperor's image with incense and wine, and blaspheme Christ. If they followed these commands, then they were allowed to leave provided they denied being or having ever been Christian. Pliny had heard it said that nothing could force a true Christian to speak ill of Christ. Indeed, when Polycarp, Bishop of Smyrna, was given the opportunity to save himself from death by cursing Christ half a century later, he told the Roman before him: 'I have been His servant for eighty-six years, and he has done nothing to dishonour me. How can I blaspheme the King who saved me?'[37]

For perhaps the first time in his life, Pliny felt truly ruffled. Roman governors in this period usually tried to avoid stirring up tension among provincials by allowing them to continue to live by their old laws instead of imposing too much of the Roman way of life upon them.[38] Governors were, however, required to maintain order; the Christians seemed to threaten that order. Pliny was so alarmed by what he had learned from the Christians during his interrogations that he decided that it was now 'even more necessary to seek the truth from two female slaves, who were called "deaconesses", by means of torture'.[39] Pliny did not need to elaborate, for it was standard practice among the Romans to take evidence from slaves accused of crimes under torture.[40] But the criminality of the Christians of this province had not been established, and there was no guaranteeing that a slave under torture would reveal anything pertinent. As Pliny told Trajan, while exacting his punishments, he 'found nothing except a depraved and unbridled *superstitio*'. It was at this point that Pliny sought Trajan's guidance. He had come to the conclusion that Christianity in Bithynia was out of control. He had been able to discern no pattern in the people brought before him. The 'Christians' were of all ages, all classes, both genders, and from all areas of the province. The 'contagion of superstition' had spread not only through the towns and villages, but through the countryside as well. This part of Pliny's letter would have given the Christians reason to rejoice. The fourth-century Christian historian Eusebius of Caesarea took the fact that non-Christians were writing of the persecutions and martyrdoms as a sign that Christianity was in good health.[41]

The destruction of the Temple of Jerusalem by Titus' forces in AD 70 had left the Jews and early Christians with no central place of worship in Judaea, 'the origin of the evil' that had spread to Rome.[42] The Romans might reasonably have supposed that the loss of the temple would presage the destruction of the faith, but the very fact that there was no centre meant that worshippers had had to adapt and spread the Word.[43] Pliny did not connect the rise of Christianity with Roman activity in the east of the empire. He sought not a cause for the growth of the strange cult but a plan to reverse it. His progress through Bithynia had shown him that there was support for the Roman gods. There was still every chance that the tide of Christianity could be stemmed, as he informed Trajan:

It seems that [the superstition] can be stopped and corrected. Certainly it's clear that the [Roman] temples which were previously empty have begun to be visited, and sacrifices which had been given up for a long time are being performed again, and the meat of sacrificial victims is being sold everywhere, though it was very rare a buyer could be found before. It's easy to conclude from this that a lot of people could be reformed, if only they had a chance to repent.[44]

The performance of Roman-style animal sacrifice would be enforced across the empire by an edict of the emperor Decius in AD 249. For the moment, Trajan was prepared to take a passive approach to the problems Pliny had identified. His response to his letter must have come as a shock to Pliny. While he had done well to examine the Christians, Trajan told him, anonymous lists of names such as he had described had no place in their world.[45] The proper way to make an accusation was face to face.[46] Alarmed by the faith Pliny had placed in anonymous accusations, Trajan determined to correct him. Pliny had been wrong to use the evidence he had. By putting his trust in potentially unscrupulous informers Pliny had acted as Regulus and so many other men had under Nero and Domitian. Trajan advised a less active course than the one Pliny had in mind. He told him that there could be no single rule for handling Christians. From now on, he said, people who were brought before him and proven guilty were to be punished. But those who honoured the Roman gods and denied being Christian now were to be pardoned. As a general rule, Christians were not to be hunted out.

Trajan may have been advocating a more moderate approach but, to some early Christians, it was frustratingly illogical. Tertullian, a Christian writer born in Carthage about half a century after Trajan issued his instructions, believed that Roman hatred of the 'name of Christians' was driven by little more than ignorance of the faith.[47] The emperor's advice to Pliny not to go after Christians but to punish those who were brought before him seemed particularly duplicitous. In saying that Christians were not to be sought out implied that they were innocent, reasoned Tertullian, while ordering them to be punished implied that they were guilty. If you condemn them, why not also seek them out? If you do not seek them out, why not also acquit them?[48] Trajan might have reduced the number of persecutions Pliny planned to carry out, but he fell short of stopping the violence altogether. Eusebius later observed that local persecutions were still commonplace in certain provinces, with some finding any excuse to bring Christians to harm.[49]

Pliny had not anticipated that his actions against the Christians might be met with reproach. Whether they did anything to diminish the trust Trajan had placed in him is impossible to say. There is no further word on the Christians in the letters and it is unclear where Pliny proceeded to next. He was in regular communication with Rome, but his life was now very much here, in Bithynia. Calpurnia was certainly still with him in the province when news arrived from Rome that her grandfather had died. Pliny tells Trajan in his very last letter that he has taken the liberty of giving her one of his official work permits so that she can find immediate passage home.[50] He has done so out of urgency, he tells Trajan, and in hope of his approval. Pliny received a letter back. 'Dearest Secundus,' Trajan began, addressing Pliny by his last name, 'you were right to have confidence in my response and ought not to have doubted it.'[51] Trajan's words, reassuring Pliny of his authority, make for rather an abrupt ending to their correspondence.

Trajan had shown that it was possible for an emperor to rule from outside Rome while he continued in his military campaigns.[52] Through his letters to Pliny, he had also demonstrated how a ruler could make his authority felt in the furthest reaches of the empire by means of trusted representatives. Pliny was in many respects the ideal example of an emperor's deputy. Over the following centuries the emperors would seek new ways to control their vast territories. Before Emperor Constantine founded his new capital at Byzantium in AD 324, and before the First Council of Nicaea convened in Bithynia to establish the Nicene Creed of the Church, the emperor Diocletian helped to establish a tetrarchy, whereby he ruled over one part of the empire and three colleagues ruled over other parts, so as to better govern Rome's diverse provinces. Pliny had come to know the nature of these faraway landscapes and remoteness of their people long before these emperors did. His encounter with the Christians presaged the change that was to come at the heart of Rome's empire. What would Pliny have made of Emperor Constantine declaring himself a believer in the 'depraved and unbridled *superstitio*' he had worked so hard to subdue? Perhaps a part of him would have felt that he had failed in his duty to maintain order in the province.

In AD 113 one of Pliny's former colleagues in the treasury replaced him in his post. Did Pliny die in the province? Or did he follow Calpurnia back to Rome? It is certain that he had died by the time Hadrian succeeded Trajan as emperor in AD 117. Pliny would have been in his early to mid-fifties at the time of his death – no older than his uncle had been when he lost his life in the shadow of Vesuvius. He had at least outlived Regulus, his old enemy, whose absence he felt more strongly than he had anticipated.

Pliny left behind the makings of his own biography. Through his letters and speeches he had presented his life as falling in two distinct phases. After the uncertain times of Domitian came the glorious years under Trajan; it was not in Pliny's interest to dwell on the fact that he had climbed the senatorial ladder in the service of a despised emperor. Pliny's writings, as well as the sometimes exaggerated accounts of his historian friends, were what shaped the reputation of Domitian after his death. Through both his friendship with Tacitus and Suetonius and his own experience of watching the Roman people desecrate monuments across the city, Pliny anticipated how Domitian would be thought of forever after.

Given that Pliny left far more of himself behind in his letters than his uncle had done in his encyclopaedia, it is surprising that Pliny the Elder remains the more celebrated of the two men today. We document our lives so attentively that we tend to assume that something of us will remain after we die. The example of Pliny the Elder suggests otherwise. He is remembered not because he wrote about himself, but because he was written about by others, especially his nephew, who might have shared his fate had he not been so concerned with completing his studies in the midst of the eruption of Vesuvius. As Pliny himself had said of his uncle, he was one of those men who had done what deserved to be written about and written what deserved to be read. Pliny the Elder's death only cemented his fame: 'look to the end', as the Greeks said. His encyclopaedia preserved the findings of many who had come before him and would concern all who came after him. The *Natural History* survived because it was not personal.

The fact that Pliny was so mindful of his own place in the world and anxious to secure a legacy for the future did not make him the antithesis of his uncle. For all he fretted about his position in Rome, what really made Pliny happy was what lay outside the city, in the fields and meadows of his estates. He was a man who saw the world through its details – of wills and inheritance, of water levels, of seasonal change. If only subconsciously, he perpetuated his uncle's celebration of Nature by embracing it in its purest forms and favouring the modest over the elaborate, his silent study over his grand porticoes, his bronze sculpture of a wrinkly old man over more distinguished masterpieces; his beetroot and snails over oysters and snow. He was a career man who escaped by discovering the world beyond.

Resurrection

When the Bishop of Vercelli visited Como in 1578 its cathedral was still unfinished. The foundations of the building had been laid in 1396, and the magnificent Gothic nave and aisles, designed by Lorenzo degli Spazi, one of the architects of the cathedral at Milan, had since been erected behind its stark facade. The cathedral honoured the Assumption of the Blessed Virgin Mary, and sculptures of the Madonna and Child, St John the Baptist, and the patron saints of Como peered down over the bishop as he approached. Far larger and more noticeable than these, however, were the sculptural niches to either side of the main portal. Each contained a statue, almost two metres tall, of a man seated and grasping a book. Both were wide-eyed, long-necked, bony-kneed, and spectacularly hirsute. One had slightly longer hair than the other, but they both wore it in tight ringlets – the older man's falling around his ears, the younger's piled up on top of his head, like a plate of snails. Around their shoulders were sober robes and *mozzetta*-style capes. Bishop Bonomio might have assumed they were holy men, but then he drew nearer and realised that they were not Christian at all. On the left sat Pliny the Elder, on the right, Pliny the Younger. They were more prominent than any of the other figures on the cathedral.[1]

They sat, solemn and contemplative, their eyes raised to

Heaven, pagans disguised as good Christian men.[2] Why erect
these, wondered Bonomio, when there are so many 'other saints'?
A local sculptor named Giovanni Rodari had completed the two
sculptures and, with the assistance of his two sons, mounted
them in their elaborate niches.[3] Decades had passed since the
Verona grievance but, faced with a choice between obeying the
local bishop's pleas to remove the sculptures as unworthy of their
place on a Christian building, and yielding to the supremacy of
the Veronese claim on the two Plinys, the people of Como
elected to keep them where they were.

Pliny, one-time persecutor of Christians, now rested like an
icon over a Christian place of worship. Had his letters to Trajan
been misplaced? Had his trials and the punishments he exacted
in Bithynia been forgotten? Not by everyone. Benedetto Giovio,
the sixteenth-century scholar who had done so much to perpetuate
the connections of Pliny and his uncle with Como against the
misplaced assertions of the Veronese, had even quoted from
Pliny's letter on the Christians in his *Historiae Patriae*. Benedetto
was still alive when two large plaques were added to the cathedral to commemorate each man's scholarship, offices, imperial
ties and, in Pliny's case, his 'immense generosity to his homeland'.
In a further display of affection, a small ancient plaque that was
discovered beneath a step in an 'unremarkable home' in Como
was built into the south wall of the building so that everyone
could remember Gaius Plinius Caecilius Secundus, their great
patron.[4]

In honouring Pliny so extravagantly on their cathedral, the
people of Como had made a choice. After all the time that had
passed since his death, they preferred to remember him for the
good he had done for his people rather than the pain he had
inflicted upon their Christian forefathers. To gloss over his final
years in Bithynia was to show him forgiveness. For all his advan-
tages in life, Pliny had proven himself capable of 'Christian'

qualities, empathising with the unfortunate and maligned philosophers, if not with the Christians themselves. The Como people's rivalry and one-upmanship with the Veronese had steadily been supplanted by an appreciation of the role Pliny had played in transforming their city. He had left Como far more illustrious than he had found it. His library, his baths, the provisions he made for the education of children – his own name – had made Comum a respectable town, and these buildings and the extensive letters that described them became the very seeds of humanist learning in the Renaissance city. They fuelled the Giovio brothers' quest to re-establish the role that both Plinys had played in their history.[5]

Pliny survived a potential backlash from the Christians. His uncle survived the attempts of humanists to discredit him. In 1492, a short time after the people of Como commissioned the Pliny statues, a physician named Niccolò Leoniceno tore into the dubious science of the *Natural History* in a tract entitled *De Plinii et aliorum medicorum in medicina erroribus*. Not only had Pliny the Elder confused Greek plant names, Leoniceno complained, he had even described the moon as larger than the earth on the basis that: 'If the earth were bigger than the moon, it would not be possible for the entire sun to be eclipsed when the moon passed between it and the earth.'[6] As if it was not serious enough that the *Natural History* had been disseminated by a modern press, its errors had crept into other scholars' books. The passage on the relative size of the earth and moon had found its way into the works of the Venerable Bede, who drew heavily on the *Natural History* in his own *De Natura Rerum* (*On the Nature of Things*) and *De Temporibus* (*On Times*).[7]

Pliny the Elder's more fanciful passages may have irritated some readers but they enchanted far more. Even scholars were eager to leap to his defence. At the same time as Leoniceno was fulminating against his methods, a Venetian humanist named

Ermolao Barbaro was preparing his *Castigationes Plinianae*, in which he claimed to correct thousands of errors made, not by Pliny the Elder, but by the copyists of his manuscripts: 'I have cured almost five thousand wounds inflicted on that work by the scribes, or at the very least shown how they might be cured.'[8] The same year, 1493, saw the publication of Pandolfo Collenuccio's *Pliniana defensio adversus Nicolai Leoniceni accusationem*, a riposte to Leoniceno's assault on the *Natural History*. Leoniceno might have prompted some readers to think more carefully before relying on what was handed down to them in ancient textbooks, but his publication did little to diminish Pliny the Elder's appeal to Renaissance men: Francis Bacon, Leonardo da Vinci, Giorgio Vasari, the great patrons of the Italian courts.

Pliny the Elder and Pliny the Younger were Renaissance men in their own time. Beneath their statues on Como Cathedral their rich lives are precised in four small panels. Pliny the Elder is in his study surrounded by books, reading, oblivious to the citizens who are massing outside his doorway. In the next frame he turns away from the volcano, aloof and untroubled as Vesuvius erupts and envelops panicking Campanians in flame. His nephew is absorbed in his reading in a study of his own. When Pliny has finished with his research he makes his way to the senate house, mounts a podium, and prepares to deliver his speech to Trajan. He takes a deep breath and begins . . .

Timeline

BC

264	First Punic War (to 241)
218	Second Punic War (to 201)
189	Triumph of Lucius Cornelius Scipio Asiaticus and 'birth of luxury' in Rome
149	Third Punic War (to 146)
106	Births of Cicero and Pompey the Great
100	Birth of Julius Caesar
74	King Nicomedes IV bequeaths Bithynia to Rome
63	Cicero becomes consul
59	Julius Caesar founds Novum Comum
42	Octavian is named son of deified Caesar
38	Octavian marries Livia and becomes stepfather to her sons Drusus and Tiberius
30	Deaths of Antony and Cleopatra
27	Octavian becomes 'Augustus' and first emperor of Rome
13	Tiberius becomes consul
9	Death of Drusus

AD

4	Augustus adopts Tiberius
6	Judaea becomes a Roman province

9	Defeat of Varus and loss of Roman legions in Germania
14	Death of Augustus and accession of Tiberius
19	Jews expelled from Rome
23/24	**Birth of Gaius Plinius Secundus (Pliny the Elder) in Comum**
37	Death of Tiberius and accession of Caligula
c.38	Birth of the poet Martial
41	Death of Caligula and accession of Claudius, who grants power over Judaea to Herod Agrippa
43	Claudius invades Britain
47	Pliny the Elder confronts the Chauci
50	Claudius adopts Nero
c.50	Pliny the Elder confronts the Chatti
54	Death of Claudius and accession of Nero
55	Death of Britannicus
c.56	Birth of Cornelius Tacitus
59	Death of Agrippina the Younger
60/61	Rebellion of Boudicca
c.62	**Birth of Gaius Plinius Caecilius Secundus (Pliny the Younger) in Comum**
64	Fire at Rome. Persecution of Christians
65	Pisonian Conspiracy; Suicides of Seneca the Younger and Lucan; Death of Poppaea
66	Thrasea Paetus condemned to death; Suicide of Petronius; Start of the Jewish War
67	Vespasian leaves for Judaea
68	Death of Nero and accession of Galba
69	'Year of the Four Emperors': Galba, Otho, Vitellius, Vespasian
70	The Temple of Jerusalem burns
c.70	Birth of Gaius Suetonius Tranquillus
73–4	Siege of Masada and conclusion of the Jewish War

79	Death of Vespasian and accession of Titus
	Eruption of Vesuvius
	Death of Pliny the Elder
80	Fire in Rome. Pliny the Younger enters the Court of One Hundred
81	Death of Titus and accession of Domitian
83	Domitian celebrates a triumph for war against the Chatti
85	Agricola recalled to Rome from Britain after Battle of Mons Graupius. Domitian's conflict with Dacia
93	Expulsion of philosophers. Stoic trials
96	Death of Domitian and accession of Nerva
c.97	Death of Pliny the Younger's first wife; Pliny the Younger falls ill
98	Death of Nerva and accession of Trajan
	Pliny the Younger, now married to Calpurnia, becomes prefect of the Treasury of Saturn
100	Pliny the Younger becomes consul and delivers his *Panegyricus*
101	Beginning of Trajan's Dacian Wars
c.103	Pliny the Younger becomes augur
c.109–13	Pliny the Younger in Bithynia and condemnation of Christians.
	Death of Pliny the Younger (c.113)
115	Trajan's Parthian campaign
117	Death of Trajan and accession of Hadrian
324	Constantine founds new capital at Byzantium

List of Illustrations

Integrated pictures

p. 41 Relief showing the earthquake from shrine in House of Lucius Caecilius Iucundus, Pompeii. *(DEA/A. DAGLI ORTI/De Agostini/Getty Images)*

p. 88 Roman coin featuring the Colosseum. *(DEA PICTURE LIBRARY/ De Agostini/Getty Images)*

p. 93 Emperor Domitian. *(© José Luiz Bernardes Ribeiro/CC BY-SA 4.0)*

p. 136 Skull, Museo Storico Nazionale dell'Arte Sanitaria, Rome. *(Photo: Flavio Russo/Historisches Nationalmuseum für die Kunst der Medizin/ dpa – Rome/Italy/Agefotostock)*

p. 147 Relief from the Arch of Titus, Rome. *(Three Lions/Hulton Archive/ Getty Images)*

p. 164 Roof tile stamped with Pliny initials. *(J. Uroz Sáez, 'Fundiary property and brick production in the high Tiber valley' in F. Coarelli and H. Patterson (eds), 2008, Fig. 14)*

p. 175 Leonardo da Vinci's drawing of Curio's Revolving Double Theatre. *(akg-images/Album)*

p. 187 Roman mosaic showing cat with bird, ducks and sea life, Pompeii, 2nd century BC, National Archaeological Museum, Naples. *(Prisma Archivo/Alamy Stock Photo)*

p. 203 Ground plan of Pliny's Tuscan villa by Karl Friedrich Schinkel. *(Historic Images/Alamy Stock Photo)*

Picture section

Silvered bronze phalera from a horse-harness, inscribed with Pliny the Elder's name. (© *The Trustees of the British Museum*)

Roman wall painting, Stabiae. (*CM Dixon/Print Collector/Getty Images*)

Wall painting from Pompeii, showing Vesuvius and Bacchus with snake. (*DEA/L. PEDICINI/De Agostini/Getty Images*)

The Euphronios Krater, *c*.515 BC, showing Sarpedon speared in the chest by Patroclus. (*Historic Collection/Alamy Stock Photo*)

Fifteenth-century manuscript showing Pliny the Elder writing in his study and a landscape. (*British Library, London, UK/© British Library Board. All Rights Reserved/Bridgeman Images*)

A cast of a victim of the Vesuvius eruption. (*Art Media/Print Collector/ Getty Images*)

Wall painting of writing materials, 1st century AD, Pompeii/National Archaeological Museum, Naples. (*Werner Forman Archive/Bridgeman Images*)

Page of letter by Pliny from late fifth (or possibly early sixth) century manuscript. (*The Morgan Library and Museum, New York. MS M.462. Purchased by J. Pierpont Morgan (1837–1913) in 1910*)

Wall painting of bird, Pompeii (© *The Trustees of the British Museum*)

Model of Pliny's Laurentine villa by Clifford Fanshawe Pember, 1940s. (*Mixed media, English School (20th century)/Ashmolean Museum, University of Oxford, UK/Bridgeman Images*)

Christian mosaic of Constantine and Justinian from Hagia Sophia Church Museum, Istanbul. (*Chris Hellier/Alamy Stock Photo*)

Trajan's Column. (*National Geographic Image Collection/Alamy Stock Photo*)

Francesco I de'Medici's private study, Palazzo Vecchio, Florence. (*Courtesy of the author*)

Empress Domitia. (*Adam Eastland Art + Architecture/Alamy Stock Photo*)

Pliny's spring, Como. (*Courtesy of the author*)

Sculpture of Pliny the Elder, Como. (*Universal Images Group North America LLC/De Agostini/Alamy Stock Photo*)

Sculpture of Pliny the Younger, Como. (*akg-images/De Agostini Picture Lib./A. Vergani*)

Endnotes

Abbreviations used in the Notes

AE: L'Année Epigraphique

CIL: Corpus Inscriptionum Latinarum (De Gruyter, Berlin and New York)

PLE: Pliny the Elder, *Natural History*

PLY: Pliny the Younger, *Letters*

Note: References to Pliny the Elder's *Natural History* follow the numbering in Mayhoff's Teubner version of the Latin text, which is helpfully available in full on Bill Thayer's website: http://penelope.uchicago.edu/Thayer/E/Roman/home.html. For Pliny the Younger's letters and *Panegyricus* I used Radice's two-volume text of 1969

PROLOGUE: *Darker than Night*

1 PLY 6.16.6; PLE 22.92–5.

2 Horace *Satires* 2.4.33.

3 Virgil *Aeneid* 6.163; 6.171–2.

4 Suetonius *Life of Augustus* 49. On Pliny the Elder's post, see: J. F. Healy, *Pliny the Elder on Science and Technology*, Oxford University Press, Oxford, 1999, pp. 22–3.

5 PLE 2.236–8.

6 PLE 3.62; 14.22; 14.34.

7 PLE 3.41.

8 Plutarch (*Crassus* 9) describes Spartacus and his allies making ladders from vines; Appian (*Civil Wars* 1.116) explicitly names the mountain as Vesuvius.

9 Strabo *Geography* 5.4.8. On fires blazing on Vesuvius 'in ancient times', see Vitruvius *De Architectura* 2.6.2. See also Diodorus Siculus *Library of History*, 4.21.5, who writes of Vesuvius bearing signs of the fires it put forth 'in ancient times' like Etna in Sicily.

10 V. Arnó, C. Principe, M. Rosi, R. Santacroce, A. Sbrana, and M. F. Sheridan, 'Eruptive History', in *Somma-Vesuvius*, 114, Vol. 8, edited by R. Santacroce, Consiglio nazionale delle ricerche, Rome, 1987; H. Sigurdsson, 'Mount Vesuvius Before the Disaster', p. 30 in W. F. Jashemski and F. G. Meyer (eds), *The Natural History of Pompeii*, Cambridge University Press, Cambridge, 2002. A particularly large eruption of Vesuvius is thought to have occurred in around 1600 BC. As Sigurdsson notes: 'a period of quiescence of 1,400 to 4,000 years' has tended to precede each Plinian eruption historically. The longer Vesuvius is dormant, the more catastrophic its next eruption may be (see J-M. Bardintzeff and A. McBirney, *Volcanology*, Jones and Bartlett, Sudbury, Massachusetts, 2000, p. xv).

11 See H. Sigurdsson and S. Carey, 'The Eruption of Vesuvius in AD 79', in Jashemski and Meyer (eds), *Natural History of Pompeii*, p. 44, for the evidence of the initial explosion.

12 P. Roberts, *Life and Death in Pompeii and Herculaneum*, British Museum, London, 2013, p. 284.

13 Sigurdsson and Carey, 'Eruption of Vesuvius', in Jashemski and Meyer (eds), *Natural History of Pompeii*, pp. 48, 58.

14 PLY 6.16.9.

15 PLY 6.16.10.

16 The so-called 'Plinian' phase, see H. Sigurdsson, S. Cashdollar, and S. R. J. Sparks, 'The Eruption of Vesuvius in AD 79: Reconstruction from Historical and Volcanological Evidence', *American Journal of Archaeology*, Vol. 86, No. 1, January 1982, pp. 39, 48.

17 Sigurdsson et al., 'The Eruption of Vesuvius in AD 79', p. 47.

18 Pliny the Elder said that to put a statue of a man on a high column was to elevate him above other mortals (PLE 34.27).

19 PLY 6.16.12.

20 PLY 6.16.13.

21 PLY 6.16.13; 6.16.19; 3.5.7.

22 As has been discovered through excavations at Villa Ariadne and Villa di Varano in Stabiae: see Sigurdsson et al., 'The Eruption of Vesuvius in AD 79', p. 40; Sigurdsson and Carey, 'Eruption of Vesuvius', in Jashemski and Meyer (eds), *Natural History of Pompeii*, p. 61.

23 PLY 6.20.3.

24 Tacitus *Annals* 15.22.

25 Seneca *Natural Questions* 6.10.

26 Seneca *Natural Questions* 6.27–9.

27 The date of 5 February, AD 63, is provided by Seneca the Younger (*Natural Questions* 6.1) shortly after the earthquake. Tacitus (*Annals* 15.22), writing decades later, appears to favour a date in late AD 62. For a short overview of the difficulties of the date see N. Monteix, 'Urban Production and the Pompeian Economy', in A. Wilson and M. Flohr (eds), *The Economy of Pompeii*, Oxford University Press, Oxford, 2017, p. 210. On the destruction and rebuilding of Pompeii see W. F. Jashemski, 'The Vesuvian Sites Before AD 79: The Archaeological, Literary, and Epigraphical Evidence', in Jashemski and Meyer (eds), *Natural History of Pompeii*, pp. 8–10. For earthquakes not in winter: see Seneca *Natural Questions* 6.1.

28 In the sixth century BC, Thales of Miletus believed that the earth was balanced on water. In its ebb and flow, he suggested, the water caused the earth to quake; see Seneca *Natural Questions* 6.6.

29 PLE 2.192. A fuller explanation of the theory I draw on is provided by Seneca the Younger in *Natural Questions* 6.

30 Seneca *Natural Questions* 6.12–13, adducing the arguments of Greek scholars including Aristotle, Archelaus and Theophrastus.

31 PLY 6.16.16. On the formation of pumice see E. De Carolis and G. Patricelli, *Vesuvius, AD 79: The Destruction of Pompeii and Herculaneum*, J. Paul Getty Museum, LA, 2003, p.12.

32 PLY 6.20.3–4.

33 PLY 6.16.17.

34 Sigurdsson and Carey, 'Eruption of Vesuvius', in Jashemski and Meyer (eds), *Natural History of Pompeii*, p. 61.

35 On the collapse of the column and release of pyroclastic flows, see R. S. J. Sparks and L. Wilson, 'A model for the formation of ignimbrite by gravitational column collapse', *Journal of the Geological Society*, Vol. 132, July 1976, pp. 441–51.

36 J. Berry, *The Complete Pompeii*, Thames and Hudson, London, 2013, p. 27.

37 Asphyxiation by ash, as Sigurdsson and Carey observe ('Eruption of Vesuvius' in Jashemski and Meyer (eds), *Natural History of Pompeii*, p. 49), was the cause of death of many victims of the 1980 eruption of Mount St Helens in Washington State, and was likely also to have killed Pliny the Elder. Other theories for his cause of death have included a heart attack or heart disorder, or apoplexy. J. Bigelow, 'On the Death of Pliny the Elder', *Memoirs of the American Academy of Arts and Sciences*, Vol. 6, No. 2, 1859, pp. 223–7; R. M. Haywood, 'The Strange Death of the Elder Pliny', *Classical Weekly*, Vol. 46, No. 1, November 1952, pp. 1–3; and H. C. Lipscomb and R. M. Haywood, 'The Strange Death of the Elder Pliny', *Classical Weekly*, Vol. 47, No. 5, January 1954, p. 74, make for lively reading.

38 PLY 6.20.7.

39 PLY 6.20.9.

40 As suggested by Sigurdsson and Carey in 'Eruption of Vesuvius', Jashemski and Meyer (eds), *Natural History of Pompeii*, pp. 50, 62.

41 PLY 6.20.12.

42 PLY 6.20.14–15.

43 Ps-Seneca *Hercules Oetaeus* 1111, 1114–1117; A. N. Sherwin-White, *The Letters of Pliny: A Historical and Social Commentary*, Clarendon

Press, Oxford, 1966, p. 380; and F. G. Downing, 'Cosmic Eschatology in the First Century: "Pagan", Jewish and Christian', *L'Antiquité Classique*, Vol. 64, 1995, p. 106, the latter of whom detects the influence of Epicureanism in Pliny's interpretation of the scene.

44 PLE 7.73.

45 Virgil *Aeneid* 6.426–9.

46 Dio Cassius *Roman History* 66.23.4.

47 Dio Cassius *Roman History* 66.23.7–9.

48 PLY 6.20.16.

49 PLY 6.20.18.

ONE: *Roots and Trees*

1 PLY 3.5.10.

2 On who was reading Pliny's letters in later antiquity see A. Cameron, 'The Fate of Pliny's Letters in the Late Empire', *Classical Quarterly*, Vol. 15, No. 2, November 1965, pp. 289–98. As Cameron notes, some of the blame for the conflation of the two Plinys lay with Jerome, who in the late fourth century produced a translation and continuation of Bishop Eusebius of Caesarea's Greek *Chronicon*, a history of time from the birth of Abraham to the present day, which featured 'Plinius Secundus' as an 'orator and distinguished historian from Novum Comum [Como in northern Italy] whose many inspired works still survive: he perished while visiting Vesuvius' (Jerome *Chronicle* S.a.109).

3 Giovanni de Matociis, *Brevis adnotatio de duobus Pliniis* (early fourteenth century) – text reproduced in E. T. Merrill, 'On the Eight-Book Tradition of Pliny's Letters in Verona', *Classical Philology*, Vol. 5, No. 2, April 1910, pp. 186–8. S. B. McHam, 'Renaissance Monuments to Favourite Sons', *Renaissance Studies*, Vol. 19, No. 4, September 2005, p. 468 and n.62 discusses de Matociis on the Plinys.

4 E. A. Lowe and E. K. Rand (eds), *A Sixth-Century Fragment of the Letters of Pliny the Younger*, Carnegie Institution of Washington,

Washington, 1922, inspected the ancient folios, now in New York's Pierpoint Morgan Library, and established the arguments for viewing them as part of the Paris manuscript used in Venice by Aldus Manutius. See especially Rand, p. 41, and on the dating, Lowe, pp. 13–15. The leaves are now thought to date to the late fifth century. They contain letters from Pliny's second and third books. The manuscript Aldus Manutius used came from the Abbey of Saint Victor in Paris. Pieces of five ancient manuscripts of Pliny the Elder's *Natural History* still survive (see L. D. Reynolds and N. G. Wilson (eds), *Texts and Transmission: A Survey of the Latin Classics*, Oxford University Press, Oxford and New York, 2005, p. 309), the fullest of which also dates to the fifth century. The inclusion of excerpts of the work in medical books and other compendia helped to keep Pliny the Elder's name alive.

5 This manuscript of Pliny's letters, arranged over eight books, had been found by Guarino Guarini in either Venice or Verona in 1419. The first printed edition of Pliny's letters was produced by Ludovicus Carbone in Venice in 1471. On the eight-, nine- and ten-book traditions of Pliny's letters see D. Johnson, 'The Manuscripts of Pliny's Letters', *Classical Philology*, Vol. 7, No. 1, January 1912, pp. 66–75. And on the history of the manuscript tradition see Reynolds and Wilson (eds), *Texts and Transmission*, pp. 316–22.

6 Attr. Suetonius *Life of Pliny the Elder* 1. See M. Reeve, 'The *Vita Plinii*', pp. 207–8, in R. K. Gibson and R. Morello (eds), *Pliny the Elder: Themes and Contexts*, Brill, Leiden, 2011.

7 B. Giovio, *Historiae Patriae*, 1629, Como New Press, 1982, Vol. 2, pp. 237–40. Flavio Biondo was an architectural historian, Lorenzo Valla a talented Latinist and Niccolò Perotti a rhetorician. Petrarch owned a near-complete copy of the *Natural History* from the thirteenth century.

8 The sculptures are thought to have been erected upon the Loggia del Consiglio in Verona in 1493. See McHam's 'Renaissance Monuments to Favourite Sons', pp. 482–3, and *Pliny and the*

Artistic Culture of the Italian Renaissance, Yale University Press, New Haven; London, 2013, pp. 157–8, on the rivalry.

9 Giovio, *Historiae Patriae*, Vol. 2, 237–40.

10 PLE 16.5.

11 H. G. Coffin, R. H. Brown, R. J. Gibson, *Origin by Design*, Review and Herald Publishing Association, Hagerstown, Maryland, 2005, p. 243, citing also W. J. Fritz, 'Reinterpretation of the Depositional Environment of the Yellowstone "Fossil Forests"', *Geology*, Vol. 8, 1980, pp. 309–13.

12 Coffin et al., *Origin by Design*, pp. 242–6.

13 See H. H. Scullard, *From the Gracchi to Nero*, Routledge, London and New York, 2006, pp. 254–9 for a concise account of Augustus' plans.

14 PLY 3.5.4.

15 Tacitus *Annals* 1.69; Suetonius (*Life of Caligula* 8) cites Pliny the Elder's *German Wars* on Caligula and his birthplace.

16 See Tacitus *Annals* 1.55 on the death of Varus.

17 Tacitus *Germania* 4.

18 Tacitus *Germania* 16.

19 Tacitus *Germania* 35.

20 Tacitus *Annals* 11.18. It is generally agreed that Pliny the Elder joined Corbulo's campaign. I have consulted here the entry on Pliny the Elder in *Brill's New Pauly* (H. Cancik and H. Schneider (eds), 'Pliny the Elder', *Brill's New Pauly*, Phi-Prok, Brill, Leiden, 2007) and R. Syme ('Pliny the Procurator', *Harvard Studies in Classical Philology*, Vol. 73, 1969, pp. 205–7), who summarises Münzer, *Bonner Jahrbücher*, 104, 1899, who established the details of Pliny the Elder's three Germanic campaigns, which I follow in this book.

21 PLE 16.3.

22 Tacitus *Annals* 11.18. The leader of the Chauci, Gannascus, had formerly served with the Roman auxiliary.

23 Tacitus *Annals* 11.19.

24 Catullus *Carmina* 29.12.

25 Cancik and Schneider (eds), 'Pliny the Elder'.

26 PLE 31.20, cited by Syme, 'Pliny the Procurator', p. 206.

27 Quintilian *Institutio Oratoria* 10.1.98.

28 PLE 13.83; 7.80.

29 Tacitus *Annals* 12.28.

30 PLE 13.83.

31 Tacitus *Annals* 12.56.

32 PLE 33.63, cited by Syme, 'Pliny the Procurator', p. 206. The golden cloak is also described by Tacitus in *Annals* 12.56.

33 Suetonius *Life of Claudius* 43–4; Tacitus *Annals* 12.65–67; PLE 2.92.

34 PLE 22.92–5.

35 Suetonius *Life of Nero* 9–11.

36 Suetonius *Life of Nero* 33–5.

37 Suetonius *Life of Nero* 38.

38 Tacitus *Annals* 15.44.

39 Pliny the Younger *Panegyricus* 42.1.

40 Tacitus *Agricola* 2.

41 Tacitus *Annals* 15.49–74.

42 Tacitus *Annals* 16.18.

43 PLY 3.5.5.

44 Tacitus *Agricola* 44.

45 P. Roche, 'Pliny's Thanksgiving: An Introduction to the *Panegyricus*', p. 4, in P. Roche (ed.), *Pliny's Praise: The Panegyricus in the Roman World*, Cambridge University Press, Cambridge and New York, 2011.

46 The two letters, 10.96 and 10.97, predate Tacitus' descriptions of Nero's persecution of the Christians – see Sherwin-White, *Letters of Pliny*, p. 693.

47 PLY 10.96.8.

48 PLY 3.5.17.

49 The Roman writers were Marcus Terentius Varro and Celsus. Cato the Elder, Aristotle and Theophrastus were also important influences upon Pliny the Elder.

50 PLE 11.6.

51 PLE 2.207.

52 PLE 25.9.

53 PLE 29.85. The *Natural History* inspired numerous other reference books besides, including Vincent of Beauvais' *Speculum Maius* in the thirteenth century and Conrad Gesner's *Bibliotheca Universalis* in 1545.

54 R. P. Duncan-Jones, 'The Finances of a Senator', in R. K. Gibson and C. Whitton (eds), *The Epistles of Pliny*, Oxford University Press, Oxford, 2016, p. 91, suggests that Pliny possessed more than twice the 8 million sesterces normally deemed a reasonable capital for a senator.

55 Plutarch *Lucullus* 39.4. Like Pliny, Lucullus owned an estate near Tusculum and used it as a summer residence.

56 The first nine volumes of Pliny's letters are thought to have been released in his lifetime, but the tenth book, which contains the letters he sent Trajan and Trajan's replies, was probably published posthumously.

57 Although the ten books of Pliny's letters progress roughly chronologically, the letters within them are often out of sequence. Later letters often intersperse the sequences of earlier ones. J. Bodel, 'The Publication of Pliny's Letters', provides in pp. 13–35 of I. Marchesi (ed.), *Pliny the Book-Maker: Betting on Posterity in the Epistles*, Oxford University Press, Oxford, 2015, a useful examination of the arrangement of the letters and a summary of the attempts of Mommsen, Syme and Sherwin-White to order and date them.

TWO: *Illusions of Immortality*

1 PLY 2.1.6.

2 PLY 7.20.4.

3 PLY 2.1.8.

4 Pliny always admired a well-earned, well-structured retirement – see Letters 6.10 and 3.1.

5 PLY 6.10.3.

6 PLY 7.33.1. Tacitus probably used Pliny's account of the eruption to write a section of his *Histories* that is now lost.

7 PLY 6.16.1.

8 PLY 6.20.20.

9 PLY 6.16.22.

10 Sigurdsson et al., 'The Eruption of Vesuvius in AD 79', p. 44.

11 U. Eco, *The Limits of Interpretation*, Indianapolis Press, Bloomington, Indianapolis, 1994, p. 136.

12 Francis Bacon, Letter to the Earl of Arundel and Surrey, *The Letters and The Life of Francis Bacon*, edited by J. Spedding, Longmans, Green, Reader, and Dyer, London, 1874, 7.550. A. Doody quotes from and discusses Bacon's letter in her book on the reception of Pliny the Elder's *Natural History – Pliny's Encyclopedia: The Reception of the Natural History*, Cambridge University Press, Cambridge and New York, 2010, pp. 32–3. Doody observes that Bacon was reflecting on Pliny's description of his uncle in his second letter on the eruption. This letter of Bacon is also discussed in relation to Pliny the Elder by L. Jardine and A. Stewart, *Hostage to Fortune: The Troubled Life of Francis Bacon*, Victor Gollancz, London, 1998, pp. 502–8 (work cited in Doody, *Pliny's Encyclopedia*, p. 33) and by G. Darley, *Vesuvius: The Most Famous Volcano in the World*, Profile, London, 2011, pp. 38–9.

13 John Aubrey, *Life of Francis Bacon*, *'Brief Lives', chiefly of Contemporaries: set down by John Aubrey, between the years 1669 & 1696, edited from the Author's MSS*, by Andrew Clark, Vol. 1, Clarendon Press, Oxford, 1898, pp. 75–6.

14 Francis Bacon, Letter to the Earl of Arundel and Surrey, in J. Spedding (ed.), *The Letters and The Life of Francis Bacon*, 7.550.

15 Aubrey, *Life of Francis* Bacon, in Clark (ed.), Vol. 1, pp. 75–6. Aubrey was here recording the account of Bacon's former secretary Thomas Hobbes.

16 Doody, *Pliny's Encyclopedia*. Writing on the causes of Bacon's death, L. Jardine and A. Stewart (*Hostage to Fortune*, pp. 504–8) have suggested that Bacon had been taking opiates in an attempt to extend his life when he fell ill. The fact that Bacon's fingers were too 'disjointed' [numb] to hold a pen is, they argue, evidence that he died from 'an overdose of inhaled nitre or opiates'.

17 Francis Bacon, Letter to the Earl of Arundel and Surrey, 7.550.

18 On some of the eyewitness accounts of the eruption of 1631 see J. E. Everson, 'The melting pot of science and belief: studying Vesuvius in seventeenth-century Naples', *Renaissance Studies*, Vol. 26, No. 5, November 2012, pp. 691–727.

19 Sir William Hamilton, Letter to the Right Honourable the Earl of Morton, President of the Royal Society, 29 December 1767, *Observations on Mount Vesuvius, Mount Etna, and Other Volcanos: In a Series of Letters to the Royal Society*, T. Cadell, London, 1773, Letter II, p. 25.

20 Sir William Hamilton, Letter to the Right Honourable the Earl of Morton, 29 December 1767, *Observations on Mount Vesuvius*, 1773, Letter II, p. 27. There was a handsome display of pictures from Hamilton's *Campi Phlegraei* at the 'Volcanoes' exhibition at the Bodleian in Oxford in spring 2017.

21 See D. Camardo, 'Herculaneum from the AD 79 eruption to the medieval period: analysis of the documentary, iconographic and archaeological sources, with new data on the beginning of exploration at the ancient town', *Papers of the British School at Rome*, Vol. 81, 2013, pp. 328–37.

22 Sir William Hamilton, Letter to Mathew Maty, M. D. Secretary to the Royal Society, 4 October 1768, *Observations on Mount Vesuvius*, Letter III, pp. 48–9.

23 E. Dwyer, *Pompeii's Living Statues*, University of Michigan Press, Ann Arbor, 2010, p. 26; S. L. Dyson, *In Pursuit of Ancient Pasts*, Yale University Press, New Haven and London, 2006, p. 49.

24 For the range of dates given by the manuscripts see M. Borgongino

and G. Stefani, 'Intorno alla data dell'eruzione del 79 d.C.', *Rivista di Studi Pompeiani*, Vol. 12/13, 2001–2, p. 178.

25 Berry, *Complete Pompeii*, p. 20.

26 Description based on the findings outlined by Borgongino and Stefani, 'Intorno alla data dell'eruzione del 79 d.C.', pp. 177–215.

27 Though, as Roberts notes, it is strange that this warmer clothing was also found on bodies indoors (Roberts, *Life and Death in Pompeii*, p. 278).

28 R. Abdy, 'The Last Coin in Pompeii: A Re-evaluation of the Coin Hoard from the House of the Golden Bracelet', *Numismatic Chronicle*, Vol. 173, 2013, pp. 79–83. Cf. G. Stefani and M. Borgongino, 'Ancora sulla data dell'eruzione', *Rivista di Studi Pompeiani*, Vol. 18, 2007, pp. 204–6.

29 G. A. Rolandi, A. Paone, M. di Lascio, G. Stefani, 'The 79 AD eruption of Somma: The relationship between the date of the eruption and the southeast tephra dispersion', *Journal of Volcanology and Geothermal Research*, Vol. 169, 2007, pp. 87–98. In 2018, a charcoal graffito was discovered at Pompeii bearing the date of 17 October. Given that charcoal does not survive for long, the inscription has been taken as evidence that the eruption took place later that month. Like so much of the evidence, however, it fails to offer proof of when exactly in AD 79 Vesuvius erupted.

30 See Dio Cassius *Roman History* 66.21, where it is said that the eruption took place in the waning of the year, or 'late autumn'.

31 PLY 5.8.8; 1.18.3.

32 Tacitus *Dialogus* 38.

33 On decrees and edicts and the development of Roman law see A. M. Riggsby, *Roman Law and the Legal World of the Romans*, Cambridge University Press, New York, 2010, especially pp. 25–39.

34 PLY 6.12.2.

35 See Tacitus *Dialogus* 20.

36 PLY 9.26.4.

37 As the years went by the court grew steadily noisier and less salubrious,

or at least, Pliny became increasingly aware of its shortcomings. See PLY 2.14.

38 PLY 6.33.8.

39 PLY 1.2.2–4.

40 PLY 1.20.22–3.

41 PLY 1.20.3.

42 Homer *Iliad* 3.221–2; PLY 1.20–2.

43 Homer *Odyssey* 19.204–9.

44 PLY 1.20.16.

45 Quintilian *Institutio Oratoria* 11.3.

46 PLY 1.20.17.

47 PLY 1.20.14–15.

48 Tacitus *Histories* 4.42; Pliny (PLY 2.20.13) says that Regulus rose from poverty to great wealth.

49 Juvenal *Satires* 4.140–3 (assuming it is the same Montanus); Tacitus *Histories* 4.42. The unfortunate victim was Piso, who was nominated as successor to Galba, one of the 'four emperors' of AD 69. According to Pliny, the legacy-hunting Regulus also conned Piso's widow Verania, the daughter of a former governor of Britain.

50 PLY 1.5.14.

51 PLY 2.20.7–8.

52 PLY 4.7.4.

53 PLY 1.5.13 *expalluit notabiliter*, 'grew paler than usual'.

54 PLY 2.19.

55 PLY 6.2.2.

56 PLY 2.20.14.

57 PLY 4.2.5.

58 Martial *Epigrams* 1.12.1–2; 1.82.1; PLY 6.2.4.

THREE: *To Be Alive is to Be Awake*

1 PLE 17.210.

2 PLY 3.5.

3 Suetonius *Life of Vespasian* 4.

4 On the Jewish revolt against Rome see M. Goodman, *The Ruling Class of Judaea*, Cambridge University Press, Cambridge, 1987. The most remarkable document from this period is Claudius' letter of AD 41 to the Alexandrians in which he promoted peace and reaffirmed Jewish rights.

5 As B. Levick explains in *Vespasian*, Routledge, London and New York, 2016, pp. xiii–xiv, the capture of Jerusalem must have been 'a prime objective' of Vespasian's campaign, but he needed first to pacify the surrounding territories.

6 Josephus *Jewish War* 3.342–408. The book was translated into Greek and published at Rome.

7 S. Schama observes in *The Story of the Jews: Finding the Words (1000 BCE–1492 CE)*, Bodley Head, London, 2013, p. 299, that the collective suicide of the Jews at Masada and martyrdoms under Hadrian later inspired debates over whether suicide might ever be chosen over forced transgression. On the Jews' arguments that suicide would be in keeping with established *nomoi*, see R. Gray, *Prophetic Figures in Late Second Temple Jewish Palestine*, Oxford University Press, New York and Oxford, 1993, pp. 48–50.

8 Tacitus *Histories* 1.11.

9 Suetonius *Life of Titus* 1. As B. W. Jones observes in *The Emperor Domitian*, Routledge, London and New York, 1992, p. 8, this honour was ordinarily reserved for sons of foreign princes but could also be conferred upon eminent Italians.

10 Suetonius *Life of Titus* 7.

11 Suetonius *Life of Titus* 3.

12 On the trappings and their connection to Pliny the Elder see I. Jenkins, P. Craddock, and J. Lambert, 'A Group of Silvered-Bronze Horse-Trappings from Xanten ("Castra Vetera")', *Britannia*, Vol. 16, 1985, pp. 141–64.

13 Jenkins, Craddock, and Lambert, 'A Group of Silvered-Bronze Horse-Trappings from Xanten ("Castra Vetera")', p. 157.

14 PLE 5.73.

15 PLE 12.111.

16 Suetonius *Life of Vespasian* 21.

17 Suetonius *Life of Vespasian* 16.

18 From the lost biography of Pliny the Elder, attributed to Suetonius.

19 Suetonius *Life of Vespasian* 23.

20 PLE Preface 18.

21 PLY 3.5.8.

22 PLE 7.167.

23 PLE Preface 18.

24 Red Figure Calyx Krater by Euphronios, *c*.515 BC.

25 PLE Preface 3.

26 Dio Cassius *Roman History* 66.24; Suetonius *Life of Titus* 8.

27 PLY 5.8.3 citing Virgil *Georgics* 3.9–10.

28 Martial, quoted by Pliny in Letter 3.21.

29 PLY 3.21.2.

30 PLY 3.5.15.

31 PLY 1.15. 'Dancing girls' from Cadiz were notorious (see Martial *Epigrams* 5.78); the satirist Juvenal knew just how much they aroused their audiences with their moves (see Juvenal *Satires* 11.162–6).

32 On Pliny's balanced diet and balanced life see E. Gowers, *The Loaded Table: Representations of Food in Roman Literature*, Clarendon Press, Oxford, 1993, pp. 267–78.

33 PLE 20.64. Lettuces could be sown at any time of year, but Pliny the Elder recommended doing so upon the winter solstice (PLE 19.130–1).

34 PLY 7.3.2–5.

35 PLE 19.55.

36 M. de Montaigne, 'Of Ancient Customs', translated by Charles Cotton, p. 58 in *Michel de Montaigne Selected Essays*, edited by W. C. Hazlitt, Dover Publications Ltd, New York, 2011. Montaigne's reference to snow and wine is cited by H. N. Wethered, *A Short History of Gardens*, Methuen & Co., London, 1933, p. 85.

37 S. Bakewell, *How to Live: A Life of Montaigne in One Question and Twenty Attempts at an Answer*, Vintage Books, London, 2011, p. 29. Montaigne sourced his quotation from PLE 2.25.

38 PLE 32.64.

39 See A. Wallace-Hadrill, 'Pliny the Elder and Man's Unnatural History', *Greece & Rome*, Vol. 37, No. 1, April 1990, p. 87.

40 PLE 9.105.

41 PLE 32.63.

42 PLE 9.107; 11.129.

43 PLE 32.60.

44 PLE 9.107–9.

45 PLE 2.189.

46 PLE 32.60.

47 PLE 9.168–9.

48 PLE 32.59.

49 PLE 32.64–5.

50 PLE 9.104.

51 PLY 2.9.4. S. E. Hoffer suggests in *The Anxieties of Pliny the Younger* (Scholars Press, Atlanta, 1999, p. 26), that Septicius Clarus shared Pliny's distaste for these extravagant suppers, but was obliged to dine elsewhere to court a patron, perhaps to develop support for his nephew.

52 Scriptores Historiae Augustae *Hadrian* 11.3. This source dates to the fourth century AD.

53 AE 1953.73.

54 PLY 1.24; 3.8. On some of Pliny's lacklustre friends see R. Syme, 'Pliny's Less Successful Friends', *Roman Papers*, Vol. 2, edited by E. Badian, Clarendon Press, Oxford, 1991, pp. 477–95.

55 Suetonius was probably sitting on the drafts of his *De viris illustribus*, which in the fourth century AD would inspire Jerome's work of the same title. For the arguments for the work in question being the *De viris illustribus* see, for example, T. J. Power, 'Pliny, Letters 5.10 and the Literary Career of Suetonius', *Journal of Roman*

Studies, Vol. 100, 2010, p. 141ff. Suetonius also wrote a work on Nature, the so-called *Prata*, which is now fragmentary.

56 PLY 5.10.2.

57 PLY 5.9.2.

58 Artemidorus of Ephesus *On the Interpretation of Dreams* 1.79.

59 PLY 1.18.4. The words were originally spoken by Hector in Homer *Iliad* 12.243.

60 Homer *Odyssey* 19.560–7.

61 Virgil *Aeneid* 6.896.

62 PLY 1.18.1; Homer *Iliad* 1.63.

63 Homer *Iliad* 2.1–40.

FOUR: *Solitary as an Oyster*

1 Catullus *Carmina* 14.15.

2 Martial *Epigrams* 14.1.

3 Statius *Silvae* 1.6. Pliny the Elder criticised his contemporaries who travelled to Georgia and Numidia in search of fowl and suffered the heat of Ethiopia when there were perfectly good views from the windows at home – PLE 19.52.

4 PLY 2.17.22.

5 Charles Dickens, *A Christmas Carol*, Stave I.

6 PLY 2.17.2.

7 The layers as found in the test trench are described by A. Claridge, 'Report on excavations at the imperial vicus 1995–1998', Laurentine Shore Project, Royal Holloway, University of London, 2010 (https://www.royalholloway.ac.uk/laurentineshore), p. 9.

8 R. A. Lanciani, *Wanderings in the Roman Campagna*, Constable & Co., London, 1909, pp. 307–11, citing Varro *De re rustica* 3.13.2–3 and an inscription (CIL VI 8583) that lists Tiberius' freedman Tiberius Claudius Speculator as *procurator Laurento ad elephantos*; *collegio saltuariorum* – AE 1920 no. 122. Lanciani's book is cited by and available in extract via the Royal Holloway

Laurentine Shore Project. It was a role of aediles to stage such spectacles.

9 PLE 8.1.

10 PLE 8.44.

11 PLE 8.5–7.

12 Lanciani, *Wanderings in the Roman Campagna*, pp. 306, 311. The estates of Castelfusano, Castelporziano, and Capocotta were based here.

13 My description is based on both PLY 2.17 and the findings of the Laurentine Shore Project at Royal Holloway, University of London, on the archaeology of the *Vicus*, as outlined in their online resource and illustrations at https://www.royalholloway.ac.uk/laurentineshore

14 PLY 4.6.2.

15 PLY 1.9.6.

16 Virgil *Aeneid* 7.59–63. On the ancient origins of Laurentum and the *Aeneid* see N. Purcell, 'Discovering a Roman Resort-Coast: The Litus Laurentinum and the Archaeology of Otium' via https://intranet.royalholloway.ac.uk/classics/research/laurentine-shore-project/documents/pdf/litus-laurentinum-english-version.pdf, 1998, especially p. 10.

17 T. C. A. de Haas, *Fields, Farms and Colonists*, Vol. 1, Barkhuis and Groningen University Library, Groningen, 2011, p. 206.

18 PLY 2.17.7.

19 At the top of one tower was a dining room with a wide view over the water. There have been many attempts to find Pliny's house at Laurentum; some have 'found' it at Grotte di Piastra (S. P. Ricotti, 'La Villa Laurentina di Plinio il Giovane: un ennesima ricostruzione', *Lunario Romano*, 1983, pp. 229–51); others in the area of the so-called Villa di Plinio, 'La Palombara' – see Lanciani, *Wanderings in the Roman Campagna*, on Sachetti (1713); others at Tor Paterno in Castelporziano. Cardinal Barberini drew the ruins he found at Tor Paterno – see I. Campbell, *Ancient Roman Topography and Architecture*, Vol. 2 of *The Paper Museum of*

Cassiano Del Pozzo (20 Parts in 3 Series, Royal Collection Trust, 1996–), the Royal Collection and Warburg Institute in association with Harvey Miller Publishers, London, 2004, p. 669.

20 Varro said that the solstice, *solstitium,* was so-named because it was the time the sun, *sol,* came to a halt, *sistere* (*de Lingua* 6.8).

21 PLY 8.7.1.

22 PLY 7.20.3.

23 Hoffer, *Anxieties of Pliny the Younger,* p. 29 n.1. Pliny was legally permitted to free a fifth of his slaves up to total of one hundred. See also Duncan-Jones, 'The Finances of a Senator', p. 97 n.56 with earlier bibliography on this point.

24 PLY 1.21.2; 8.16.

25 PLY 2.17.24.

26 PLY 7.21.1–2.

27 PLY 7.21; P. R. du Prey, *The Villas of Pliny: From Antiquity to Posterity,* University of Chicago Press, Chicago and London, 1994, p. 283.

28 Lanciani, *Wanderings in the Roman Campagna,* p. 318 notes the discovery of clay weights.

29 PLE 30.19.

30 PLE 11.145, and Cicero *Ars Oratoria* 138; PLE 11.139.

31 For a discussion of the phrase in Latin poetry see J. Glenn, 'The Blinded Cyclops: Lumen Ademptum (Aen. 3.658)', *Classical Philology,* Vol. 69, No. 1, January 1974, pp. 37–8.

32 On the lamps discovered at the site, many of which date to the first century AD, see G. G. Fernández, 'Le Lucerne', pp. 149–53, in P. Braconi, and J. Uroz Sáez (eds), *La Villa Di Plinio il Giovane a San Giustino,* Quattroemme, Perugia, 1999.

33 The seven stars of the Pleiades were imagined to be the daughters of Atlas. Their names were Halcyone, Merope, Celaeno, Electra, Sterope, Taygete, and Maia. But as the writer Aratus said, while 'certainly no star has perished from the sky unobserved', only six were usually visible to the human eye (Aratus *Phaenomena* 259).

34 PLE 2.41.

35 PLE 7.190.

36 PLE 7.188.

37 PLE 7.131.

38 PLE 2.14.

39 Lucretius *De Rerum Natura* 4, especially 4.30–43; 55–64; 724–67.
Pliny quotes from the poem in letter 4.18.

40 PLE 2.28; 2.98.

41 PLE 2.108–9; Cicero *On Divination* 2.14. Garlands of pennyroyal
could be hung in bedrooms to relieve headaches, according to
Varro, PLE 20.152.

42 PLY 7.27.1. Pliny the Elder had also heard stories of ghosts, PLE
7.179.

43 PLY 7.27.5.

44 D. Felton also compares Pliny's ghost story to Dickens's description
of Marley's ghost. See *Haunted Greece and Rome: Ghost Stories from
Classical Antiquity*, University of Texas Press, Austin, 1998, pp. 91–2.

45 A. Lang, *The Works of Charles Dickens in Thirty-four Volumes
(Gadshill Edition), with Introductions, General Essay, And Notes*
Vol. XVIII: *Christmas Books*, Charles Scribner's Sons, New York,
1898, pp. vi–vii. Lang's words are cited by Felton, *Haunted Greece
and Rome*, p. 91.

46 W. C. Dendy, *The Philosophy of Mystery*, Longman, Orme, Brown,
Green, & Longmans, London, 1841, listed in J. H. Stonehouse
(ed.), *Catalogue of the Library of Charles Dickens from Gadshill*,
Piccadilly Fountain Press, London, 1935, p. 27.

FIVE: *The Gift of Poison*

1 PLY 2.11.

2 Justinian *Digest* 48.11 on the Julian law on Extortion (Macer *Public
Prosecution* Book I).

3 PLY 4.16.2.

4 *Brevitas* could mean as few as two water clocks – see Sherwin-

White, *Letters of Pliny*, p. 132 and PLY 6.2.4–5. Tacitus *Dialogus* 38 (cited in *Letters of Pliny*, p. 134) refers to a limit placed on the length of speeches. Even fellow lawyers were now complaining about long speeches: 'Who has the patience for those hefty volumes?' – Tacitus *Dialogus* 20.

5 Juvenal *Satires* 1.49–50.

6 PLY 2.12.

7 PLY 2.11.23.

8 PLE 13.9.

9 PLE 33.148 with Livy *Ab urbe condita* 37.59.

10 PLE 14.2.

11 Pliny the Elder was discussing Eastern medicines and their popularity over the natural kitchen garden remedies he preferred (PLE 24.5).

12 Tacitus *Annals* 1.11.

13 See especially A. Goldsworthy, *Pax Romana*, Weidenfeld & Nicolson, London, 2016, pp. 174–84.

14 Suetonius *Life of Domitian* 2.

15 Dio Cassius *Roman History* 66.26.2–3; Philostratus *Life of Apollonius of Tyana* 6.32.2. There was also a Jewish legend that Titus died after a gnat entered his brain. Contrary to Dio's account, Suetonius (*Life of Domitian* 2.3) says that it was when Vespasian died that Domitian hesitated over whether or not to bestow a double bounty upon the army.

16 PLE 29.10.

17 PLE 32.58–9.

18 Suetonius *Life of Titus* 11.

19 Suetonius *Life of Domitian* 3; Pliny *Panegyricus* 48.3–5. Hutchinson compares the Ciceronian language of the beast with the image of blood-licking from Polybius 7.13.6 on the tyrant Philip V – G. O. Hutchinson, 'Politics and the Sublime in the *Panegyricus*', p. 129 in P. Roche (ed.), *Pliny's Praise: The Panegyricus in the Roman World*, Cambridge University Press, Cambridge and New York, 2011.

20 Pliny *Panegyricus* 48.3–5; 90.5.

21 Pliny *Panegyricus* 49.

22 Suetonius *Life of Domitian* 1.1. The house on the Quirinal Hill was later converted into the temple of Gens Flavia, which was struck by lightning in AD 96, the year of Domitian's death. Domitian's remains and those of his niece Julia were later deposited there; see Suetonius *Life of Domitian* 17.3.

23 Pliny *Panegyricus* 48.3–5.

24 Martial *Epigrams* 4.14; On Silius Italicus' praise of Domitian's poetry, see for example *Punica* 3.621.

25 Silius Italicus *Punica* 3.607; Suetonius *Life of Domitian* 6.1; Tacitus *Agricola* 39.

26 Tacitus *Germania* 30.

27 See Syme, 'Pliny's Less Successful Friends', pp. 477–95; Tacitus *Annals* 12.27–8.

28 P. Southern, *Domitian: Tragic Tyrant*, Routledge, London and New York, 2013, pp. 80–2. As Southern notes here: 'The reasons for the war and the course it took are not attested in any ancient source.'

29 Tacitus *Agricola* 39.

30 See Dio Cassius *Roman History* 67.6–7.

31 PLY 4.11; Suetonius *Life of Domitian* 8.4–5.

32 Cf. Dio Cassius *Roman History* 67.3; Plutarch *Numa* 10.4–7.

33 PLY 4.11.6.

34 Plutarch *Numa* 10.5.

35 PLE 10.171.

36 Hesiod *Works and Days* 586–8; 524–5. E. Campanile, 'Ἀνόστεος ὅν πόδα τένδει', in A. Etter, (ed.), *O-o-pe-ro-si*, Festschrift für Ernst Risch zum 75 Geburtstag, de Gruyter, Berlin and New York, 1986, pp. 355–62.

37 Suetonius *Life of Domitian* 22; Juvenal *Satires* 2.32–33; PLY 4.11.

38 PLY 4.11.11.

39 Suetonius *Life of Domitian* 8 9. Cf. Dio Cassius *Roman History* 67.1.

40 PLY 4.11.11. Domitian was surprisingly lenient after the senator confessed his guilt. Suetonius (*Life of Domitian* 8.4) says that

Cornelia's 'lovers' were clubbed to death, while Licinianus escaped owing to uncertainty over his involvement even after witnesses were tortured.

41 PLY 4.11.5.

42 PLY 4.11.12. The quote comes from Homer *Iliad* 18.20, and was used by Pliny's teacher, the orator Quintilian (*Institutio Oratoria* 10.1.49), as a good example of brevity, as noted by B. Radice, trans., Pliny the Younger, *Letters and Panegyricus*, Harvard University Press, Cambridge, MA and London, 1969, Vol. 1, p. 272.

43 Dio Cassius *Roman History* 67.13 says that Herennius Senecio stood for no office after that of quaestor.

44 Suetonius *Life of Domitian* 10.3.

45 On Pliny the Elder as Stoic see M. Beagon, *Roman Nature: The Thought of Pliny the Elder*, Clarendon Press, Oxford, 1992, pp. 94–5, who believes that his 'view of life springs from a mainly Stoic outlook'. On some of the Stoic elements of his beliefs see also M. Griffin, 'The Elder Pliny on Philosophers', in E. Bispham and G. Rowe (eds), with E. Matthews, *Vita Vigilia Est: Essays in Honour of Barbara Levick*, Institute of Classical Studies, London, 2007, pp. 91–100.

46 T. Morgan, *Literate Education in the Hellenistic and Roman Worlds*, Cambridge University Press, Cambridge, 1998, pp. 33; 50–89. On the invention and development of encyclopaedias, see R. Fowler, 'Encyclopaedias: Definitions and Theoretical Problems', pp. 3–30 (and pp. 27–9 on first attested use of the word), in P. Binkley (ed.), *Pre-modern Encyclopaedic Texts*, Brill, Leiden, New York and Cologne, 1997.

47 PLE 2.4.

48 PLY 3.5.6.

49 Diogenes Laertius *Lives of the Eminent Philosophers* 7.1.3. On Zeno and Stoicism see especially H. A. K. Hunt, *A Physical Interpretation of the Universe: The Doctrines of Zeno the Stoic*, Melbourne University Press, Carlton, 1976.

50 PLY 7.31.2.

51 C. E. Lutz, *Musonius Rufus: 'The Roman Socrates'*, Yale University Press, New Haven, 1947; Musonius Rufus was a tutor of Epictetus. On Musonius' teachings see J. T. Dillon, *Musonius Rufus and Education in the Good Life*, Dallas; University Press of America, Lanham, Boulder, New York and Oxford, 2004.

52 Tacitus *Histories* 3.81.

53 Dio Chrysostom *Orations* 31.122.

54 PLY 1.10.5.

55 Philostratus *Life of Apollonius of Tyana* 1.13.3.

56 Philostratus *Life of Apollonius of Tyana* 8.7.34.

57 PLY 1.10.6; Euphrates cited in Epictetus *Discourses* 4.8.

58 See Dio Cassius *Roman History* 65.13; contrast Musonius Rufus, who said the beard should be left to grow (*Discourses* 21).

59 Seneca *Epistles* 103.5.

60 Musonius Rufus *Discourses* 9. He went into exile twice under Nero and once under Vespasian. Philostratus (*Life of Apollonius of Tyana* 7.16.2) said that Musonius Rufus had opposed Nero's rule. He was apparently very resourceful. During one of his exiles, it was said, he was sent to Gyara, an island in the northern Cyclades, which lacked a water supply, and discovered a spring.

61 PLY 3.11.5.

62 Musonius Rufus *Discourses* 18b.

63 Dillon, *Musonius Rufus and Education in the Good Life*, pp. 20–21.

64 PLE 33.2; 2.158–9.

65 PLE 17.96.

66 PLE 33.1

67 PLE 7.1–4.

68 PLE 2.27; 2.156–7; 7.167–8. Cf. PLE 18.3. On Mithridates and antidotes (below) see A. Mayor, *The Poison King*, Princeton University Press, Princeton and Oxford, 2010.

69 Seneca the Younger *Epistles* 58.36.

70 PLE 14.51.

71 Tacitus *Annals* 15.64.

72 Dio Cassius *Roman History* 69.8.13.

73 PLY 1.22.2.

74 PLY 1.10.4.

75 Sherwin-White, *Letters of Pliny*, p. 136; PLY 1.22.1; 6.20.7.

SIX: *Pliniana*

1 The phrase that has fallen into popular parlance is divorced from its earlier context: Seneca *Epistles* 87.22–5, later discussed by Augustine.

2 PLE 2.103–4. Pliny the Elder was speaking here of the constellations restricting the reach of some elements, and encouraging the growth of others.

3 Ovid *Fasti* 2.151–2.

4 PLE 7.134.

5 D. Camardo, 'Herculaneum from the AD 79 eruption to the medieval period', p. 305, notes that vegetation returned slowly to Pompeii – around twenty years after the eruption, according to recent research.

6 PLE 21.2.

7 A. E. Housman, *A Shropshire Lad*, 2.

8 PLE 15.102.

9 PLE 15.103. J. Reynolds, 'The Elder Pliny and His Times', p. 10 in R. French and F. Greenaway (eds), *Science in the Early Roman Empire: Pliny the Elder, his Sources and Influence*, Croom Helm, London and Sydney, 1986, who suggests that someone of Pliny's name introduced a new variety of tree.

10 PLE 15.104.

11 PLY 2.17.14–15.

12 The first figs come in August in Horace *Epistles* 1.7.5.

13 Hesiod *Works and Days* 679–87.

14 PLY 9.40.3.

15 PLE 2.122.

16 PLE 15.74–5.

17 PLE 12.4–5.

18 PLE 23.117ff and 8.209. '111 observations' – J. Bostock and H. T. Riley (eds), *The Natural History of Pliny*, Vol. 4, Henry G. Bohn, London, 1856, pp. 502–7.

19 PLE 8.209: Pliny the Elder attributed to Marcus Apicius the method of increasing the size of goose or sow livers by cramming them with dried figs.

20 PLY 1.24.4.

21 PLY 1.7.6.

22 Martial *Epigrams* 3.45.

23 PLY 7.3.2–5; 7.9.7–8.

24 PLY 1.13.1.

25 Suetonius *Life of Titus* 8.1.

26 PLY 1.13.4–5.

27 PLY 5.12; 5.3.9.

28 PLY 5.3.5.

29 Suetonius *Life of Caesar* 73.

30 PLY 1.16.5; 4.14.4.

31 PLY 1.2.6.

32 PLY 4.27

33 PLY 4.25.

34 A. E. Housman, *The Name and Nature of Poetry*, Leslie Stephen Lecture, Cambridge University Press, Cambridge, 1933.

35 See, for example, Housman's letter, dated 26 June 1906, to James Duff Duff, author of *C. Plini Caecili secundi epistularum liber sextus*, on PLY 6.8.6 (A. E. Housman, *The Letters of A.E. Housman* Vol. 1, edited by A. Burnett, Clarendon Press, Oxford, 2007, p. 197).

36 PLY 7.4.2.

37 PLY 4.14.2; 7.4.4; 8.

38 PLY 4.14.3–4.

39 Sherwin-White, *Letters of Pliny*, pp. 71, 559, argues that Pliny married three times and that Calpurnia was his third wife. Pliny

speaks of two marriages in Letter 10.2 but it is uncertain whether his marriage to Calpurnia had taken place by this point. There is no evidence in his letters of a wife prior to the (unnamed) daughter of Pompeia Celerina to whom he was married before Calpurnia. I am inclined to think that Pliny married only twice.

40 Radice, *Pliny: Letters and Panegyricus*, Vol 1, p. xv, is among the scholars who date the death of Pliny's previous wife to AD 97, citing letter 9.13.4. R. K. Gibson and R. Morello (*Reading the Letters of Pliny the Younger: An Introduction*, Cambridge University Press, Cambridge and New York, 2012, p. 32) suggest that Pliny remarried in or before AD 98. I also believe that Pliny remarried very soon after her death and that Calpurnia is the second of the two wives Pliny mentions to Trajan in Letter 10.2. This letter dates to the early part of his rule – AD 98, according to Sherwin-White (*Letters of Pliny*, p. 557). In this letter Pliny writes of how he longed to have children in the past and is still longing to now. I believe this letter post-dates Calpurnia's miscarriage.

41 PLY 4.19.8.

42 PLY 1.14.8.

43 PLY 4.19.5.

44 On Pliny's erotic vocabulary in Letter 7.5 see A. R. de Verger, 'Erotic Language in Pliny, Ep. VII 5', *Glotta* 74, B., 1/2. H., 1997/98, pp. 114–16.

45 PLY 7.4.6.

46 PLY 7.4.

47 See W. Fitzgerald, *Catullan Provocations*, University of California Press, Berkeley, LA and London, 1995, pp. 44–6.

48 PLY 7.9.

49 PLY 2.17.3.

50 PLE 11.11–14.

51 PLE 2.232; Leonardo da Vinci, *The Literary Works of Leonardo da Vinci*, edited by J. P. Richter, Phaidon, New York, 1970, Vol. II.1029 (also 1031).

52 PLY 4.30.4.

53 R. Holmes, *Shelley: The Pursuit*, Weidenfeld and Nicolson, London, 1974, pp. 328–9. The quotes are from the preface of Mary Shelley's *Frankenstein*.

54 Shelley, *Rosalind and Helen*, line 6. See J. Bieri, *Percy Bysshe Shelley: A Biography*, University of Delaware Press, Newark, 2005, pp. 61, 73.

55 Mary Shelley, *The Last Man* (1826), H. J. Luke, Jr. (ed.), University of Nebraska Press, Lincoln and London, 1993, p. 314. The description of the Pliniana in the novel is cited by R. G. Grylls, *Mary Shelley: A Biography*, Haskell House, New York, 1969, p. 95. Mary Shelley's description of the Pliniana in *The Last Man* was inspired by her own visit to the Pliniana and the waterfall, which she recounts in her Journals, 11 April 1818: M. Shelley, *The Journals of Mary Shelley, 1814-1844*, edited by P. R. Feldman and D. Scott-Kilvert, Clarendon Press, Oxford, 1987, Vol 1., p. 204.

56 Holmes, *Shelley*, p. 30.

57 C. Clairmont, *The Journals of Claire Clairmont*, edited by M. K. Stocking, Harvard University Press, Cambridge, MA, 1968 – Journal entry 12 April 1818, p. 91, cited by Holmes, *Shelley*, p. 418.

58 I draw here on Holmes, *Shelley*, pp. 417–18; 421; 471–2, who suggests that the Shelleys' failure to acquire the Villa Pliniana might have been linked to a curious incident involving a pistol. Shelley is thought to have fathered a child with one of his servants while he was at Como. Holmes suggests that the pistol incident might be understood in light of Shelley's probable impregnation of Elise, the servant.

59 Mary Shelley, *Rambles in Germany and Italy*, Edward Moxon, London, 1844, Vol. 1, p. 89 (15 August 1840); cited by L. Morrison and S. L. Stone, *A Mary Shelley Encyclopaedia*, Greenwood Press, Connecticut and London, 2003, p. 343.

60 Shelley, *Prometheus Unbound*, 1667–70.

61 PLY 6.30.

62 Dio Cassius *Roman History* 68.15.

63 Martial *Epigrams* 7.47. In this poem Martial rejoices in Licinius Sura's narrow escape from death. In *Epigram* 1.49, meanwhile, Martial celebrates Licinius Sura's coming to Spain.

64 Pliny may not have been familiar with the curious wine-pouring automata of Philon of Byzantium which were powered by similar siphon mechanisms.

65 PLY 5.6.36–7.

SEVEN: *The Shadow of Verona*

1 W. Pater, *The Renaissance*, Macmillan & Co., London, 1873, p. 153.

2 PLY 8.20.5.

3 See Livy *Ab urbe condita* 33.36.

4 Information retrieved at the baths and museum at Viale Lecco, Como.

5 CIL V 5279. See F. Sacchi, 'Como romana: Gli aspetti monumentali della città e del surburbio', in G. Luraschi (ed.), *Storia di Como*, Storia di Como, Como: Luglio, 2013, Vol. 1, pp. 154–5.

6 A. Sartori, *Le Iscrizioni Romane*, Musei Civici Como, Como, 1994, p. 37. See also T. Mommsen, *Gesammelte Schriften*, Vol. 4, Weidmann, Berlin, 1906, pp. 394–5, who suggests that this Lucius Caecilius Cilo was Pliny's father, and that of the sons named in the inscription, Publius Caecilius Secundus was Pliny as he was known prior to his adoption. Sherwin-White (*Letters of Pliny*, p. 70) believes that Lucius Caecilius Cilo is rather 'a collateral relation' of Pliny.

7 It is possible that the baths at Viale Lecco, Como, were those Pliny bestowed upon the town; see G. Luraschi, *Storia di Como*, Vol. 1, p. 30.

8 PLY 5.11.2.

9 CIL V, Suppl. 747. This inscription was discovered in Como in the late nineteenth century – A. Sartori, *Le Iscrizioni Romane*, pp. 34–5. Lucius Caecilius Secundus dedicated the temple in the name of his

daughter, Caecilia, so if he was Pliny's father, then Pliny had a sister whom he never mentioned in his letters. She might have died young.

10 The portrait head of Augustus as Chief Priest dates to the first century BC and was acquired by Paolo Giovio. It is on display at the Museo Civico in Como. A number of suggestions have been made for the location of the forum, but the argument for Piazza San Fedele remains the most persuasive. See particularly the discussion of S. Maggi, 'L'urbanistica di Como romana', pp. 131–47 in Luraschi (ed.), *Storia di Como*, Vol. 1.

11 Remains of the building have been discovered on the corner between Viale Varese and Via Benzi in Como – information retrieved from Museo Civico, Como.

12 PLY 1.3.1; see Catullus *Carmina* 2.

13 PLY 2.8.2.

14 Marble relief sculpture dated to the second half of the first century AD and discovered on Piazza San Fedele, probable site of the forum. If Pliny looked up from this frieze to the panel above it, then he would have seen a more familiar panorama. Young men of his social class, the equestrians, parade in ceremonial procession on horseback, as he himself might well have had done in his youth.

15 PLY 1.3.1.

16 G. Luraschi, *Aspetti Di Vita Pubblica Nella Como Dei Plini*, Società Archeologica Comense, Como, 1986, p. 6 n.5; *Storia di Como*, Vol. 1, p. 31; 'La villa romana di Via Zezio in Como', *Rivista Como*, No. 3, 1976, pp. 24ff.

17 I. N. De Agostini, *La sezione romana del museo archeologico di Como*, Musei Civici, Como, 2006, pp. 49–52.

18 PLE 36.189, Museo Civico, Como.

19 De Agostini, *La sezione romana del museo archeologico di Como*, pp. 50–1.

20 Giovio, *Historiae Patriae*, Vol. 2, p. 232. See T. C. Price Zimmerman, *Paolo Giovio: The Historian and the Crisis of Sixteenth-Century Italy*, Princeton University Press, New Jersey, 1995, pp. 161, 338 n.125.

21 P. L. Rubin, *Giorgio Vasari: Life and History*, Yale University Press, New Haven and London, 1995, pp. 109–10 on Paolo Giovio's advice to Giorgio Vasari about the publication without portraits. The second edition of the *Lives*, published in 1568, did include portraits.

22 Price Zimmerman, *Paolo Giovio*, p. 188. On the portraits see also M. W. Gahtan (ed.), *Giorgio Vasari and the Birth of the Museum*, Routledge, London and New York, 2016, pp. 81, 94 n.4.

23 PLY 2.15.

24 On the lack of evidence for regular large-scale productions of drama in Rome in this period see G. Manuwald, *Roman Republican Theatre*, Cambridge University Press, Cambridge, 2011, p. 119.

25 PLY 9.7.4.

26 See Price Zimmerman, *Paolo Giovio* p. 161 on Giovio's rather opportunistic description of his museum's site as having been that of a 'Plinian' villa.

27 Not the famous hotel but the Rockefeller Foundation located behind it.

28 Giovio, *Historiae Patriae*, Vol. 2, p. 249.

29 This must be the fragment now in the Museo Civico at Como – CIL V 5221. See Sartori, *Le Iscrizioni Romane*, p. 56.

30 There have been several attempts to identify the Plinius of the inscription as a correspondent of Pliny. While residents of sixteenth-century Bellagio conjectured that Pliny wrote to him about the studies of his uncle, R. Syme ('Consular Friends of the Elder Pliny', *Roman Papers* Vol. 7, edited by A. R. Birley, Clarendon Press, Oxford, 1991, p. 510 n.104) suggests that this Plinius may have been the Sabinianus (a 'Sa' is visible in the fragment) addressed in PLY 9.21 and 9.24.

31 *In iugo huis prom fuit villa Plinii quam Tragediam appellare solebat* at Bellagio. And *hic olim Villa Plinii quam Comediam appellare solebat* at Lenno – Ortelius, Map of Lake Como, *Theatrum orbis terrarum* (cited also by P. R. du Prey, *The Villas of Pliny*, pp. 4–6)

– and also Gibson and Morello, *Reading the Letters of Pliny the Younger*, p. 200, who discuss further the appeal of Bellagio and Lenno as locations of Pliny's villas with views of one another.

32 Many tourists have glimpsed what they believe to be Roman remains beneath the bay at Lenno. See for example T. W. M. Lund, *The Lake of Como*, Kegan Paul, London; Trübner & Co. Ltd, Trench, 1910, p. 66.

EIGHT: *Portrait of a Man*

1 PLY 5.7.3.

2 PLY 3.6.2–3.

3 PLE 34.6.

4 Martial *Epigrams* 9.59.

5 Petronius *Cena Trimalchionis* 50.

6 PLE 34.34; 33.148.

7 PLE 35.151–2.

8 PLE 35.5. Cf. PLY 2.7.7.

9 In 2017 an Italian newspaper helped to launch a crowd-funding project to conclude once and for all whether this was indeed the skull of Pliny the Elder. Some of the scientists who carried out investigations on Ötzi the Iceman, the mummified corpse discovered in the Alps in 1991, have been approached to examine the isotopes in the tooth enamel. See A. Cionci, 'Il cranio di Plinio il Vecchio perso nei meandri della burocrazia', *La Stampa*: newspaper article, published online on 25 August 2017.

10 F. Russo and F. Russo, *79 d.C Rotta su Pompei (Indagine sulla Scomparse di un Ammiraglio)*, Edizioni Scientifiche e Artistiche, Naples, 2007, p. 21.

11 Russo and Russo, *79 d.C Rotta su Pompei*, p. 23.

12 M. J. Becker and J. M. Turfa, *The Etruscans and the History of Dentistry*, Routledge, London and New York, 2017, p. 322 on the skull and non-matching mandible. See D. J. Waarsenburg,

'Archeologisch Nieuws verzorgd door het Nederlands Institut te Rome: De Schedel van Plinius Maior', *Hermeneus: Tijdshrift voor Antieke Cultuur* 63e, No. 1, February 1991, pp. 39–43 on the difficulties surrounding the identification of the skull and inconsistencies in Matrone's account of the excavation. As Waarsenburg notes, groundwater hampered the extraction of objects from the site.

13 Tacitus *Dialogus* 29.

14 Darwin owned the 1601 edition of the *Natural History* – C. Darwin, *The Correspondence of Charles Darwin* Vol. 4: 1847–50, edited by F. Burkhardt and S. Smith, Cambridge University Press, Cambridge, 1988, pp. 457, 485. Darwin and the Plinian Society – J. Browne, *Charles Darwin, Voyaging, Volume I of a Biography*, Pimlico, London, 2003, pp. 72–80.

15 Charles Darwin, *The Descent of Man, and Selection in Relation to Sex*, D. Appleton and Company, New York, 1876, pp. 115, 123–4.

16 PLY 4.7.7.

17 Martial *Epigrams* 6.38; PLY 4.2.1.

18 PLY 4.2.3.

19 PLY 6.6.3.

20 Quintilian *Institutio Oratoria* 1.1.1.

21 PLY 6.6.3.

22 Tacitus *Dialogus* 34–5.

23 Petronius *Satyrica* 1.1.

24 PLY 4.13.8.

25 PLY 7.18.

26 Hoffer in *Anxieties of Pliny the Younger*, pp. 95–6, calculated that Pliny's gift (of 500,000 sesterces or 30,000 sesterces annual income) could have provided for the education of only about 150 children, a small proportion of Comum's total population. Duncan-Jones, 'The Finances of a Senator', p. 101 suggests that it supported 175 boys and girls in total.

27 Six per cent calculation – Radice, *Pliny: Letters and Panegyricus,* Vol. 1, p. 522 n.2.

28 CIL V 5278.

29 PLY 1.8.9.

30 Luraschi, *Storia di Como,* p. 31. After Pliny died a magnificent inscription (CIL V 5262) was erected in the town to commemorate the full range of his achievements and benefactions. A sixth of it survives at Milan (there is a copy of it in the Museo Civico at Comum). Radice (*Pliny: Letters and Panegyricus,* Vol. 2, p. 549) suggests that the inscription 'evidently stood over the baths at Comum'.

31 PLY 1.8.2–5; on Pliny's library see T. K. Dix, 'Pliny's Library at Comum', *Libraries & Culture,* Vol. 31, No. 1, Reading & Libraries I, Winter 1996, pp. 85–102.

NINE: *The Death of Principle*

1 From V. S. Vernon Jones's 1912 translation.

2 PLE 10.81.

3 PLE 10.141–2.

4 PLE 9.20–3.

5 Herodotus *Histories* 1.24.

6 PLY 9.33.8. See PLE 9.26 for Pliny the Elder's version of the dolphin story.

7 On Pliny's dolphin story see C. L. Miller, 'The Younger Pliny's Dolphin Story ("Epistulae" IX 33): An Analysis', *Classical World,* Vol. 60, No. 1, September 1966, pp. 6–8.

8 PLE 7.23; 7.16.

9 PLY 6.24.

10 PLE 26.139–47; 28.241–3; 30.113–18.

11 PLE 30.116; Hippocrates *Prorrhetikon* II, Kühn, 1825, I, p. 207.

12 The Arch of Titus was probably completed under Domitian; see D. E. E. Kleiner, *Roman Sculpture,* Yale University Press, New Haven and London, 1992, pp. 183–5.

13 PLY 3.16; Martial *Epigrams* 1.13.

14 PLY 3.16.6. Martial also observed that suicide could be used to achieve fame.

15 PLY 3.16.5.

16 PLY 8.22.3.

17 Tacitus *Annals* 16.22; accusations against Thrasea were brought by Cossutianus Capito, who was bitter because Thrasea had formerly assisted in having him prosecuted for extortion.

18 Plutarch later drew on Thrasea Paetus' biography of Cato when he wrote his own *Life of Cato*. Thrasea Paetus' text was based on a treatise by Munatius (Plutarch *Cato the Younger* 37).

19 M. Griffin (*Nero: The End of a Dynasty*, Routledge, London and New York, 2001, p. 173) notes that the Stoics' moral disapproval of Nero's behaviour was political in so far as they condemned tyranny. See especially pp. 171–7 on the relevance of Stoicism to these men's fates.

20 Dio Cassius *Roman History* 65.12.2; on Helvidius' philosophical upbringing see Tacitus *Histories* 4.5.

21 Tacitus says that when the young Arulenus Rusticus had hoped to try to save Thrasea Paetus from being condemned, Thrasea had told him to save himself; his career was just beginning. Suetonius (*Life of Domitian* 10.3) is alone in stating that Arulenus wrote both biographies.

22 PLY 9.13.2.

23 PLY 7.19.

24 PLY 7.19.7; Suetonius *Life of Domitian* 10.3.

25 Dio Cassius *Roman History* 67.16.1.

26 Tacitus *Histories* 1.1. On the dilemma Tacitus and Pliny faced and Pliny's efforts to align himself with the Stoics, see C. Whitton, '"Let us tread our path together": Tacitus and the Younger Pliny', in V. E. Pagán (ed.), *A Companion to Tacitus*, Wiley-Blackwell, Chichester, West Sussex; Malden, MA, 2012, p. 353.

27 Tacitus *Agricola* 45.

28 See J. A. Shelton, *The Women of Pliny's Letters*, Routledge, Oxford and New York, 2013, p. 69. J. M. Carlon (*Pliny's Women: Constructing Virtue and Creating Identity in the Roman World*, Cambridge University Press, Cambridge and New York, 2009, p. 19) notes that 'Pliny's silence, like that of his fellow senators, assured their condemnation . . .', and A. R. Birley (*Hadrian: The Restless Emperor*, Routledge, Abingdon and New York, 1997, p. 29) observes that the senators were 'obliged to vote for the death sentence against Helvidius, Rusticus and Senecio'.

29 Tacitus *Agricola* 45.

30 Tacitus *Agricola* 2.

31 PLY 7.19.6.

32 Suetonius *Life of Domitian* 10.4.

33 Suetonius *Life of Domitian* 3.1; Martial *Epigrams* 11.13.

34 Dio Cassius *Roman History* 67.3; Suetonius (*Life of Domitian* 10.1) suggested that Domitian had one of Paris's protégés killed because he reminded him of Paris.

35 Suetonius *Life of Domitian* 10.3.

36 Dio Cassius *Roman History* 67.13.3; all the philosophers left in Rome, Dio said, were banished again – which may refer to an earlier banishment by Domitian, or perhaps rather to banishments under Nero and Vespasian.

37 See B. W. Jones, *The Emperor Domitian*, pp. 120–3.

38 Juvenal *Satires* 7.86–9.

39 Eusebius *Church History* 3.17.

40 'On a very slight suspicion': Suetonius *Life of Domitian* 15.1; atheism/Judaism: Dio Cassius *Roman History* 67.14.

41 Dio Cassius *Roman History* 67.14.

42 Eusebius *Church History* 3.19–20, quoting Hegesippus, a second-century AD writer. Jones (*The Emperor Domitian*, p. 117) suggests that Domitian's persecution of Christians was largely a myth.

43 Tertullian *Apology* 5.4.

44 PLY 1.5.

45 PLE 8.215.

46 PLY 1.5.3.

47 PLY 7.19.10.

48 PLY 3.11.3.

49 Dio Cassius *Roman History* 67.1; Pliny *Panegyricus* 90.5; PLY 3.11.3.

TEN: *The Imitation of Nature*

1 PLY 5.6.19.

2 PLY 4.1.4.

3 PLY 5.6.6–7.

4 J. Boyle, Earl of Orrery, *The Letters of Pliny the Younger with Observations on Each Letter; And an Essay on Pliny's Life, addressed to Charles Lord Boyle*, James Bettenham for Paul Vaillant, London, 1752, p. 350.

5 PLY 5.6.46.

6 Cato *On Agriculture* 1.1. On the healthy climate see PLY 8.1.

7 PLE 8.227.

8 S. Black, J. Browning, and R. Laurence, 'From Quarry to Road: The Supply of Basalt for Road Paving in the Tiber Valley', in F. Coarelli and H. Patterson (eds), *Mercator Placidissimus: The Tiber Valley in Antiquity*, Quasar, Rome, 2008, pp. 715–17. The basalt came from volcanic regions including Mount Vulsini, on Lake Bolsena, and Lake Bracciano. The basalt repaving dates to the first/second century AD.

9 J. Uroz Sáez, 'Fundiary property and brick production in the high Tiber valley', in Coarelli and Patterson (eds), *Mercator Placidissimus*, p. 124.

10 G. F. Gamurrini, 'Le Statue della Villa di Plinio in Tuscis', in W.

Helbig (ed.), *Strena Helbigiana*, B. G. Teubner, Leipzig, 1900, p. 95 and n.5; more tiles stamped with Pliny's initials were discovered in the late twentieth century.

11 Uroz Sáez, 'Fundiary property and brick production in the high Tiber valley', p. 124.

12 PLY 9.6.

13 Suetonius *Life of Domitian* 4.

14 I. K. McEwen, 'Housing Fame: In the Tuscan Villa of Pliny the Younger', *RES: Anthropology and Aesthetics*, No. 27, spring 1995, p. 18. The restoration was completed under Trajan.

15 PLY 10.74.

16 On Pliny the Elder and rings see R. Hawley, 'Lords of the Rings: Ring-Wearing, Status, and Identity in the Age of Pliny the Elder', in Bispham and Rowe (eds), *Vita Vigilia Est*, pp. 103–11.

17 Tacitus *Germania* 31.

18 PLE 33.21.

19 PLE 33.8.

20 The room was intended *servire per una guardaroba di cose rare et pretiose, et per valuta, et per arte* . . . (V. Borghini, *Lo Stanzino del Principe in Palazzo Vecchio: i concetti, le immagini, il desiderio*, edited by M. Dezzi Bardeschi, *Le Lettere*, Florence, 1980. *Invenzione* I, p. 31).

21 I examined Francesco de Medici's *Studiolo*, including the use of Pliny the Elder's descriptions of rings, in detail in my doctoral thesis (2013). On the recreation of *Natural History* in this room see also S. J. Schaefer, *The Studiolo of Francesco I de'Medici in the Palazzo Vecchio in Florence*, PhD Thesis, Bryn Mawr College, Pennsylvania, 1976.

22 The first Italian translation of Pliny the Elder's *Natural History* was by Cristoforo Landino and printed at Venice by Nicolas Jenson in 1476. There were 1025 copies printed; a rare copy, on parchment, is now in the Bodleian Library at Oxford (Arch.G b.6).

23 Christopher Columbus, as McHam notes (*Pliny and the Artistic*

IN THE SHADOW OF VESUVIUS

Culture of the Italian Renaissance, p. 149), owned a copy of Cristoforo Landino's translation. This was the 1489 edition, printed at Venice and now housed in the Biblioteca Colombina in Seville; see the inventory of Columbus's books in S. A. Bedini (ed.), *The Christopher Columbus Encyclopaedia*, Vol. 1, Macmillan, London, 1992, p. 421.

24 Rubin (*Giorgio Vasari*, p. 304) observes that Vasari uses the word *effigie* in the 1550 edition of his book. He may have chosen the word after reading Landino's translation of the *Natural History*.

25 The British Library, Harley 2677 f.1, *c*.1457–8, illustrated by Andrea da Firenze. The British Library also holds a beautiful edition (Harley 2676) by Hubertus with Medici coat of arms from *c*.1467.

26 PLE 9.119.

27 PLE 33.8.

28 Filippo Villani, *Liber de civitatis florentiae famosis civibus* (1381–2), edited by G. C. Galletti, Joannes Mazzoni, Florence, 1847, p. 35.

29 PLE 35.79.

30 PLE 35.65.

31 See L. Freedman, 'Titian and the Classical Heritage', in P. Meilman (ed.), *The Cambridge Companion to Titian*, Cambridge University Press, Cambridge, 2004, p. 193.

32 Dolce's *Aretino* – L. Dolce, *Dolce's Aretino and Venetian Art Theory of the Cinquecento*, edited by M. W. Roskill, University of Toronto Press, Toronto, Buffalo, NY, London, 2000, pp. 96–7.

33 PLY 5.6.22.

34 On the painting fragments at the estate see R. E. Tébar, 'Gli Intonaci', in Braconi and Uroz Sáez (eds), *La Villa Di Plinio il Giovane a San Giustino*, p. 64.

35 J. C. M. Villora, 'Le Terrecotte Architettoniche', in Braconi and Sáez, *La Villa Di Plinio il Giovane a San Giustino*, pp. 52–3.

36 PLE 7.10.

37 PLY 4.19.7.

ELEVEN: A *Difficult, Arduous, Fastidious Thing*

1 PLY 7.5.1.

2 PLY 9.36.2.

3 PLY 9.10.3.

4 PLY 7.20.6.

5 PLY 9.10.1.

6 PLY 1.6.2.

7 According to the calculation of Uroz Sáez, 'Fundiary property and brick production in the high Tiber valley', pp. 132–3. Uroz Sáez includes in this total the adjacent plot Pliny is planning to buy in Letter 3.19.

8 Other entertainments held in the Colosseum included candlelit gladiator fights and mock 'sea' battles over a flooded stage.

9 See especially R. Edwards, 'Hunting for Boars with Pliny and Tacitus', *Classical Antiquity*, Vol. 27, No. 1, April 2008, pp. 35–58 on the association between the Marcus Aper of Tacitus' *Dialogus* and Pliny's 'three boars'. On the *Dialogus* and Pliny see W. Dominik, 'Tacitus and Pliny on Oratory', in W. Dominik and J. Hall (eds), *A Companion to Roman Rhetoric*, Wiley-Blackwell, Chichester, West Sussex and Malden, MA, 2010, pp. 323–38.

10 Tacitus *Dialogus* 5–10.

11 PLY 9.10.2.

12 PLY 6.17.5.

13 PLY 1.9.4.

14 PLE 36.117. On Pliny the Elder and Curio's theatre see C. Schultze, 'Making a Spectacle of Oneself: Pliny on Curio's Theatre', in Bispham and Rowe (eds), *Vita Vigilia Est*, pp. 127–45.

15 P. Fane–Saunders, *Pliny the Elder and the Emergence of Renaissance Architecture*, Cambridge University Press, New York, 2016, pp. 246–7.

16 PLY 7.30.3.

17 On the treasury see F. Millar, 'The Aerarium and its Officials under the Empire', *Journal of Roman Studies*, Vol. 54, Parts 1 and 2, 1964, pp. 39–40.

18 CIL V 5667.

19 PLY 1.10.9.

20 Suetonius *Life of Domitian* 14.

21 Suetonius *Life of Domitian* 17.

22 Suetonius *Life of Domitian* 14.

23 A. M. Ward, F. M. Heichelheim and C. A. Yeo (A *History of the Roman People*, Routledge, London and New York, 2016, p. 326) describe Stephanus entering the conspiracy as a 'devoted former butler' of Domitilla.

24 It was said that a storm put out Domitian's funeral pyre and dogs tore apart his semi-burned corpse.

25 Tacitus *Histories* 4.41; 44; see Levick, *Vespasian*, p. 49.

26 Pliny *Panegyricus* 34.

27 PLY 1.5.1.

28 PLY 7.27.12–16.

29 PLY 9.13.2.

30 PLY 9.13.6.

31 PLY 1.5.15.

32 PLY 9.13.21.

33 Tacitus *Agricola* 3.

34 PLY 4.22.7.

35 *Epitome de Caesaribus* 12.8. The Praetorian Guard are said to have seized both the *cubicularius* or chamberlain Parthenius and Petronius Secundus, one of the praetorian prefects. On the frustration of the Guard see also Dio Cassius *Roman History* 68.8. Cf. Pliny *Panegyricus* 6.2.

36 See J. D. Grainger, *Nerva and the Roman Succession Crisis of AD 96–99*, Routledge, London and New York, 2003, p. 89 on the dilemma Nerva faced over when to adopt a successor.

37 On the complex machinations which might have been taking

place among the Guard and behind the scenes see W. Eck, 'An Emperor is Made: Senatorial Politics and Trajan's Adoption by Nerva in 97', in G. Clark and T. Rajak (eds), *Philosophy and Power in the Graeco-Roman World: Essays in Honour of Miriam Griffin*, Oxford University Press, Oxford and New York, 2002, pp. 211–26. See also Grainger, *Nerva and the Roman Succession Crisis of AD 96–99*, pp. 90–9.

38 Pliny *Panegyricus* 8.1.

39 PLY 9.13.21.

40 PLY 7.19.4.

41 PLY 9.13.25.

42 PLY 1.10.10.

TWELVE: *Head, Heart, Womb*

1 PLE 7.191. In late May a fertility rite known as the Ambarvalia honoured Ceres.

2 PLY 9.39.

3 PLY 6.30.4.

4 A. Marzano (*Roman Villas in Central Italy: A Social and Economic History*, Brill, Leiden and Boston, 2007, p. 110) explains that the villa was built by Granius Marcellus; pottery finds, but not building materials, predate his ownership. Establishing a precedent for Pliny, this magistrate had fired thousands of tiles bearing his name, more than 300 of which have since been recovered from the plain and from as far as ten kilometres away, at Parnacciano and Mazzano; see Uroz Sáez, 'Fundiary property and brick production in the high Tiber valley', p. 128. Gamurrini ('Le Statue della Villa di Plinio in Tuscis', p. 97) made the link between these tiles, Pliny's statues, and the two men named Granius mentioned by Tacitus. In Letter 10.8.1 Pliny says that the statues of the emperors had been passed down *per plures successiones*. The idea that his are the same statues owned by Granius Marcellus is uncertain but

very compelling and is proposed by Gamurrini, pp. 93–7; Sherwin-White, *Letters of Pliny*, pp. 322–3; and A. J. Woodman, 'Tacitus and the contemporary scene', in A. J. Woodman (ed.), *The Cambridge Companion to Tacitus*, Cambridge University Press, Cambridge, 2009, pp. 34–5.

5 CIL XI 5264 names Granius as a *duovir quinquennalis* of Hispellum. See Marzano, *Roman Villas in Central Italy*, p. 110.

6 Tacitus *Annals* 1.74.

7 Tacitus *Annals* 6.38; Uroz Sáez ('Fundiary property and brick production in the high Tiber valley', pp. 128–9) suggests that the estate passed to Granius' son Granius Marcianus and then into imperial hands when he committed suicide.

8 Uroz Sáez, 'Fundiary property and brick production in the high Tiber valley', p. 131.

9 Jean Hardouin cited in E. Allain, *Pline le jeune et ses héritiers*, Fontemoing, Paris, 1902, Vol. 3, pp. 282–91. The inscription was recorded by the sixteenth-century Augustinian monk Onofrio Panvinio in his *In Fastorum Libros Commentarii* and later adduced by Gamurrini ('Le Statue della Villa di Plinio in Tuscis', p. 98), whose theory of Pliny the Elder recovering the property is developed by Uroz Sáez ('Fundiary property and brick production in the high Tiber valley', pp. 130–1; and in Braconi and Uroz Sáez (eds), *La Villa Di Plinio il Giovane a San Giustino*, pp. 194–5).

10 Pliny *Panegyricus* 52.

11 Pliny *Panegyricus* 51.

12 Suetonius *Life of Domitian* 5; Dio Cassius 66.24. See P. Roche, 'The Panegyricus and the Monuments of Rome', in P. Roche (ed.), *Pliny's Praise*, p. 46.

13 Pliny *Panegyricus* 52.4–5; see also Suetonius *Life of Domitian* 23. Domitian is said to have allowed only gold and silver sculptures of a certain weight to be dedicated to him on the Capitoline Hill (see Suetonius *Life of Domitian* 13).

14 PLY 10.5.1; 7.1.4. Sherwin-White (*Letters of Pliny*, p. 566) dates

Letter 10.5, in which Pliny writes of being ill 'last year', to between mid-AD 98 and 99. In Letter 10.8, Pliny describes how his ill health delayed work on the temple.

15 PLY 7.1.3.

16 PLE 29.11.

17 PLE 29.28.

18 PLE 29.25; 33.116.

19 PLE 29.27.

20 PLE 29.26.

21 PLE 26.12.

22 PLE 20.42–3; 26.14.

23 A handful of bricks survive from the complex with the letters *CAESAR*. See Braconi and Uroz Sáez, 'La Villa Di Plinio il Giovane a San Giustino', in Coarelli and Patterson (eds), *Mercator Placidissimus*, p. 114. A piece of mosaic floor found at Pliny's Tuscan villa consisted of black and white tiles arranged in triangular patterns with a chequered border; it has been dated to the end of the first century AD/first half of the second century AD, which coincides precisely with Pliny's dates; see A. G. Catalá, 'Mosaici', in Braconi and Uroz Sáez (eds), *La Villa Di Plinio il Giovane a San Giustino*, pp. 121–5.

24 PLY 7.1.6.

25 PLY 10.5; 10.6; 6.3.

26 PLY 7.26.1.

27 PLY 2.8.2.

28 1 Peter 1:7.

29 PLY 7.26.4.

30 PLE 7.41.

31 A male foetus, on the other hand, was said to move on the fortieth day after conception.

32 See, for example, PLE 28.70, and R. Flemming, 'Women, Writing and Medicine in the Classical World', *Classical Quarterly*, Vol. 57, No. 1, May 2007, particularly pp. 273–4, on Pliny the Elder's

lack of distinction between the two professions. On matters of gynaecological health in the *Natural History* see A. Richlin, 'Pliny's Brassiere: Roman Medicine and the Female Body', in L. K. McClure (ed.), *Sexuality and Gender in the Classical World*, Blackwell, Oxford, 2002, pp. 225–52.

33 PLE 7.64.

34 PLY 8.11.3.

35 Tacitus *Annals* 16.8.

36 PLY 8.10.

37 It is impossible to know whether the illness that led Calpurnia to travel to Campania was the result of her miscarriage, or another illness entirely, but I believe it is likely that she went there to recover after her loss.

38 Statius *Silvae* 4.4.81–2. To the historian Dio Cassius (*Roman History* 66.21), writing in the third century AD, the mountain now resembled an amphitheatre, its centre burned out but its slopes once again covered in vineyards. Even then the crater continued to belch forth smoke, fire, and ash.

39 Camardo, 'Herculaneum from the AD 79 eruption to the medieval period', p. 305.

40 PLY 6.30.

41 PLY 6.28.

42 PLY 6.4.1–2.

43 PLY 6.4.4.

44 PLY 6.4.5; 6.7.

45 R. Steele and J. Addison, *The Tatler*, Vol. 3, John Sharpe, London, 1804, pp. 180–6. The original article was published in 1709–10 and is cited by C. Whitton and R. Gibson, 'Readers and Readings of Pliny's *Epistles*', in Gibson and Whitton (eds), *The Epistles of Pliny*, p. 9.

46 PLY 7.5.2.

47 PLE 26.100.

48 Several of these remedies for gout were included in the *Medicina*

Plinii that was compiled from the medical passages of the *Natural History* in the fourth century AD.

49 PLY 1.12.

50 PLY 1.12.8; see Hoffer, *Anxieties of Pliny the Younger*, pp. 141–8.

51 PLY 1.12.12.

THIRTEEN: *After the Solstice*

1 Cicada: PLE 11.107; Vines: PLE 16.104.

2 PLE 10.80.

3 PLE 21.56; 18.265.

4 PLE 18.295.

5 PLE 18.267.

6 PLE 8.133.

7 PLE 18.72.

8 PLE 18.295.

9 PLE 18.97; 18.296–8.

10 Outbuildings and square: Braconi and Uroz Sáez, 'La Villa Di Plinio il Giovane a San Giustino', p. 115, and Braconi, 'La Villa di Plinio a San Giustino', pp. 35–6.

11 PLY 4.6.2.

12 PLY 7.30.3; 9.37.2.

13 PLE 18.36.

14 PLE 18.11.

15 Hesiod *Works and Days* 303–9.

16 PLY 10.8.5.

17 PLY 2.4.3.

18 PLY 3.19.8.

19 PLY 5.6.10; PLE 18.181. Sherwin-White (*Letters of Pliny*, p. 322) used the similarities of their descriptions of the soil as further evidence that Pliny inherited the Tuscan estate from his uncle.

20 Horace *Satires* 2.6.4–5.

21 PLE 18.9.

22 Hesiod *Works and Days* 43–4.

23 PLY 3.19.

24 Carlon, *Pliny's Women*, p. 120, suggests that Pliny had tutelary control over Pompeia Celerina's funds.

25 Carlon, *Pliny's Women*, p. 122, notes that Letter 1.4, in which Pliny describes visiting Pompeia Celerina's properties, almost definitely post-dates the death of his first wife. Even under Trajan, Pliny was still assisting Pompeia by requesting that her relative, Caelius Clemens, be transferred to Bithynia; when Trajan granted the favour, Pliny thanked him for being so generous to his 'whole household' (PLY 10.51.2).

26 PLY 5.6.4.

27 PLE 15.3.

28 PLE 15.8.

29 See J. M. Vidal, 'Mercantile trade in the Upper Tiber Valley: the villa of Pliny the Younger "in Tuscis"', in Coarelli and Patterson (eds), *Mercator Placidissimus*, pp. 231–3.

30 Vidal ('Mercantile trade in the Upper Tiber Valley', p. 232) describes the abundance of amphorae for preserved fish products imported from Cadiz and surrounding areas and found at Pliny's estate.

31 PLY 5.6.29.

32 PLE 14.13.

33 PLE 14.10.

34 Columella *On Agriculture* 3.3.8.

35 Propertius *Elegies* 4.2.

36 PLY 9.20.

37 Braconi and Uroz Sáez, 'La Villa Di Plinio il Giovane a San Giustino', p. 115: Pliny either extended the existing equipment or created it new.

38 Seneca *Epistles* 83.

39 PLE 14.137.

40 PLE 14.141.

41 PLE 14.8.

42 Suetonius *Life of Domitian* 7.2.

43 PLE 14.134.

44 PLE 14.134.

45 Vidal, 'Mercantile trade in the Upper Tiber Valley', p. 228.

46 Vidal, 'Mercantile trade in the Upper Tiber Valley', pp. 227–35; Marzano, *Roman Villas in Central Italy*, p. 111 n.45, on so-called Spello amphorae (Altotiberina 1 and 2 amphorae).

47 PLY 2.6.

48 PLE 14.91.

49 PLY 2.6.4–5.

50 Juvenal *Satires* 7.119–21, also cited by Vidal, 'Mercantile trade in the Upper Tiber Valley', p. 228.

51 P. Braconi, 'Territorio e Paesaggio Dell'Alta Valle Del Tevere in Età Romana', in Coarelli and Patterson (eds), *Mercator Placidissimus*, p.100.

52 Marzano, *Roman Villas in Central Italy*, p. 111 n.45.

53 Vidal, 'Mercantile trade in the Upper Tiber Valley', pp. 227–8.

FOURTEEN: *Life in Concrete*

1 PLE 3.54.

2 PLY 5.6.12.

3 PLY 8.17.2–5.

4 PLY 9.16; 8.15.

5 PLY 4.6; 10.8.5.

6 *Epitome De Caesaribus* 12.10–12. This account was written hundreds of years after the event.

7 Tacitus *Agricola* 3.

8 PLY 10.1.

9 Pliny *Panegyricus* 4.

10 *Epitome De Caesaribus* 1.6; P. Garnsey, *Famine and Food Supply in the Graeco-Roman World: Responses to Risk and Crisis*, Cambridge University Press, Cambridge, 1993, p. 231.

11 Pliny *Panegyricus* 30.2.

12 Pliny *Panegyricus* 29.3–4.

13 PLY 4.8.5.

14 PLE 7.117.

15 AE 1972. The statue was dedicated by one Marcus Cassius Comicus. The base still survives and is on display in the Museo Civico at Como.

16 PLY 3.18.1.

17 Pliny *Panegyricus* 59.2.

18 Tacitus *Annals* 1.1; Pliny *Panegyricus* 2.2.

19 Pliny *Panegyricus* 35.1.

20 PLY 3.18.10.

21 A. N. Sherwin-White, 'Pliny, the Man and His Letters', *Greece & Rome*, Vol. 16, No. 1, April 1969, p. 77 described the speech as 'terrible'.

22 Pliny *Panegyricus* 52.1.

23 Pliny *Panegyricus* 49.6. Suetonius (*Life of Domitian* 21), by contrast, remembered Domitian's banquets as generous and not prolonged. On the juxtapositions and a close literary analysis of the speech, see R. Rees, 'To Be and Not to Be: Pliny's Paradoxical Trajan', *Bulletin of the Institute of Classical Studies*, Vol. 45, 2001, pp. 149–68.

24 Pliny *Panegyricus* 46.4.

25 See D. H. Sick, 'Ummidia Quadratilla: Cagey Businesswoman or Lazy Pantomime Watcher?', *Classical Antiquity*, Vol. 18, No. 2, October 1999, p. 334 on Pliny's struggle in this passage on pantomimes.

26 Pliny *Panegyricus* 17.

27 Pliny *Panegyricus* 13.

28 Dio Cassius *Roman History* 68.13–14.

29 PLY 8.4.2.

30 Pliny *Panegyricus* 12.4.

31 On this obscure post, which might have involved directing some river traffic as well as managing Rome's sewers, see B. Campbell, *Rivers and the Power of Ancient Rome*, University of North Carolina Press, North Carolina, 2012, pp. 318–19.

32 PLY 6.31.13.

33 PLY 6.31.17.

34 PLE 35.166.

35 M. D. Jackson, S. R. Mulcahy, H. Chen, Y. Li, Q. Li, P. Cappelletti and H. Wenk, 'Phillipsite and Al-tobermorite mineral cements produced through low-temperature water-rock reactions in Roman marine concrete', *American Mineralogist*, Vol. 102, (7), 2017, pp. 1435–50.

36 Pliny *Panegyricus* 75.2.

37 PLY 3.7.5.

38 PLY 3.7.13 on Herodotus *Histories* 7.45.

39 PLY 3.7.15. See also PLY 1.3.4.

40 PLY 5.5.4.

41 PLE Preface 12–13.

42 PLY 3.18.

43 Pliny's *Panegyricus* was preserved separately from his letters, in a manuscript known as the *XII Panegyrici Latini* (Pan Latin X(2)). It considerably predates the other eleven speeches in that collection. The next earliest speech after Pliny's *Panegyricus* dates to almost two hundred years later.

FIFTEEN: *Depraved Belief*

1 On Pliny's role, and on Book 10 of his letters as a collection, see G. Woolf, 'Pliny's Province', pp. 93–108, in T. Bekker-Nielsen (ed.), *Rome and the Black Sea Region*, Aarhus University Press, Aarhus, 2006.

2 PLY 10.15.

3 PLE 36.2.

4 PLY 10.17A.

5 Tacitus *Annals* 3.33–4 cited in Shelton, *The Women of Pliny's Letters*, p. 24.

6 Hoffer, *Anxieties of Pliny the Younger*, p. 12, observes that 'the

system of political patronage seems to have acted as a disincentive to child-rearing'.

7 See Power, 'Pliny, Letters 5.10 and the Literary Career of Suetonius', p. 158.

8 PLY 10.2; 2.13.8.

9 PLY 10.94; 10.95.

10 PLY 10.78.

11 B. Levick ('Pliny in Bithynia – and What Followed', *Greece & Rome*, Vol. 26, No. 2, October 1979, pp. 125–30) argues that the focus placed on work here might have been in recognition of Bithynia's growing importance to the empire.

12 See, for example, PLY 4.9; 5.20; 6.13; 7.6; 7.10.

13 PLE 11.242.

14 PLY 10.17B.

15 PLY 10.18.2.

16 On the tension that could arise from this arrangement see F. Millar, 'Trajan: Government by Correspondence', in *Government, Society, and Culture in the Roman Empire*, Vol. 2, edited by H. M. Cotton, and G. M. Rogers, University of North Carolina Press, Chapel Hill and London, 2004, p. 25.

17 PLY 2.12.6.

18 Millar, 'Trajan: Government by Correspondence', pp. 35–40.

19 PLY 10.23.

20 PLY 10.40.3.

21 PLY 10.40.3; see also PLY 10.18, in which Trajan rejects Pliny's request for land surveyors; on suspected instances of Trajan's voice versus his secretary's in the letters, and the history of scholarship thereof, see A. N. Sherwin-White, 'Trajan's Replies to Pliny: Authorship and Necessity', *Journal of Roman Studies*, Vol. 52, Pts 1 and 2, 1962, pp. 114–19.

22 PLY 10.61; 10.41–2.

23 PLY 10.33.

24 PLY 10.34.

25 See Millar, 'Trajan: Government by Correspondence', p. 39 on Pliny encountering Christians in the remote part of the province.

26 Tacitus *Annals* 15.44; Suetonius *Life of Claudius* 25.4 with Orosius *History Against the Pagans* 7.6.15–16. The crucifixion of Christ had helped to quell the 'deadly belief' for a time, but by the mid first century 'It would have been difficult to shut them out of the city without causing riots among the crowd' (Dio Cassius *Roman History* 60.6.6).

27 On *cognitio* see Sherwin-White, *Letters of Pliny*, p. 695.

28 PLY 10.96.1.

29 Tacitus *Annals* 15.44.

30 PLY 10.96.3.

31 See G. E. M. de Ste. Croix, *Christian Persecution, Martyrdom, and Orthodoxy*, edited by M. Whitby and J. Streeter, Oxford University Press, Oxford and New York, 2006, especially pp. 110–11. PLY 10.96.7.

33 See V. A. Alikin, *The Earliest History of the Christian Gathering*, Brill, Boston and Leiden, 2010, p. 36.

34 Dio Cassius *Roman History* 60.6.6.
    Minucius Felix *Octavius* 8.4, also cited by S. Benko, *Pagan Rome and the Early Christians*, Indiana University Press, Bloomington, Indianapolis, 1984, p. 10.

36 Tertullian *de Resurrectione Carnis* 47, also cited by J. Ker, 'Nocturnal Writers in Imperial Rome: The Culture of Lucubratio', *Classical Philology*, Vol. 99, No. 3, July 2004, p. 240, who discusses the use of the word *lucubratio* for nocturnal Christian prayer versus Roman night-writing.

37 *Martyrdom of Polycarp* 9.3. Polycarp's refusal to blaspheme Christ is also mentioned in light of Pliny's procedure by both Benko, *Pagan Rome and the Early Christians*, p. 10 and L. W. Hurtado, *Lord Jesus Christ: Devotion to Jesus in Earliest Christianity*, William B. Eerdmans Publishing Company, Michigan, Cambridge, 2003, p. 609.

38 See Goldsworthy, *Pax Romana*, on the so-called *pax Romana*.

39 PLY 10.96.8.

40 Justinian *Digest* 48.18. See also W. W. Buckland, *The Roman Law of Slavery*, Cambridge University Press, Cambridge, 1970, p. 87 on the torture of slaves while extracting evidence.

41 Eusebius *Church History* 3.18.

42 Tacitus *Annals* 15.44.

43 See N. E. Pasachoff and R. J. Littman, *A Concise History of the Jewish People*, Rowman & Littlefield Publishers Inc., Lanham, Boulder, New York, Toronto, Oxford, 2005, pp. 86–9 on the impact of the loss of the shrine on Judaism. Hadrian later built a temple to Jupiter on the site.

44 PLY 10.96.9–10.

45 PLY 10.97.

46 Benko, *Pagan Rome and the Early Christians*, p. 10.

47 Tertullian *Apology* 1.4–5.

48 Tertullian *Apology* 2.8.

49 Eusebius *Church History* 3.33.2. See Sherwin-White, *Letters of Pliny*, p. 692.

50 PLY 10.120.

51 PLY 10.121.

52 See Millar, 'Trajan: Government by Correspondence', pp. 25–41 on the precedent set by Trajan's absence from Rome, his 'government by correspondence' with Pliny, and the challenges of sending messages over such a wide empire.

EPILOGUE: *Resurrection*

1 C. F. Ciceri, *Selva di Notizie Autentiche Risguardanti La Fabbrica della Cattedrale di Como con altre memorie patrie*, Eredi Caprani, Como, 1811, pp. 110–14.

2 On the representation of Pliny the Elder and Pliny the Younger as Christian saints on Como Cathedral see McHam, 'Renaissance Monuments to Favourite Sons', pp. 480–1.

3 It is uncertain whether the sculptures of the two Plinys, which date to around 1480, were completed by Giovanni Rodari or his two sons. The sons seem to have completed the sculpture niches. Their names are still visible on the plaque beneath the sculpture of Pliny the Elder.

4 CIL V 5263.

5 When Benedetto died, his tomb was placed inside the cathedral. The *Historiae Patriae*, speeches, and poems, the plaque proclaims, 'do not allow Benedetto Giovio to die'.

6 PLE 2.49.

7 See F. Wallis, *Bede: The Reckoning of Time, translated, with intro-duction, notes and commentary*, Liverpool University Press, Liverpool, 1999, pp. 78–9.

8 E. Barbaro, *Castigationes Plinianae*, Hermolaus Barbarus, Venice, 1493, p. 1. On Leoniceno and Barbaro and the *Natural History*, see B. W. Ogilvie, *The Science of Describing: Natural History in Renaissance Europe*, University of Chicago Press, Chicago and London, 2008, pp. 121–33 and G. Williams, *Pietro Bembo on Etna: The Ascent of a Venetian Humanist*, Oxford University Press, New York, 2017, pp. 139–44.

Select Bibliography

Primary Sources
(Note: The 'Loeb' volumes cited below contain English translations alongside the Greek or Latin text)

Appian, *Roman History*, trans. H. White, Loeb Classical Library, Vol. 3, William Heinemann Ltd, London and G. P. Putnam's Sons, New York, 1933

Aratus, *Phaenomena*, trans. G. R. Mair, Loeb Classical Library, William Heinemann, London and G. P. Putnam's Sons, New York, 1921

Artemidorus, *Oneirocritica*, edited by D. E. Harris-McCoy, Oxford University Press, Oxford, 2012

Aubrey, J., *'Brief Lives', chiefly of Contemporaries: set down by John Aubrey, between the years 1669 & 1696, edited from the Author's MSS*, by Andrew Clark, Vol. 1, Clarendon Press, Oxford, 1898

Bacon, F., *The Letters and the Life of Francis Bacon*, edited by J. Spedding, Vol. 7, Longmans, Green, Reader, and Dyer, London, 1874

Barbaro, E., *Castigationes Plinianae*, Hermolaus Barbarus, Venice, 1493

Bede, *De Natura Rerum* and *De Temporibus*, trans. C. B. Kendall and F. Wallis, Liverpool University Press, Liverpool, 2010

Borghini, V., *Lo Stanzino del Principe in Palazzo Vecchio: i concetti, le immagini, il desiderio,* edited by M. Dezzi Bardeschi, Le Lettere, Florence, 1980

Cato, *De Agri Cultura,* edited by A. Mazzarino, B. G. Teubner, Leipzig, 1962

Catullus, *Carmina,* edited by R. A. B. Mynors, Clarendon Press, Oxford, 1958

Ciceri, C. F., *Selva di Notizie Autentiche Risguardanti La Fabbrica della Cattedrale di Como con altre memorie patrie,* Eredi Caprani, Como, 1811

Cicero, *De Divinatione,* edited by O. Plasberg and W. Ax, B. G. Teubner, Stuttgart, 1965

Clairmont, C., *The Journals of Claire Clairmont,* edited by M. K. Stocking, Harvard University Press, Cambridge, MA, 1968

Collenuccio, P., *Pliniana defensio adversus Nicolai Leoniceni accusationem,* Andreas Belfortis, Ferrara, 1493

Columella, *Res Rustica,* edited by R. H. Rodgers, Oxford University Press, Oxford, 2010

Darwin, C., *The Descent of Man: And Selection in Relation to Sex:* D. Appleton and Company, New York, 1876

———*The Correspondence of Charles Darwin,* Vol. 4, 1847–50, edited by F. Burkhardt and S. Smith, Cambridge University Press, Cambridge, 1988

Dickens, C., *Letters of Charles Dickens, 1833–70,* edited by G. Hogarth and M. Dickens, Cambridge University Press, Cambridge, 2011

Dio Cassius, *Roman History,* edited by E. Gros, Librairie De Firmin Didot Frères, Paris, 1867

Dio Chrysostom, *Orations,* edited by J. de Arnim, Weidmann, Berlin, 1893

Diodorus Siculus, *Library of History,* edited by I. Bekker, L. Dindorf and F. Vogel, B. G. Teubner, Leipzig, 1888–90

Diogenes Laertius, *Lives of the Eminent Philosophers,* trans. R. D. Hicks, Harvard University Press, Cambridge, 1972

Dolce, L., *Dolce's Aretino and Venetian Art Theory of the Cinquecento,* edited by M. W. Roskill, University of Toronto Press, Toronto, Buffalo, NY, London, 2000

Epictetus, *Discourses*, trans. W. A. Oldfather, Loeb Classical Library, William Heinemann, London and G. P. Putnam's Sons, New York, 1928

Eusebius, *The Ecclesiastical History*, Vol. 1, trans. K. Lake, Loeb Classical Library, William Heinemann, London and G. P. Putnam's Sons, New York, 1926

Giovio, B., *Historiae Patriae*, Vol. 2, 1629; New Press, Como, 1982

Hamilton, W., *Observations on Mount Vesuvius, Mount Etna, and Other Volcanos: In a Series of Letters to the Royal Society*, T. Cadell, London, 1773

Herodotus, *Histories*, trans. A. D. Godley, Loeb Classical Library, Harvard University Press, Cambridge, MA and London, 2004

Hesiod, *Works and Days*, edited by F. Solmsen, Clarendon Press, Oxford, 1990

Hippocrates, *Magni Hippocratis Opera Omnia*, Vol. 1, edited by D. C. G. Kühn, Carl Knobloch, Leipzig, 1825

Homer, *Odyssey*, edited by T. W. Allen, Clarendon Press, Oxford, 1917

———*Iliad*, edited by D. B. Munro and T. W. Allen, Clarendon Press, Oxford, 1920

Horace, *Satires*, trans. A. Palmer, Loeb Classical Library, Harvard University Press, Cambridge, MA and Macmillan, London, 1899

———*Epistles*, Book I, edited by R. Mayer, Cambridge University Press, Cambridge, 1994

Housman, A. E., *The Name and Nature of Poetry*, Leslie Stephen Lecture, Cambridge University Press, Cambridge, 1933

———*A Shropshire Lad*, Dover Publications Inc., New York, 1990

———*The Letters of A. E. Housman*, Vol. 1, edited by A. Burnett, Clarendon Press, Oxford, 2007

Jerome, *Chronicle*, edited by R. Pearse et al., Ipswich, 2005: *http://*

www.tertullian.org/fathers/jerome_chronicle_02_part1.htm

Josephus, *The Jewish War*, trans. H. St John Thackeray, Loeb Classical Library, Harvard University Press, Cambridge, MA and London, 1928

Juvenal, *Juvenal and Perseus*, trans. and edited by S. M. Braund, Loeb Classical Library, Harvard University Press, Cambridge, MA and London, 2004

Leonardo da Vinci, *The Literary Works of Leonardo da Vinci*, Vol. 2, edited by J. P. Richter, Phaidon, New York, 1970

Leoniceno, N., *De Plinii et aliorum medicorum in medicina erroribus*, Laurentius de Rubeis, Ferrara, 1492

Livy, *Ab urbe condita*, Vols 9–10, edited by A. Drakenborg, Societas Wuertembergica, Stuttgart, 1824–5

Lucretius, *De Rerum Natura*, trans. W. H. D. Rouse, Loeb Classical Library, Harvard University Press, Cambridge, MA and London, 2002

Martial, *Epigrams*, edited by W. M. Lindsay, Clarendon Press, Oxford, 1929

de Matociis, G., *Brevis adnotatio de duobus Pliniis* (text reproduced in E. T. Merrill, 'On the Eight-Book Tradition of Pliny's Letters in Verona', *Classical Philology*, Vol. 5, No. 2, April 1910, pp. 175–88)

Minucius Felix, *Octavius*, trans. G. H. Rendall, Loeb Classical Library, Harvard University Press, Cambridge, MA and London, 2003

de Montaigne, M., 'Of Ancient Customs', trans. Charles Cotton in W. C. Hazlitt, edited and trans., *Michel de Montaigne Selected Essays*, Dover Publications Ltd, New York, 2011

Musonius Rufus, *Reliquiae*, edited by O. Hense, Teubner Press, Leipzig, 1905

Orosius, *History Against the Pagans*, edited by C. Zangemeister, C. Geroldi filium, Vienna, 1882

Ovid, *Fasti*, Vol. 1, edited and trans. J. G. Frazer, Macmillan and Co. Ltd, London, 1929

— — —*Metamorphoses*, edited by R. J. Tarrant, Clarendon Press, Oxford and New York, 2004

Panvinio, O., *In Fastorum Libros Commentarii*, Erasmiana Vincentii Valgrisii, Venice, 1558

Petronius, *Satyrica*, edited by A. Ernout, Les Belles Lettres, Paris, 1922

Philostratus, *The Life of Apollonius of Tyana*, Vols 1–2, edited and trans. C. P. Jones, Loeb Classical Library, Harvard University Press, Cambridge, MA and London, 2005

Pliny the Younger, *Letters and Panegyricus*, Vols 1 and 2, trans. B. Radice, Harvard University Press, Cambridge, MA and London, 1969

Pliny the Elder, *Natural History*, via Bill Thayer's website: http://penelope.uchicago.edu/Thayer/E/Roman/home.html

Plutarch, *Lives*, trans. B. Perrin, Loeb Classical Library, Harvard University Press, Cambridge, MA and William Heinemann, London, 1914

Polycarp, *Polycarp's Epistle to the Philippians and The Martyrdom of St. Polycarp*, edited by P. Hartog, Oxford University Press, Oxford, 2013

Propertius, *Elegies*, edited and trans. G. P. Gould, Loeb Classical Library, Harvard University Press, Cambridge, MA and London, 1999

Quintilian, *Institutio Oratoria*, Vols 1–2, edited by M. Winterbottom, Clarendon Press, Oxford, 1970

Scriptores Historiae Augustae, trans. D. Magie, Loeb Classical Library, William Heinemann, London and G. P. Putnam's Sons, New York, 1922–1932

Seneca the Younger, *Opera*, Vol. 1, edited by F. Haase, B. G. Teubner, Leipzig, 1893

— — —*Epistles* Vols 1–3, trans. J. Henderson, R. M. Gummere, Loeb Classical Library, Harvard University Press, Cambridge, MA and London, 2006

Ps. Seneca, *Hercules Oetaeus*, in *The Ten Tragedies of Seneca*, trans. W. Bradshaw, Swan Sonnenschein & Co., London, 1902

Sextus Aurelius Victor (attr.), *Epitome de Caesaribus*, edited by F. Pichlmayr, B. G. Teubner, Leipzig, 1911

Shelley, M., *Rambles in Germany and Italy*, Vol. 1, Edward Moxon, London, 1844

———*The Journals of Mary Shelley, 1814–1844*, Vol. 1, edited by P. R. Feldman and D. Scott-Kilvert, Clarendon Press, Oxford, 1987

———*The Last Man*, 1826, edited by H. J. Luke Jr., University of Nebraska Press, Lincoln and London, 1993

———*Frankenstein or The Modern Prometheus*, edited by D. L. Macdonald and K. Scherf, Broadview, Ontario, 2012

Shelley, P. B., *The Works of*, Edward Moxon, London, 1847

Silius Italicus, *Punica*, Vol. 1, trans. J. D. Duff, Loeb Classical Library, William Heinemann Ltd, London and Harvard University Press, Cambridge, MA, 1934

Statius, *Silvae*, Vols 1–2, edited by H. Frère and H. J. Izaac, Les Belles Lettres, Paris, 1961

Strabo, *Geography*, edited by A. Meineke, B. G. Teubner, Leipzig, 1877

Suetonius, *Lives of the Caesars*, edited by M. Ihm, B. G. Teubner, Leipzig, 1833

Tacitus, *Histories*, edited by W. A. Spooner, Macmillan & Co., London and New York, 1891

———*Annals*, edited by C. D. Fisher, Clarendon Press, Oxford, 1906

———*Germania* and *Agricola*, edited by J. H. Sleeman, Cambridge University Press, Cambridge, 1914

———*Dialogus de Oratoribus*, edited by F. C. Wick, I. B. Paravia, Turin, 1917

Tertullian, *De Resurrectione Carnis*, edited by G. B. Lindner, Dörffling & Franke, Leipzig, 1858

———*Apology*, trans. T. R. Glover, Loeb Classical Library, Harvard University Press, Cambridge, MA and London, 2003

Varro, *De Lingua Latina*, trans. R. G. Kent, Loeb Classical Library, Harvard University Press, Cambridge, MA and William Heinemann Ltd, London, 1951

———*De Re Rustica*, On Agriculture, trans. W. D. Hooper and H. B. Ash, Loeb Classical Library, Harvard University Press, Cambridge, MA and London, 1993

Villani, Filippo, *Liber de civitatis florentiae famosis civibus*, 1381–2, edited by G. C. Galletti, Joannes Mazzoni, Florence, 1847

Virgil, *Georgics*, trans. A. S. Way, Macmillan and Co. Ltd, London, 1912

———*Aeneid*, Vols 1–2, edited by R. D. Williams, Bristol Classical Press, London, 2004

Vitruvius, *De Architectura*, trans. F. Granger, Loeb Classical Library, Harvard University Press, Cambridge, MA and London, 1998

Secondary Sources

Abdy, R., 'The Last Coin in Pompeii: A Re-evaluation of the Coin Hoard from the House of the Golden Bracelet', *Numismatic Chronicle*, Vol. 173, 2013, pp. 79–83

De Agostini, I. N., *La sezione romana del museo archeologico di Como*, Musei Civici, Como, 2006

Alikin, V. A., *The Earliest History of the Christian Gathering*, Brill, Boston and Leiden, 2010

Allain, E., *Pline le jeune et ses héritiers*, Vol. 3, Fontemoing, Paris, 1902

Arnó, V., C. Principe, M. Rosi, R. Santacroce, A. Sbrana, and M. F. Sheridan, 'Eruptive History', in *Somma-Vesuvius*, 114, Vol. 8, edited by R. Santacroce, Consiglio nazionale delle ricerche, Rome, 1987, pp. 53–103

Bakewell, S., *How to Live: A Life of Montaigne in One Question and Twenty Attempts at an Answer*, Vintage Books, London, 2011

Bardintzeff, J-M., and A. McBirney, *Volcanology*, Jones and Bartlett, Sudbury, Massachusetts, 2000

Beagon, M., *Roman Nature: The Thought of Pliny the Elder*, Clarendon Press, Oxford, 1992

Becker, M. J., and J. M. Turfa, *The Etruscans and the History of Dentistry*, Routledge, London and New York, 2017

Bedini, S. A. (ed.), *The Christopher Columbus Encyclopaedia*, Vol. 1, Macmillan, London, 1992

Bekker-Nielsen, T. (ed.), *Rome and the Black Sea Region*, Aarhus University Press, Aarhus, 2006, especially G. Woolf, 'Pliny's Province', pp. 93–108

Benko, S., *Pagan Rome and the Early Christians*, Indiana University Press, Bloomington, Indianapolis, 1984

Bennett, J., *Trajan: Optimus Princeps*, Routledge, London, 1997

Bergmann, B., 'Visualising Pliny's villas', *Journal of Roman Archaeology*, Vol. 8, 1995, pp. 406–20

Berry, J., *The Complete Pompeii*, Thames and Hudson, London, 2013

Bieri, J., *Percy Bysshe Shelley: A Biography*, University of Delaware Press, Newark, 2005

Bigelow, J., 'On the Death of Pliny the Elder', *Memoirs of the American Academy of Arts and Sciences*, Vol. 6, No. 2, 1859, pp. 223–7

Binkley, P. (ed.), *Pre-modern Encyclopaedic Texts*, Brill, Leiden, New York and Cologne, 1997, especially R. Fowler, 'Encyclopaedias: Definitions and Theoretical Problems', pp. 3–30

Birley, A. R., *Hadrian: The Restless Emperor*, Routledge, Abingdon and New York, 1997

———*Onomasticon to the Younger Pliny: Letters and Panegyric*, Saur, Munich, 2000

Bispham, E., and G. Rowe (eds), with E. Matthews, *Vita Vigilia Est: Essays in Honour of Barbara Levick*, Institute of Classical Studies, London, 2007, especially M. Beagon, 'Situating Nature's Wonders in Pliny's Natural History', pp. 19–40; E. Bispham, 'Pliny the Elder's Italy', pp. 41–67; M. Griffin, 'The Elder Pliny on Philosophers', pp. 85–101; R. Hawley, 'Lords of the Rings: Ring-Wearing, Status, and Identity in the Age of Pliny the Elder', pp. 103–11; G. Herbert-Brown, 'Scepticism, Superstition, and the Stars: Astronomical Angst in Pliny the Elder', pp. 113–26; C. Schultze, 'Making a Spectacle of Oneself: Pliny on Curio's Theatre', pp. 127–45

Borgongino, M., and G. Stefani, 'Intorno alla data dell'eruzione del 79 d.C.', *Rivista di Studi Pompeiani*, Vols 12–13, 2001–2, pp. 177–215

Bostock, J., and H. T. Riley (eds), *The Natural History of Pliny*, Vol. 4, Henry G. Bohn, London, 1856

Boyle, J., Earl of Orrery, *The Letters of Pliny the Younger with Observations on Each Letter; And an Essay on Pliny's Life, addressed to Charles Lord Boyle*, James Bettenham for Paul Vaillant, London, 1752

Braconi, P., and J. Uroz Sáez (eds), *La Villa Di Plinio il Giovane a San Giustino*, Quattroemme, Perugia, 1999, especially P. Braconi, 'La Villa di Plinio a San Giustino', pp. 21–42; A. G. Catalá, 'Mosaici', pp. 121–5; G. G. Fernández, 'Le Lucerne', pp. 149–53; R. B. García, '*Gli Oggetti di Metallo*', pp. 173–4; A. M. P. Navarro, 'Terra Sigillata Italica', pp. 67–102; J. Uroz Sáez, '*Domini* e Proprietà Agraria', pp. 191–207; J. Uroz Sáez, 'I bolli laterizi', pp. 43–50; R. E. Tébar, 'Gli Intonaci', pp. 61–5; J. M. Vidal, 'Anfore e Relazioni Commerciali', pp. 103–12; J. C. M. Villora, 'Le Terrecotte Architettoniche', pp. 51–60

Browne, J., *Charles Darwin, Voyaging, Volume I of a Biography*, Pimlico, London, 2003

Bruère, R. T., 'Tacitus and Pliny's Panegyricus', *Classical Philology*, Vol. 49, No. 3, July 1954, pp. 161–79

Buckland, W. W., *The Roman Law of Slavery*, Cambridge University Press, Cambridge, 1970

Bulwer-Lytton, E., *The Last Days of Pompeii*, Richard Bentley, London, 1834

Calvino, I., *The Literature Machine*, translated from the Italian by Patrick Creagh, Vintage, London, 1997, especially 'Man, the Sky, and the Elephant'

Camardo, D., 'Herculaneum from the AD 79 eruption to the medieval period: analysis of the documentary, iconographic and archaeological sources, with new data on the beginning of exploration at the ancient town', *Papers of the British School at Rome*, Vol. 81, 2013, pp. 303–40, 414

Cameron, A., 'The Fate of Pliny's Letters in the Late Empire', *Classical Quarterly*, Vol. 15, No. 2, November 1965, pp. 289–98

Campanile, E., 'Ἀνόστεος ὅν πόδα τένδει', in A. Etter (ed.), *O-o-pe-ro-si*, Festschrift für Ernst Risch zum 75 Geburtstag, de Gruyter, Berlin and New York, 1986, pp. 355–62

Campbell, B., *Rivers and the Power of Ancient Rome*, University of North Carolina Press, North Carolina, 2012

Campbell, I., *Ancient Roman Topography and Architecture*, Vol. 2 of *The Paper Museum of Cassiano Del Pozzo* (20 Parts in 3 Series, Royal Collection Trust, 1996–), the Royal Collection and Warburg Institute in association with Harvey Miller Publishers, London, 2004

Cancik, H., and H. Schneider (eds), 'Pliny the Elder', *Brill's New Pauly*, Phi-Prok, Brill, Leiden, 2007

Carey, S., *Pliny's Catalogue of Culture: Art and Empire in the* Natural History, Oxford University Press, Oxford and New York, 2003

Carlon, J. M., *Pliny's Women: Constructing Virtue and Creating Identity in the Roman World*, Cambridge University Press, Cambridge and New York, 2009

De Carolis, E., and G. Patricelli, *Vesuvius, AD 79: The Destruction of Pompeii and Herculaneum*, J. Paul Getty Museum, Los Angeles, 2003

Cionci, A., 'Il cranio di Plinio il Vecchio perso nei meandri della burocrazia', *La Stampa*: newspaper article, published online on 25 August 2017

Claridge, A., 'Report on excavations at the imperial vicus 1995–1998', Laurentine Shore Project, Royal Holloway, University of London, 2010 (https://www.royalholloway.ac.uk/laurentineshore)

Clark, G., and T. Rajak (eds), *Philosophy and Power in the Graeco-Roman World: Essays in Honour of Miriam Griffin*, Oxford University Press, Oxford and New York, 2002, especially W. Eck, 'An Emperor is Made: Senatorial Politics and Trajan's Adoption by Nerva in 97', pp. 211–26

Cleere, H. (ed.), *Approaches to the Archaeological Heritage*, Cambridge University Press, Cambridge, 1984

Coarelli, F., and H. Patterson (eds), *Mercator Placidissimus: The Tiber Valley in Antiquity*, Quasar, Rome, 2008, especially S. Black, J. Browning, and R. Laurence, 'From Quarry to Road: The Supply of Basalt for Road Paving in the Tiber Valley', pp. 705–30; P. Braconi, 'Territorio e Paesaggio Dell'Alta Valle Del Tevere in Età Romana', pp. 87–104; P. Braconi and J. Uroz Sáez, 'La Villa Di Plinio il Giovane a San Giustino', pp. 105–21; R. Esteve, 'Le Produzioni Ceramiche di Epoca Repubblicana nell'alta Valle del Tevere', pp. 143–88; C. Migliorati, '*Tifernum Tiberinum*: Ipotesi per L'Identificazione del Porto Fluviale', pp. 379–86; J. Uroz Sáez, 'Fundiary property and brick production in the high Tiber valley', pp. 123–42; J. M. Vidal, 'Mercantile trade in the Upper Tiber Valley: the villa of Pliny the Younger "in Tuscis"', pp. 215–49; A. Wilson, 'Villas, Horticulture and Irrigation Infrastructure in the Tiber Valley', pp. 731–68

Coffin, H. G., R. H. Brown, and R. J. Gibson, *Origin by Design*, Review and Herald Publishing Association, Hagerstown, Maryland, 2005

Colp Jr, R., '"I was a born naturalist": Charles Darwin's 1838 Notes about Himself', *Journal of the History of Medicine and Allied Sciences*, Vol. 35, No. 1, January 1980, pp. 8–39

Darley, G., *Vesuvius: The Most Famous Volcano in the World*, Profile, London, 2011

Dickens, C. (ed.), *The Library of Fiction, or Family Story-Teller*, Vol. 2, Chapman and Hall, London, 1837, especially A. Campbell, 'The Rival Colours', pp. 153–60

Dillon, J. T., *Musonius Rufus and Education in the Good Life*, Dallas; University Press of America, Lanham, Boulder, New York and Oxford, 2004

Dix, T. K., 'Pliny's Library at Comum', *Libraries & Culture*, Vol. 31, No. 1, Reading & Libraries I, Winter 1996, pp. 85–102

Dominik, W., and J. Hall (eds), *A Companion to Roman Rhetoric*, Wiley-Blackwell, Chichester, West Sussex and Malden, MA, 2010, especially W. Dominik, 'Tacitus and Pliny on Oratory', pp. 323–38

Doody, A., *Pliny's Encyclopedia: The Reception of the Natural History*, Cambridge University Press, Cambridge and New York, 2010

Downing, F. G., 'Cosmic Eschatology in the First Century: "Pagan", Jewish and Christian', *L'Antiquité Classique*, Vol. 64, 1995, pp. 99–109

Dwyer, E., *Pompeii's Living Statues*, University of Michigan Press, Ann Arbor, 2010

Dyson, S. L., *In Pursuit of Ancient Pasts*, Yale University Press, New Haven and London, 2006

Eco, U., *The Limits of Interpretation*, Indianapolis Press, Bloomington, Indianapolis, 1994

Edwards, R., 'Hunting for Boars with Pliny and Tacitus', *Classical Antiquity*, Vol. 27, No. 1, April 2008, pp. 35–58

Everson, J. E., 'The melting pot of science and belief: studying Vesuvius in seventeenth-century Naples', *Renaissance Studies*, Vol. 26, No. 5, November 2012, pp. 691–727

Fane-Saunders, P., *Pliny the Elder and the Emergence of Renaissance Architecture*, Cambridge University Press, New York, 2016

Farrar, L., *Ancient Roman Gardens*, History Press, Stroud, Gloucestershire, 2011

Felton, D., *Haunted Greece and Rome: Ghost Stories from Classical Antiquity*, University of Texas Press, Austin, 1998

Fitzgerald, W., *Catullan Provocations*, University of California Press, Berkeley, LA and London, 1995

Flemming, R., 'Women, Writing and Medicine in the Classical World', *Classical Quarterly*, Vol. 57, No. 1, May 2007, pp. 257–79

Frazer, A. (ed.), *The Roman Villa: Villa Urbana*, Philadelphia, University of Pennsylvania, 1998

French, R., and F. Greenaway (eds), *Science in the Early Roman Empire: Pliny the Elder, his Sources and Influence*, Croom Helm, London and Sydney, 1986, especially J. Reynolds, 'The Elder Pliny and His Times', pp. 1–10; R. French, 'Pliny and Renaissance Medicine', pp. 252–81

Fritz, W. J., 'Reinterpretation of the Depositional Environment of the Yellowstone "Fossil Forests"', *Geology*, Vol. 8, 1980, pp. 309–13

Gahtan, M. W. (ed.), *Giorgio Vasari and the Birth of the Museum*, Routledge, London and New York, 2016

Garnsey, P., *Famine and Food Supply in the Graeco-Roman World: Responses to Risk and Crisis*, Cambridge University Press, Cambridge, 1993

Gibson, R. K., and R. Morello, *Reading the Letters of Pliny the Younger: An Introduction*, Cambridge University Press, Cambridge and New York, 2012

———(eds), *Pliny the Elder: Themes and Contexts*, Brill, Leiden, 2011, especially M. Reeve, 'The *Vita Plinii*', pp. 207–22

Gibson, R. K., and C. Whitton (eds), *The Epistles of Pliny*, Oxford University Press, Oxford, 2016, especially C. Whitton and R. Gibson, 'Readers and Readings of Pliny's *Epistles*', pp. 1–48; R. P. Duncan-Jones, 'The Finances of a Senator', pp. 89–106

Glenn, J., 'The Blinded Cyclops: Lumen Ademptum (Aen. 3.658)', *Classical Philology*, Vol. 69, No. 1, January 1974, pp. 37–8

Goldsworthy, A., *Pax Romana*, Weidenfeld & Nicolson, London, 2016

Goodman, M., *The Ruling Class of Judaea*, Cambridge University Press, Cambridge, 1987

Gowers, E., *The Loaded Table: Representations of Food in Roman Literature*, Clarendon Press, Oxford, 1993

Grainger, J. D., *Nerva and the Roman Succession Crisis of AD 96–99*, Routledge, London and New York, 2003

Gray, R., *Prophetic Figures in Late Second Temple Jewish Palestine*, Oxford University Press, New York and Oxford, 1993

Griffin, M., *Nero: The End of a Dynasty*, Routledge, London and New York, 2001

–––'The Younger Pliny's debt to Moral Philosophy', *Harvard Studies in Classical Philology*, Vol. 103, 2007, pp. 451–81

Grylls, R. G., *Mary Shelley: A Biography*, Haskell House, New York, 1969

de Haas, T. C. A., *Fields, Farms and Colonists*, Vol. 1, Barkhuis and Groningen University Library, Groningen, 2011

Hales, S., and J. Paul (eds), *Pompeii in the Public Imagination from its Rediscovery to Today*, Oxford University Press, Oxford and New York, 2011

Hardy, E. G., *C Plinii Caecilii Secundi Epistulae – Ad Traianum Imperatorem cum eiusdem responsis*, Macmillan and Co., London and New York, 1889

Harris, J., *Pompeii Awakened: A Story of Rediscovery*, I. B. Tauris, London and New York, 2014

Harris, W. V., 'Roman Opinions about the Truthfulness of Dreams', *Journal of Roman Studies*, Vol. 93, 2003, pp. 18–34

Haywood, R. M., 'The Strange Death of the Elder Pliny', *Classical Weekly*, Vol. 46, No. 1, November 1952, pp. 1–3

Healy, J. F., *Pliny the Elder on Science and Technology*, Oxford University Press, Oxford, 1999

–––*Pliny the Elder, Natural History, A Selection, translated with an introduction and notes*, Penguin, London, 2004

Heaney, S., *Death of a Naturalist*, Faber and Faber, London, 1991

315

Helbig, W. (ed.), *Strena Helbigiana*, B. G. Teubner, Leipzig, 1900, especially G. F. Gamurrini, 'Le Statue della Villa di Plinio in Tuscis', pp. 93–8

Henderson, J., 'Knowing Someone Through Their Books: Pliny on Uncle Pliny ("Epistles" 3.5)', *Classical Philology*, Vol. 97, No. 3, July 2002, pp. 256–84

Hoffer, S. E., *The Anxieties of Pliny the Younger*, Scholars Press, Atlanta, 1999

— — — 'Divine Comedy? Accession Propaganda in Pliny, "Epistles" 10.1–2 and the "Panegyric"', *Journal of Roman Studies*, Vol. 96, 2006, pp. 73–87

Holmes, R., *Shelley: The Pursuit*, Weidenfeld and Nicolson, London, 1974

Horrell, D. G., *Becoming Christian: Essays on 1 Peter and the Making of Christian Identity*, Bloomsbury, London, New Delhi, New York and Sydney, 2013

Hunt, H. A. K., *A Physical Interpretation of the Universe: The Doctrines of Zeno the Stoic*, Melbourne University Press, Carlton, 1976

Hunt, J. D. (ed.), *The Italian Garden: Art, Design and Culture*, Cambridge University Press, Cambridge and New York, 2006

Hurtado, L. W., *Lord Jesus Christ: Devotion to Jesus in Earliest Christianity*, William B. Eerdmans Publishing Company, Michigan, Cambridge, 2003

Isager, J., *Pliny on Art and Society*, Odense University Press, Odense, 1990

Jackson, M. D., S. R. Mulcahy, H. Chen, Y. Li, Q. Li, P. Cappelletti, and H. Wenk, 'Phillipsite and Al-tobermorite mineral cements produced through low-temperature water-rock reactions in Roman marine concrete', *American Mineralogist*, Vol. 102, (7), 2017, pp. 1435–50

Jardine, L., and A. Stewart, *Hostage to Fortune: The Troubled Life of Francis Bacon*, Victor Gollancz, London, 1998

Jashemski, W. F., and F. G. Meyer (eds), *The Natural History of*

Pompeii, Cambridge University Press, Cambridge, 2002, especially W. F. Jashemski, 'The Vesuvian Sites Before AD 79: The Archaeological, Literary, and Epigraphical Evidence', pp. 6–28; H. Sigurdsson, 'Mount Vesuvius Before the Disaster', pp. 29–36; H. Sigurdsson and S. Carey, 'The Eruption of Vesuvius in AD 79', pp. 37–64

Jenkins, I., P. Craddock, and J. Lambert, 'A Group of Silvered-Bronze Horse-Trappings from Xanten ("Castra Vetera")', *Britannia*, Vol. 16, 1985, pp. 141–64

Johnson, D., 'The Manuscripts of Pliny's Letters', *Classical Philology*, Vol. 7, No. 1, January 1912, pp. 66–75

Johnson, G. J., 'De "conspiratione delatorum": Pliny and the Christians Revisited', *Latomus* T. 47, Fasc. 2, April–June 1988, pp. 417–22

Jones, B. W., *The Emperor Domitian*, Routledge, London and New York, 1992

Kemp, M., *Leonardo da Vinci: The Marvellous Works of Nature and Man*, Oxford University Press, Oxford, 2006

Ker, J., 'Nocturnal Writers in Imperial Rome: The Culture of Lucubratio', *Classical Philology*, Vol. 99, No. 3, July 2004, pp. 209–42

Kleiner, D. E. E., *Roman Sculpture*, Yale University Press, New Haven and London, 1992

Lanciani, R. A., *Wanderings in the Roman Campagna*, Constable & Co., London, 1909

Lang, A., *The Works of Charles Dickens in Thirty-four Volumes (Gadshill Edition), with Introductions, General Essay, And Notes Vol XVIII: Christmas Books*, Charles Scribner's Sons, New York, 1898

Levick, B., 'Pliny in Bithynia – and What Followed', *Greece & Rome*, Vol. 26, No. 2, October 1979, pp. 119–31

–––– *Vespasian*, Routledge, London and New York, 2016

Lipscomb, H. C., and R. M. Haywood, 'The Strange Death of the

Elder Pliny', *Classical Weekly*, Vol. 47, No. 5, January 1954, p. 74

Lloyd, G. E. R., *Science, Folklore and Ideology*, Cambridge University Press, Cambridge, New York and Melbourne, 1983

Lowe, E. A., and E. K. Rand (eds), *A Sixth-Century Fragment of the Letters of Pliny the Younger*, Carnegie Institution of Washington, Washington, 1922

Lund, T. W. M., *The Lake of Como*, Kegan Paul, London; Trübner & Co. Ltd, Trench, 1910

Luraschi, G., 'La villa romana di Via Zezio in Como', *Rivista Como*, No. 3, 1976

———*Aspetti Di Vita Pubblica Nella Como Dei Plini*, Società Archeologica Comense, Como, 1986

———*Vita pubblica nella Como dei Plini*, Società Archeologica Comense, Como, 1986

———(ed.), *Storia di Como*, Vol. 1, Como, Storia di Como: Luglio, 2013, especially: S. Maggi, 'L'urbanistica di Como romana', pp. 131–47; F. Sacchi, 'Como romana: Gli aspetti monumentali della città e del surburbio', pp. 149–82

Lutz, C. E., *Musonius Rufus: 'The Roman Socrates'*, Yale University Press, New Haven, 1947

McClure, L. K. (ed.), *Sexuality and Gender in the Classical World*, Blackwell, Oxford, 2002, especially A. Richlin, 'Pliny's Brassiere: Roman Medicine and the Female Body', pp. 225–52

McEwen, I. K., 'Housing Fame: In the Tuscan Villa of Pliny the Younger', *RES: Anthropology and Aesthetics*, No. 27, spring 1995, pp. 11–24

McHam, S. B., 'Renaissance Monuments to Favourite Sons', *Renaissance Studies*, Vol. 19, No. 4, September 2005, pp. 458–86

———*Pliny and the Artistic Culture of the Italian Renaissance*, Yale University Press, New Haven; London, 2013

Manuwald, G., *Roman Republican Theatre*, Cambridge University Press, Cambridge, 2011

Marchesi, I. (ed.), *Pliny the Book-Maker: Betting on Posterity in the Epistles*, Oxford University Press, Oxford, 2015, especially J. Bodel, 'The Publication of Pliny's Letters', pp. 13–105

Marzano, A., *Roman Villas in Central Italy: A Social and Economic History*, Brill, Leiden and Boston, 2007

Mayor, A., *The Poison King: The Life and Legend of Mithridates, Rome's Deadliest Enemy*, Princeton University Press, Princeton and Oxford, 2010

Meilman, P. (ed.), *The Cambridge Companion to Titian*, Cambridge University Press, Cambridge, 2004, especially L. Freedman, 'Titian and the Classical Heritage', pp. 183–202

Merrill, E. T., 'On the Eight-Book Tradition of Pliny's Letters in Verona', *Classical Philology*, Vol. 5, No. 2, April 1910, pp. 175–88

Millar, F., 'The Aerarium and its Officials under the Empire', *Journal of Roman Studies*, Vol. 54, Parts 1 and 2, 1964, pp. 33–40

– – –*Government, Society, and Culture in the Roman Empire*, Vol. 2, edited by H. M. Cotton and G. M. Rogers, University of North Carolina Press, Chapel Hill and London, 2004, especially 'Trajan: Government by Correspondence', pp. 23–46

Miller, C. L., 'The Younger Pliny's Dolphin Story ("Epistulae" IX 33): An Analysis', *Classical World*, Vol. 60, No. 1, September 1966, pp. 6–8

Miller, J. F., and A. J. Woodman, (eds), *Latin Historiography and Poetry in the Early Empire*, Brill, Leiden and Boston, 2010, especially C. Newlands, 'The Eruption of Vesuvius in the *Epistles* of Statius and Pliny', pp. 105–21

Mommsen, T., *Gesammelte Schriften*, Vol. 4, Weidmann, Berlin, 1906

Morello, R., and A. D. Morrison (eds) *Ancient Letters: Classical and Late Antique Epistolography*, Oxford University Press, Oxford and New York, 2007, especially W. Fitzgerald, 'The Letter's the Thing (in Pliny, Book 7)', pp. 191–210

Morgan, T., *Literate Education in the Hellenistic and Roman Worlds*, Cambridge University Press, Cambridge, 1998

Morrison, L., and S. L. Stone, A *Mary Shelley Encyclopaedia*, Greenwood Press, Connecticut and London, 2003

Murphy, T., *Pliny the Elder's Natural History: The Empire in the Encyclopaedia*, Oxford University Press, Oxford, 2004

Noreña, C. F., 'The Social Economy of Pliny's Correspondence with Trajan', *American Journal of Philology*, Vol. 128, No. 2, summer 2007, pp. 239–77

Ogilvie, B. W., *The Science of Describing: Natural History in Renaissance Europe*, University of Chicago Press, Chicago and London, 2008

Pagán, V. E. (ed.), A *Companion to Tacitus*, Wiley-Blackwell, Chichester, West Sussex; Malden, MA, 2012, especially C. Whitton, '"Let us tread our path together": Tacitus and the Younger Pliny', pp. 345–68

Pasachoff, N., and R. J. Littman, A *Concise History of the Jewish People*, Rowman & Littlefield Publishers, Inc., Lanham, Boulder, New York, Toronto, Oxford, 2005

Pater, W., *The Renaissance*, Macmillan & Co., London, 1873

Pitcher, R. A., 'The Hole in the Hypothesis: Pliny and Martial Reconsidered', *Mnemosyne*, Vol. 52, No. 5, October 1999, pp. 554–61

Power, T. J., 'Pliny, Letters 5.10 and the Literary Career of Suetonius', *Journal of Roman Studies*, Vol. 100, 2010, pp. 140–62

Power, T., and R. K. Gibson (eds), *Suetonius The Biographer*, Oxford University Press, Oxford, 2014, especially R. K. Gibson, 'Suetonius and the *uiri illustres* of Pliny the Younger', pp. 199–230.

du Prey, P. R., *The Villas of Pliny: From Antiquity to Posterity*, University of Chicago Press, Chicago and London, 1994

Price Zimmerman, T. C., *Paolo Giovio: The Historian and the Crisis of Sixteenth-Century Italy*, Princeton University Press, New Jersey, 1995

Purcell, N., 'Discovering a Roman Resort-Coast: The Litus Laurentinum and the Archaeology of Otium', via the Laurentine Shore Project at Royal Holloway, University of London online, 1998

— — —'Pliny (1) the Elder, 23/4–79 CE', entry in *Oxford Classical Dictionary*, http://classics.oxfordre.com, published March 2016

Radice, B., 'Pliny and the "Panegyricus"', *Greece & Rome*, Vol. 15, No. 2, October 1968, pp. 166–72

Rawson, B., and P. Weaver (eds), *The Roman Family in Italy: Status, Sentiment, Space*, Clarendon Press, Oxford; Humanities Research Centre, Canberra, 1999, especially W. Eck, 'Rome and the Outside World: Senatorial Families and the World They Lived in', pp. 73–100

Rees, R., 'To Be and Not to Be: Pliny's Paradoxical Trajan', *Bulletin of the Institute of Classical Studies*, Vol. 45, 2001, pp. 149–68

Reynolds, L. D., and N. G. Wilson (eds), *Texts and Transmission: A Survey of the Latin Classics*, Oxford University Press, Oxford and New York, 2005

Ricotti, S. P., 'La Villa Laurentina di Plinio il Giovane: un ennesima ricostruzione', *Lunario Romano*, 1983, pp. 229–51

Riggsby, A. M., *Roman Law and the Legal World of the Romans*, Cambridge University Press, New York, 2010

Roberts, P., *Life and Death in Pompeii and Herculaneum*, British Museum, London, 2013

Roche, P. (ed.), *Pliny's Praise: The Panegyricus in the Roman World*, Cambridge University Press, Cambridge and New York, 2011, especially P. Roche, 'Pliny's Thanksgiving: An Introduction to the *Panegyricus*', pp. 1–28; P. Roche, 'The Panegyricus and the Monuments of Rome', pp. 45–66; G. O. Hutchinson, 'Politics and the Sublime in the *Panegyricus*', pp. 125–41; C. F. Noreña, 'Self-fashioning in the *Panegyricus*', pp. 29–44

Rolandi, G., A. Paone, M. di Lascio, and G. Stefani, 'The 79 AD eruption of Somma: The relationship between the date of the eruption and the southeast tephra dispersion', *Journal of Volcanology and Geothermal Research*, Vol. 169, 2007, pp. 87–98

Rowe, C., and M. Schofield (eds), *The Cambridge History of Greek and Roman Political Thought*, Cambridge University Press, Cambridge, 2000, especially M. Griffin, 'Seneca and Pliny', pp. 532–58

Rubin, P. L., *Giorgio Vasari: Life and History*, Yale University Press, New Haven and London, 1995

Russo, F., and F. Russo, *79 d.C Rotta su Pompei (Indagione sulla Scomparse di un Ammiraglio)*, Edizioni Scientifiche e Artistiche, Naples, 2007

de Ste. Croix, G. E. M., *Christian Persecution, Martyrdom, and Orthodoxy*, edited by M. Whitby and J. Streeter, Oxford University Press, Oxford and New York, 2006

Sartori, A., *Le Iscrizioni Romane*, Musei Civici Como, Como, 1994

Scarth, A., *Vulcan's Fury: Man Against the Volcano*, Yale University Press, New Haven and London, 1999

———*Vesuvius: A Biography*, Terra, Hertfordshire, 2009

Schaefer, S. J., *The Studiolo of Francesco I de'Medici in the Palazzo Vecchio in Florence*, PhD Thesis, Bryn Mawr College, Pennsylvania, 1976

Schama, S., *The Story of the Jews: Finding the Words (1000 BCE–1492CE)*, Bodley Head, London, 2013

Scullard, H. H., *From the Gracchi to Nero*, Routledge, London and New York, 2006

Shelton, J-A., *The Women of Pliny's Letters*, Routledge, Oxford and New York, 2013

Sherwin-White, A. N., 'Trajan's Replies to Pliny: Authorship and Necessity', *Journal of Roman Studies*, Vol. 52, Parts 1 and 2, 1962, pp. 114–25

———*The Letters of Pliny: A Historical and Social Commentary*, Clarendon Press, Oxford, 1966

———'Pliny, the Man and His Letters', *Greece & Rome*, Vol. 16, No. 1, April 1969, pp. 76–90

Sherwin-White, A. N., and S. Price, 'Pliny (2) the Younger, c. 61–c. 112 CE', entry in *Oxford Classical Dictionary*, http://classics. oxfordre.com, published March 2016

Sick, D. H., 'Ummidia Quadratilla: Cagey Businesswoman or Lazy Pantomime Watcher?', *Classical Antiquity*, Vol. 18, No. 2, October 1999, pp. 330–48

Sigurdsson, H., S. Cashdollar, and S. R. J. Sparks, 'The Eruption of Vesuvius in AD 79: Reconstruction from Historical and Volcanological Evidence', *American Journal of Archaeology*, Vol. 86, No. 1, January 1982, pp. 39–51

de Simone, G. F., 'On the shape of Vesuvius before AD 79 (and why it should matter to modern archaeologists)', *Rivista di Studi Pompeiani*, Vol. 25, 2014, pp. 201–5

Southern, P., *Domitian: Tragic Tyrant*, Routledge, London and New York, 2013

Sparks, R. S. J., and L. Wilson, 'A model for the formation of ignimbrite by gravitational column collapse', *Journal of the Geological Society*, Vol. 132, July 1976, pp. 441–51

Steele, R., and J. Addison, *The Tatler*, Vol. 3, John Sharpe, London, 1804

Stefani, G., and M. Borgongino, 'Ancora sulla data dell'eruzione', *Rivista di Studi Pompeiani*, Vol. 18, 2007, pp. 204–6

Stonehouse, J. H. (ed.), *Catalogue of the Library of Charles Dickens from Gadshill*, Piccadilly Fountain Press, London, 1935

Syme, R., 'The Friend of Tacitus', *Journal of Roman Studies*, Vol. 47, No.1/2, 1957, pp. 131–5

———*Tacitus*, Clarendon Press, Oxford, 1958

———'Pliny and the Dacian Wars', *Latomus* T. 23, Fasc 4, 1964, pp. 750–9

———'Pliny the Procurator', *Harvard Studies in Classical Philology*, Vol. 73, 1969, pp. 201–36

———'Ummidius Quadratus, Capax Imperii', *Harvard Studies in Classical Philology*, Vol. 83, 1979, pp. 287–310

———'The Travels of Suetonius Tranquillus', *Hermes*, Vol. 209, Bd., H. 1, 1981, pp. 105–17

———'Juvenal, Pliny and Tacitus', *Roman Papers*, Vol. 3, edited by A. R. Birley, Clarendon Press, Oxford, 1984, pp. 1135–57

———'Consular Friends of the Elder Pliny', *Roman Papers*, Vol. 7, edited by A. R. Birley, Clarendon Press, Oxford, 1991, pp. 496–511

———'People in Pliny', *Roman Papers*, Vol. 2, edited by E. Badian, Clarendon Press, Oxford, 1991, pp. 694–723

———'Pliny's Early Career', *Roman Papers*, Vol. 7, edited by A. R. Birley, Clarendon Press, Oxford, 1991, pp. 551–67

———'Pliny's Less Successful Friends', *Roman Papers*, Vol. 2, edited by E. Badian, Clarendon Press, Oxford, 1991, pp. 477–95

———'The Ummidii', *Roman Papers*, Vol. 2, edited by E. Badian, Clarendon Press, Oxford, 1991, pp. 659–93

Tanzer, H. H., *The Villas of Pliny the Younger*, Columbia University Press, New York, 1924

de Verger, A. R., 'Erotic Language in Pliny, Ep. VII 5', *Glotta* 74, B., 1/2. H., 1997/98, pp. 114–16

Waarsenburg, D. J., 'Archeologisch Nieuws verzorgd door het Nederlands Institut te Rome: De Schedel van Plinius Maior', *Hermeneus: Tijdshrift voor Antieke Cultuur* 63e, No. 1, February 1991, pp. 39–43

Wallace-Hadrill, A., *Suetonius: The Scholar and His Caesars*, Duckworth, London, 1983

———'Pliny the Elder and Man's Unnatural History', *Greece & Rome*, Vol. 37, No. 1, April 1990, pp. 80–96

Wallis, F., *Bede: The Reckoning of Time, translated, with introduction, notes and commentary*, Liverpool University Press, Liverpool, 1999

Ward, A. M., F. M. Heichelheim, and C. A. Yeo, *A History of the Roman People*, Routledge, London and New York, 2016

Wethered, H. N., *A Short History of Gardens*, Methuen & Co., London, 1933

White, P., 'The Friends of Martial, Statius, and Pliny, and the Dispersal of Patronage', *Harvard Studies in Classical Philology*, Vol. 79, 1975, pp. 265–300

Williams, G., *Pietro Bembo on Etna: The Ascent of a Venetian Humanist*, Oxford University Press, New York, 2017

Williams, K. F., 'Pliny and the Murder of Larcius Macedo', *Classical Journal*, Vol. 101, No. 4, April–May 2006, pp. 409–24

Williams, W., *Correspondence with Trajan from Bithynia (Epistles X)*, Aris & Phillips, Warminster, 1990

Wilson, A., and M. Flohr, (eds), *The Economy of Pompeii*, Oxford University Press, Oxford, 2017, especially N. Monteix, 'Urban Production and the Pompeian Economy', pp. 209–42

Winsbury, R., *Pliny the Younger: A Life in Roman Letters*, Bloomsbury Academic, London and New York, 2015

Woodman, A. J. (ed.), *The Cambridge Companion to Tacitus*, Cambridge University Press, Cambridge, 2009, especially A. J. Woodman, 'Tacitus and the contemporary scene', pp. 31–46

Acknowledgements

While working on this book I endeavoured to pay homage to the Plinys by adapting my writing life, as they did, to the seasons, plunging myself into Pliny's snow in the bitterest winters and ploughing through his harvests in the dog days of summer (there have inevitably been moments when I have been shivering under a blanket and writing about drought). In the process I have come to know something of Pliny's temptations. Forbidden from having what is too easily within reach, I have held an oyster in my palm, pressed its shell against my nose, caressed its silky hollow, but not tasted its meat. I am horribly allergic to oysters.

I thank everyone who has sustained me through the seasons of this project. I am extremely grateful to my agent Georgina Capel, and Rachel Conway and Irene Baldoni. My editor, Arabella Pike, and copyeditor, Kate Johnson, have been wonderful, and I warmly thank them both. At HarperCollins I also thank Iain Hunt, Katherine Patrick and Marianne Tatepo.

I was very privileged to have as my first reader Barbara Levick, Emeritus Fellow in Classics at St Hilda's College, Oxford. Barbara offered a number of helpful suggestions on my text and I am so grateful to her for the time she gave me. Paul Cartledge, A. G. Leventis Senior Research Fellow of Clare College, Cambridge and A. G. Leventis Professor of Greek Culture Emeritus in the Faculty of Classics, has been a pillar of support from the beginning, and I am hugely thankful for the incisive notes he made on my manuscript.

The Plinys have sent me to many places. I'd like to thank the staff of the London Library, British Library, the Joint Library of the Hellenic and Roman Societies and Institute of Classical Studies, Senate House Library and the Bodleian. The Palazzo Vecchio in Florence and Museo Civico in Como were very accommodating. The Villa Pliniana/ Sereno Hotels on Lake Como were kind enough to provide me with private access to the building and 'Pliny's spring'. Mena Terranova of the Museo Storico dell'Arte Sanitaria in Rome updated me on progress in the investigation into the 'skull of Pliny the Elder'. The Charles Dickens Museum in London, and particularly Louisa Price, were very helpful.

Thanks also to Sir David Attenborough, Amanda Claridge, Peter Hicks, Emily Kearns, Ellida Minelli, Andrew Roberts and Greg Woolf, who answered my sometimes esoteric questions.

James Cullen was the most patient and entertaining of friends on my Italian research trips. Lucy Purcell I thank for her friendship, encouragement, and remarkable strength. Simon has been marvellously supportive.

I could not have written this book without the love and support of my parents, Amanda and Jeremy, my sister, Alice and my grandparents, Don and Wendy – to whom this book is dedicated. I am forever grateful to you all.

Index